The Black Death

D1003522

PROBLEMS IN EUROPEAN CIVILIZATION SERIES

General Editor
Merry E. Wiesner

The Black Death

Edited with an introduction by
Elizabeth A. Lehfeldt
Cleveland State University

Houghton Mifflin Company   Boston   New York

This book is dedicated to Helen Nader.

Publisher: Charles Hartford
Senior Sponsoring Editor: Nancy Blaine
Development Editor: Julie Dunn
Senior Project Editor: Carol Newman
Editorial Assistant: Trinity Peacock-Broyles
Senior Manufacturing Coordinator: Priscilla Bailey
Senior Marketing Manager: Sandra McGuire

Cover Painting: Triumph of Death of Francesco Traini, 14th Century, Galleria Nazionale, Palermo Italy/Scala/Art Resource, N.Y.

Credits appear on page 205, which constitutes an extension of the copyright page.

Copyright © 2005 by Houghton Mifflin Company. All rights reserved.

No part of this work may be reproduced or transmitted in any form or by any means, electronic or mechanical, including photocopying and recording, or by any information storage or retrieval system without the prior written permission of the copyright owner unless such copying is expressly permitted by federal copyright law. With the exception of non-profit transcription in Braille, Houghton Mifflin is not authorized to grant permission for further uses of copyrighted selections reprinted in this text without the permission of their owners. Permission must be obtained from the individual copyright owners as identified herein. Address requests for permission to make copies of Houghton Mifflin material to College Permissions, Houghton Mifflin Company, 222 Berkeley Street, Boston, MA 02116-3764.

Printed in the U.S.A.

Library of Congress Control Number: 2003110141

ISBN: 0-618-46342-9

23456789-QWE-08 07 06 05

Contents

Preface

The Black Death is a topic that has long fascinated students of history. Images of pestilence and plague capture the imagination, prompting a host of questions. Particularly in the twenty-first century as doctors, scientists, and even politicians grapple with the implications of AIDS, SARS, and the spread of other infectious diseases, fourteenth-century epidemic disease does not seem so far removed from our modern experiences. And so we wonder how Europeans confronted high death tolls, disruptions to trade and commerce, events that challenged their faith, and socioeconomic dislocations. Historians have posed various answers to these questions. Whatever the nuances within their arguments, many of them conclude that the Black Death ushered in a series of changes. Particularly since it reappeared throughout the early modern period, the disease made its impact known across a spectrum of experience, ranging from the political to the cultural to the economic. Finally, recent hypotheses about the disease's identity—was it really bubonic plague?—have reexcited interest in this subject and have already begun to generate new scholarship and reevaluations of existing work.

This volume addresses some of the major themes and debates in the study of the fourteenth-century outbreak of bubonic plague and encompasses an examination of society, culture, religion, politics, and economics. Part I examines the vexing question of whether Europe was already in a period of decline before the disease's ravages. To what extent was the experience of plague shaped by the years of famine and socioeconomic disruption that preceded it? Part II discusses one of the most contested debates in the field: the identity of the disease. Recent questions about whether the disease *was* bubonic plague have stimulated wide-ranging historical investigations of epidemiology, ecology, and climate. Parts III and IV turn to the response to and impact of the disease's course in fourteenth-century Europe. Part III focuses on the complexity of religious reactions. The works excerpted in this part enter the scholarly debate about the extent to which Europeans responded irrationally and despairingly to the disease, offering counterinterpretations that emphasize their resourcefulness and resiliency. Part IV engages the tension between stability and disorder, looking at how Europe's major institutions—the medical establishment, universities, municipalities, and the Church—weathered the experience of epidemic disease. Finally, the readings in Part V evaluate the extent to which the plague changed the socioeconomic life of fourteenth-century Europe. Did the plague mark a critical turning point, or did the status quo ultimately prevail?

In highlighting these major debates and themes, the volume showcases the work of a host of influential scholars and excerpts both old and new studies. David Herlihy, for example, entered the debate about the role of the plague in understanding late medieval Europe as early as the 1960s. His sustained scholarly engagement is demonstrated by the inclusion here of an excerpt from his posthumous *The Black Death and the Transformation of the West* (1997), a work in which he continued to wrestle with how to interpret the plague's impact. John Hatcher is another historian whose work has shaped major questions surrounding the disease. In particular, his article excerpted here reopens a pivotal question in plague historiography: Did the fortunes of English peasants change as a result of the demographic upheaval of 1348? He argues that a recent tendency in plague studies to downplay the extent to which the plague improved the lot of peasants needs to be reconsidered. The work of another influential scholar, Samuel K. Cohn, represents perhaps the most controversial challenge to plague scholarship. Cohn has posited that the fourteenth-century disease that attacked Europe was not bubonic plague. His interpretation has already sparked lively debate. In addition, this volume contains both "classic" pieces of scholarship and newer works. The inclusion of both best illustrates the ongoing debates in the field, since some newer work has been written in response to longstanding interpretations. This in turn demonstrates that the study of the plague has not ceased to excite the historical imagination.

I owe various debts of gratitude to those who have shaped my own fascination with this topic and the subsequent preparation of this book. First and foremost, I thank Helen Nader (to whom I dedicate this work), who developed and taught a course on the Black Death at Indiana University and then gave me the opportunity to teach it. Merry Wiesner, the series editor, supported the inclusion of a volume on the Black Death, nurtured and helped strengthen my prospectus, and offered other useful suggestions along the way. The volume's reviewers—Lorraine Attreed (College of the Holy Cross), Robert F. Berkhofer III (Western Michigan University), Sherri Olson (University of Connecticut), and Lisa Wolverton (University of Oregon)—offered cogent, insightful, and indispensable comments, corrections, and suggestions. At Houghton Mifflin, Nancy Blaine's enthusiastic and careful reading and advice strengthened the book's conceptualization and Julie Dunn's prompt and unfailingly helpful advice and guidance made the book's development a thoroughly enjoyable experience. The invaluable production assistance of Carol Newman, Trinity Peacock-Broyles, and Linda Sykes has improved the text and visual presentation of this volume.

Elizabeth A. Lehfeldt

Editor's Preface
to Instructors

There are many ways to date ourselves as teachers and scholars of history: the questions that we regard as essential to ask about any historical development, the theorists whose words we quote and whose names appear in our footnotes, the price of the books that we purchased for courses and that are on our shelves. Looking over my own shelves, it struck me that another way we could be dated was by the color of the oldest books we owned in this series, which used to be published by D. C. Heath. I first used a "Heath series" book—green and white, as I recall—when I was a freshman in college and taking a modern European history course. That book, by Dwight E. Lee on the Munich crisis, has long since disappeared, but several Heath books that I acquired later as an undergraduate are still on my shelves. Those that I used in graduate school, including ones on the Renaissance and Reformation, are also there, as are several I assigned my students when I first started teaching or have used in the years since. As with any system of historical periodization, of course, this method of dating a historian is flawed and open to misinterpretation. When a colleague retired, he gave me some of his even older Health series books, in red and black, which had actually appeared when I was still in elementary and junior high school, so that a glance at my shelves might make me seem ready for retirement.

The longevity of this series, despite its changing cover design and its transition from D. C. Heath to Houghton Mifflin, could serve as an indication of several things. One might be that historians are conservative, unwilling to change the way they approach the past or teach about it. The rest of the books on my shelves suggest that this conservatism is not the case, however, for many of the books discuss topics that were unheard of as subjects of historical investigation when I took that course as a freshman thirty years ago: memory, masculinity, visual culture, sexuality.

Another way to account for the longevity of this series is that several generations of teachers have found it a useful way for their students to approach historical subjects. As teachers, one of the first issues we confront in any course is what materials we will assign our students to read. (This decision is often, in fact, paramount, for we have to order books months before the class begins.) We may include a textbook to provide an overview of the subject matter covered in the course and often have several from which to choose. We may use a reader of original sources, or several sources in their entirety, because we feel that it is important for our students to hear the voices of people of the past directly. We may add a novel from the period, for fictional works often give one details and insights that do not emerge from other types of sources. We may direct our students to visual materials, either in books or on the Web, for artifacts, objects, and art can give one access to aspects of life never mentioned in written sources.

Along with these types of assignments, we may also choose to assign books such as those in this series, which present the ideas and opinions of scholars on a particular topic. Textbooks are, of course, written by scholars with definite opinions, but they are designed to present material in a relatively bland manner. They may suggest areas about which there is historical debate (often couched in phrases such as "scholars disagree about . . .") but do not participate in those debates themselves. By contrast, the books in this series highlight points of dispute, and cover topics and developments about which historians often disagree vehemently. Students who are used to the textbook approach to history may be surprised at the range of opinions on certain matters, but we hope that the selections in each of these volumes will allow readers to understand why there is such a diversity. Each volume covers several issues of interpretive debate and highlights newer research directions.

Variety of interpretation in history is sometimes portrayed as a recent development, but the age of this series in its many cover styles indicates that this account is not accurate. Historians have long recognized that historical sources are produced by particular individuals with particular interests and biases that consciously and unconsciously shape their content. They have also long—one is tempted to say "always"— recognized that different people approach the past differently, making choices about which topics to study, which sources to use, which developments and individuals to highlight. This diversity in both sources and methodologies is part of what makes history exciting for those of us who study it, for new materials and new approaches allow us to see things that have never been seen before, in the same way that astronomers find new stars with better tools and new ways of looking.

The variety and innovation that is an essential part of good historical scholarship allow this series both to continue and to change. Some of the volumes now being prepared have the same titles as those I read as an undergraduate, but the scholarship on that topic has changed so much in the last several decades that they had to be completely redone, not simply revised. Some of the volumes now in print examine topics that were rarely covered in undergraduate courses when the series began publication, and a few former volumes are no longer in print because the topics they investigated now show up more rarely. We endeavor to keep the series up-to-date and welcome suggestions about volumes that would prove helpful for teaching undergraduate and graduate courses. You can contact us at http://college.hmco.com.

Merry E. Wiesner

Editor's Preface to Students

History is often presented as facts marching along a timeline, and historical research is often viewed as the unearthing of information so that more facts can be placed on the timeline. Like geologists in caves or physicists using elaborate microscopes, historians discover new bits of data, which allow them to recover more of the past.

To some degree, this model is accurate. Like laboratory scientists, historians do conduct primary research, using materials in archives, libraries, and many other places to discover new things about the past. Over the last thirty years, for example, the timeline of history has changed from a story that was largely political and military to one that includes the experiences of women, peasants, slaves, children, and workers. Even the political and military story has changed and now includes the experiences of ordinary soldiers and minority groups rather than simply those of generals, rulers, and political elites. This expansion of the timeline has come in part through intensive research in original sources, which has vastly increased what we know about people of the past.

Original research is only part of what historians do, however, in the same way that laboratory or field research is only part of science. Historical and scientific information is useless until someone tries to make sense of what is happening, tries to explain why and how things developed the way they did. In making these analyses and conclusions, however, both historians and scientists often come to disagree vehemently about the underlying reasons for what they have observed or discovered, and sometimes about the observations themselves. Certain elements of those observations are irrefutable—a substance either caught fire or it did not, a person lived and died or he or she did not—but many more of them are open to debate: Was the event (whether historical or scientific) significant? Why and how did it happen? Under what circumstances might it not have happened? What factors influenced the way that it happened? What larger consequences did it have?

The books in this series focus on just those types of questions. They take one particular event or development in European history and present you with the analyses of several historians and other authors regarding this issue. In some cases the authors may disagree about what actually happened—in the same way that eyewitnesses of a traffic accident or crime may all see different things—but more often they disagree about the interpretation. Was the Renaissance a continuation of earlier ideas, or did it represent a new way of looking at the world? Was nineteenth-century European imperialism primarily political and economic in its origins and impact, or were cultural and intellectual factors more significant? Was ancient Athens a democracy worthy of emulation, an expansionary state seeking to swallow its neighbors, or both? Within each volume are often more specific points of debate, which add complexity to the main question and introduce you to further points of disagreement.

Each of the volumes begins with an introduction by the editor, which you should read carefully before you turn to the selections themselves. This introduction sets out the *historical* context of the issue, adding depth to what you may have learned in a textbook account or other reading, and also explains the *historiographical* context—that is, how historians (including those excerpted in the volume) have viewed the issue over time. Many volumes also include a timeline of events and several reference maps that situate the issue chronologically and geographically. These may be more detailed than the timelines and maps in your textbook, and consulting them as you read will help deepen your understanding of the selections.

Some of the volumes in the series include historical analyses that are more than a century old, and all include writings stretching over several decades. The editors include this chronological range not only to allow you to see that interpretations change, but also to see how lines of argument and analysis develop. Every historian approaching an issue depends not only on his or her own original research, but also on the secondary analyses of those who have gone before, which he or she then accepts, rejects, modifies, or adapts. Thus, within the book as a whole or within each section, the selections are generally arranged in chronological order; reading them in the order they are presented will allow you to get a better sense of the historiographical development and to make comparisons among the selections more easily and appropriately.

The description of the scholarly process noted above is somewhat misleading, for in both science and history, research and analysis are not sequential but simultaneous. Historians do not wander around archives looking for interesting bits of information but turn to their sources with specific questions in mind, questions that have often been developed by reading earlier historians. These questions shape where they will look, what they will pay attention to, and therefore what conclusions they will make. Thus, the fact that we now know so much more about women, peasants, or workers than we did several decades ago did not result primarily from sources on these people suddenly appearing where there had been none, but from historians, with new questions in mind, going back to the same archives and libraries that had yielded information on kings and generals. The same is true in science, of course; scientists examining an issue begin with a hypothesis and then test it through the accumulation of information, reaching a conclusion that leads to further hypotheses.

In both history and science, one's hypotheses can sometimes be so powerful that one simply cannot see what the sources or experiments show, which is one reason there is always opportunity for more research or a reanalysis of data. A scholar's analysis may also be shaped by many other factors, and in this volume the editor may have provided you with information about individual authors, such as their national origin, intellectual background, or philosophical perspective, if these factors are judged important to your understanding of their writings or points of view. You might be tempted to view certain of these factors as creating "bias" on the part of an author and thus to reduce the value of his or her analysis. It is important to recognize, however, that every historian or commentator has a particular point of view and writes at a particular historical moment; very often what scholars view as complete objectivity on their own part is seen as subjective bias by those who disagree. The central aim of this series over its forty-plus years of publication has been to help you and other students understand how and why the analyses and judgments of historians have differed and changed over time, to see that scholarly controversy is at the heart of the historical enterprise.

The instructor in your course may have provided you with detailed directions for using this book, but here are some basic questions that you can ask yourself as you read the selections:

- What is the author's central argument?
- What evidence does the author put forward to support this argument?
- What is the significance of the author's argument?
- What other interpretation might there be of the evidence that the author presents?
- How does each author's argument intersect with the others in the part? In the rest of the book?
- How convincing do you find the author's interpretation?

These questions are exactly the same as those that professional historians ask themselves, and in analyzing and comparing the selections in this book, you, too, are engaged in the business of historical interpretation.

Merry E. Wiesner

Chronology

October 1348	Medical faculty of the University of Paris issues its influential report on the origins and character of the plague
November 1348	Plague in London; the high death toll requires the creation of new cemeteries
February 1349	Massacre of at least 900 Jews in Strasbourg
August 1349	Massacre of Jews in Mainz
October 1349	Pope Clement VI outlaws the flagellant movement
1350	Pope Clement VI declares 1350 a jubilee year and offers plenary indulgences to all who make a pilgrimage to Rome
1351	Boccaccio finishes *The Decameron*
1351	Statute of Laborers passed (England)
1352	Corpus Christi College founded at Cambridge University
1377	Ragusa (present-day Dubrovnik) imposes the first plague-inspired quarantine
1381	English Peasants' Revolt
1720–1721	Plague outbreak in Marseilles; the last epidemic outbreak in western Europe; as many as 50,000 (out of a population of 100,000) die
1894	Alexandre Yersin identifies the plague bacillus

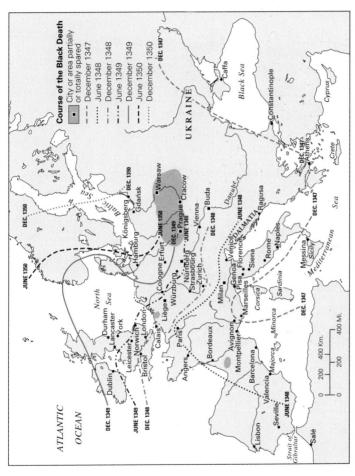

The Black Death This map demonstrates the plague's progress from 1347–1350. It spread beyond the port cities of the Mediterranean, reaching across the European continent and into the British Isles and Scandinavia.

The Black Death

Introduction

For centuries, the phenomenon of the bubonic plague epidemic that first ravaged Europe in the period 1348–1349 has captivated historians. Even the name given to this outbreak of deadly disease, the Black Death, communicates a sense of danger and intrigue. The events warrant such fascination. Although some shifts in both the socioeconomic and demographic landscapes of Europe were already in motion, the ravages of the plague transformed European life. And especially because plague outbreaks recurred throughout the late medieval and early modern periods, the experience of plague became a defining feature of life during this time. Thus, the Black Death presents itself to historians as a rich subject for historical investigation.

A modern medical understanding of plague did not emerge until the late nineteenth and early twentieth centuries. At that time, scientists identified the three critical components in understanding the disease's spread: the rat flea (*Xenopsylla cheopis*), the black rat (*Rattus rattus*), and the plague bacillus (*Yersinia pestis*). The rat flea is the vector that carries (without becoming infected itself) the bacillus. When the rat flea bites its host, the black rat, it infects the rat with plague. Plague is an enzootic disease among rat flea and rat populations in various parts of the world, including central Asia. When a disease is enzootic it exists without catastrophic results. Thus, under these circumstances, the rat flea and rats peacefully coexist without the rate of infection causing a precipitous decline in the rat population—a circumstance that would lead the rat flea to seek out another host, such as a human being. In regions like central Asia (even today) bubonic plague sometimes spills beyond its typical host population. By and large, however, the disease remains enzootic—that is, there are occasional flare-ups of the disease, but its destructive power is held in check.

In the fourteenth century, however, the situation changed as bubonic plague was introduced into western Europe and began infecting human populations. Historians postulate that the plague epidemic that began to attack Europe in 1348 came from central Asia, carried by rat fleas. The standard interpretation of the disease's introduction into Europe holds that grain shipments from central Asia carrying the black rat and its fleas (the black rat typically ate grain) introduced bubonic plague into the ports of Europe around the year 1348 (overland grain routes were also important in the spread of disease, but port cities were the primary points of introduction). Before 1348 there were reports from places in the east like Constantinople, telling of outbreaks of disease. Why, however, were human populations being attacked by a disease that typically was confined to the black rat population? The enzootic balance that had prevailed in central Asia was disrupted. Scholars have suggested that preceding the disease's spread to human populations there was a widespread rat epizootic. In other words, the plague advanced beyond its usual enzootic existence within the rat population and killed off an epidemic number of susceptible European rats. Rat fleas that had killed off their hosts turned instead to humans for sustenance, thereby infecting them. Bubonic plague also spread through its pneumonic variety that developed in some individuals who contracted the disease from infected fleas. Pneumonic plague can spread by airborne means (like the cough of an infected individual) and was almost always fatal. Thus, this manifestation of the disease dramatically heightened its ability to infect and kill.

The demographic toll of the disease was staggering. Although figures range according to region and the state of record-keeping, it is generally agreed that anywhere from one-third to one-half of the population of western Europe perished in this initial outbreak. Not surprisingly, these numbers have prompted historians to ask a range of questions, seeking to assess the reactions to and impact of such unprecedented rates of mortality. How did people respond to widespread death? How did Europeans explain—medically, religiously, and culturally—the onslaught of disease and seek to block its spread? What was the social and economic impact of such a momentous drop in the population? With so many deaths, for example, was land more readily available? Did the resulting labor shortage give women greater opportunity in the economic marketplace?

The European experience with bubonic plague in this period also challenges historians to evaluate how individuals and societies understand disease. Beyond identifying and analyzing empirical and quantitative data (for example, the number of deaths, the price of land, the actions taken by doctors and municipal authorities), there is another layer of interpretation to understanding the European response to bubonic plague. Many historians of disease contend that diseases are socially and culturally constructed—that is, specific societies and cultures interpret a specific disease in particular ways. Especially during the first outbreak of plague, for example, many Europeans blamed the disease on Jewish communities, accusing them of poisoning wells. There was no empirical evidence behind such accusations. Rather, a reaction such as this tells us very little about the spread of bubonic plague but speaks volumes about the character of Jewish-Christian relations in this period. Europeans also blamed the poor, Gypsies, and other socially marginal groups for the spread of the disease. In this way, the upheaval of disease exposed the fissures in European society. Another way of examining the cultural construction of disease is to compare the Muslim reaction to plague in the Middle East to the contemporaneous reaction in Christian areas. Although each society was coping with the same disease, the responses were different. In these ways, acknowledging the social and cultural construction of disease allows us as historians to use the experience of disease as a window into the workings of late medieval society.

Finally, beyond its immediate effects, historians have examined and debated the enduring impact of the fourteenth-century outbreak of bubonic plague. As just indicated, there were tremendous shifts in the socioeconomic landscape and cultural sensibilities of Europeans as they grappled with the disease's high demographic toll and related consequences. Yet, some historians have argued that many of these trends were already in motion and that population had already begun to decline due to a period of harsh climatic conditions that led to poor harvests and even periods of famine in the early part of the fourteenth century. Further, the overall impact of the bubonic plague epidemic must be regarded not only in the short term, but also as a recurring phenomenon. The plague reappeared in western Europe throughout the early modern era, well into the eighteenth century. On the one hand, this meant that it still had the power to wreak havoc. On the other hand, it also meant that Europeans began devising and institutionalizing ways to grapple with the disease. During the initial epidemics, for example, civic authorities often created ad-hoc commissions to regulate the spread and treatment of plague. By the early modern period, many of these commissions had become permanent boards of health and new fixtures in the growing bureaucracies of municipalities.

The Black Death, then, transcended the merely biological and epidemiological and became a phenomenon that reached into the very depths of European life, altering, and sometimes transforming, society, culture, religion, politics, and economics. Its wide-ranging impact has prompted considerable debate among historians about the character and extent of these alterations and transformations. The five sections of this volume will identify several of these scholarly debates, thus providing examples of the richness of historical inquiry in this field.

Part I examines the state of affairs in Europe before the onset of the plague. Seeking to understand the extent of demographic decline wrought by the Black Death, historians have looked to the first half of the fourteenth century to assess what changes were already taking place. In fact, many historians believe that Europe was already in the grips of a severe economic crisis—characterized by a declining population, poor harvests, and climactic changes—even before the disease's onset in 1348. The extent of this crisis and how Europeans responded to it, however, have remained a topic of heated discussion. Some scholars have argued that Europe was in the grips of a classic Malthusian tangle of population and resources. The state of agricultural productivity in the early fourteenth century could not support the existing population (which had grown dramatically in the preceding centuries). In this section, David Herlihy rejects the rigidity of that model, arguing for a greater complexity of circumstances in the preplague world. The selections by William C. Jordan and Edward Miller and John Hatcher highlight the ways in which Europeans responded to this economic crisis creatively and proactively. The responses varied widely and included the provision of charity in times of need, a rise in petty crime, and new land tenure strategies. In adopting this approach to the study of the fourteenth-century crisis, these scholars are arguing against other interpretations that depicted Europeans as helpless in the face of this agricultural crisis.

Part II examines the late medieval and modern interpretations of plague. Until quite recently all historians adhered to the idea that the disease that devastated Europe in 1348 was bubonic plague. Recent work by various scholars, however, has drawn dramatically different conclusions. Although not yet accepted as orthodox within the field and hotly contested by their critics, these investigators have postulated that the epidemic disease Europeans grappled with in the fourteenth century was *not* bubonic plague. They have argued that medieval descriptions of the disease's spread, symptoms, and other features do not conform to modern knowledge of the disease. These studies have been more hesitant in hypothesizing exactly what disease *did* attack Europe during this period (anthrax and hemorraghic plague have been suggested), but their work represents an intriguing challenge to what until recently was the most firmly entrenched piece of the puzzle: the belief that the epidemic of the fourteenth century was bubonic plague. Samuel K. Cohn's recent reassessment of the disease's identity has been controversial but also stimulating. By comparing plague data from outbreaks in India and Scotland in the modern era with the fourteenth-century evidence, he argues for marked inconsistencies that throw into question the ability to identify the medieval disease as bubonic plague. The passage by Michael McCormick comes at the question of identifying plague differently. He looks at the history and ecology of rat populations in western Europe, seeking to establish the role that they played in facilitating an outbreak of bubonic plague. The other reading in this section examines the disease in its fourteenth-century context and draws us into the world of medical practitioners and city administrators. John Henderson examines the overlap between medical and municipal understandings of plague.

Whether they know the exact identification of the disease that ravaged Europe in this period, historians are still able to assess the reactions and responses to its devastating effects. Parts III and IV offer some examples of these analyses. Part III focuses on religious and cultural reactions to the plague. The reading selections in this section focus on interpretations that break with the traditional scholarly assumption that Europeans responded to the horror of the Black Death with expressions of despair, pessimism, and irrationality. Louise Marshall's examination of the use of plague imagery, Laura Smoller's analysis of descriptions of the apocalypse, Richard Kieckhefer's interpretation of the behavior of penitential flagellants, and David Nirenberg's reconstruction of anti-Jewish hostility all seek to understand European religious responses on their own terms, without the insertion of modern prejudices and sensibilities. The final reading by Michael Dols juxtaposes Muslim reactions to plague against the aforementioned Christian reactions. Some Islamic texts of the period, for example, regarded the plague not as God's punishment (a typical Christian interpretation of the disease's virulence) but argued instead that God had sent it as a sign of his mercy and as a means of martyrdom.

Part IV turns to a discussion of how those in positions of authority responded to the plague. Not surprisingly, Europeans turned to established structures of order—the medical establishment, the university, the Church, and their local municipalities—in their quest to understand and weather the plague. And yet the disease affected these very institutions in dramatic ways. As Anna Campbell and William Courtenay demonstrate (although their conclusions differ), the plague altered the character of medical practice and the culture of university life. William Bowsky illustrates a city, Siena, in crisis, seeking to meet the demands of a populace stricken by disease. Ultimately, he argues, the socioeconomic disruptions of the period may even have threatened the traditional political order. Finally, William J. Dohar's research demonstrates how the plague's demographic toll among the clergy created a short-staffed institution struggling to meet the pastoral needs of the laity.

Part V engages the question of the plague's socioeconomic impact in the decades following the initial outbreak. For those fortunate enough to survive the plague's virulence, standards of living began to improve. Wages rose and land was more readily available. Paul Freedman and Christopher Dyer examine whether rising expectations among the peasantry created a situation ripe for revolt. John Hatcher challenges interpretations that have argued that peasants saw few improvements in their standard of living. The reading by Mavis Mate looks at how another customarily disadvantaged segment of the medieval population—women—may have benefited from the shifting circumstances of the late fourteenth century. The final selection by Harry Miskimin moves beyond the agricultural sector to examine how demographic shifts affected industrial production and market consumption.

Taken together, these five sections expose the wide-ranging impact of this outbreak of epidemic disease and reveal the complexity and richness of historical investigation. There are many lenses—political, demographic, economic, religious, cultural, social—through which scholars have examined this crisis. These varying perspectives in turn create overlapping and interdependent layers of meaning. A dramatic drop in population, for example, could have several effects. It could lead to a greater demand for labor, thereby creating a concomitant increase in wages. Yet, dramatic demographic shifts also created reactions that transcended the economic. Some have postulated, for example, that widespread infant and child mortality during plague epidemics encouraged Europeans to lavish greater attention and affection on their children. In this sense it is impossible to separate the demographic from the economic or the emotional. Thus, scholars increasingly rely on a variety of source material in reaching their conclusions. No one record can tell the whole story. As you will see in the selections that follow, a host of primary sources—paintings, parish records, chronicles—to name only some, have contributed to our modern understanding of the Black Death.

In the medieval period the vast majority of Europeans lived in rural settings where their livelihood was dependent on working the land. (Bibliotheque Nationale, Paris/AKG, London)

I Europe Before the Plague

Although the primary focus of this volume is on the impact of the Black Death, it is important to assess the state of affairs in Europe before the onset of bubonic plague. In fact, even before the momentous events of 1347–1348, Europe had experienced serious crises earlier in the fourteenth century. Poor harvests, probably brought on by unusually cold and rainy weather, had created food scarcities that resulted in famines throughout northern Europe in the period from 1315 to 1317. Chronicles from that period speak of dire circumstances, suggesting that, in their desperation, some even turned to cannibalism. Southern Europe was similarly ravaged by famine in 1339 and 1340.

Understanding the occasion and impact of famine greatly aids our comprehension of Europe's later experience with epidemic disease. For example, had population growth already begun to slow even before the demographic devastation of bubonic plague? Can the Europeans' reactions to famine help us understand their responses to the plague? How was the ability to withstand the economic and social devastation caused by epidemic disease conditioned by earlier experiences with famine? Thus, key to any comprehension of the impact of the Black Death is a thorough understanding of the socioeconomic circumstances that preceded it and a recognition that Europe may already have been in crisis before the plague added to its woes.

Europeans were certainly familiar with agricultural need and crisis. They often suffered at the hands of unpredictable weather and poor harvests and as a consequence laid up surplus grain stores. In times of famine, however, the increasingly urgent demand for food also depleted these reserves. Further, farmers not only suffered the effects of bad harvests, but they often tried to offset these calamities by consuming seed they had put aside for the next year's planting, thus jeopardizing their future agricultural security. All in all, famine could have far-reaching consequences that affected not only people's daily livelihood but also their future prosperity.

These calamitous famines stood in marked contrast to a period of dramatic economic and demographic growth and general prosperity that had begun in western Europe in the eleventh century and that continued into the thirteenth century. Beginning in the eleventh century the population of Europe began to grow dramatically. An absence of invasions (Vikings, Magyars, and Muslims had attacked western Europe in the ninth century), increasing political stability, and greater agricultural productivity (brought on by changes like the use of a new kind of plow and the switch from a two-field to a three-field planting system) spurred this demographic surge. Very quickly, this put demands on the land. The amount of land under cultivation was not sufficient to meet the needs of this expanding population. As a consequence, Europeans cleared forests, drained marshes, and expanded into frontier regions—all with the goal of putting more land to the plow.

In this context, the events of the first half of the fourteenth century probably startled Europeans all the more. Famine and epidemic disease were a shock to the system, but they provide important clues about the general slowing of expansion. Historians have postulated that Europe was experiencing a fundamental crisis of the land not being able to meet the demands of this burgeoning population. This kind of explanation is sometimes called Malthusian and is based on the writings of the clergyman Thomas Malthus (1766–1834), whose *Essay on the Principle of Population* (1798) sought to explain the delicate balance between population and resources. According to Malthus, a population ceiling was set by agricultural productivity and technological expertise. Malthus believed that population growth was destined to outstrip food supplies because whereas population grew exponentially, agriculture grew only arithmetically. Only checks—positive and preventative—on the system could avert disaster. Positive checks were forces like famine and disease. Preventative checks included controlling fertility by delaying the age of first marriage or limiting the number of births.[1] Although Malthus's ideas about population and food supply have been enormously influential in shaping the ideas of historians, in recent years, many have moved toward more subtle interpretations of this balance and the extent to which Europe stood on the brink of a crisis even before the appearance of the Black Death. The readings in this section, then, illuminate the complexity of this crisis (and even the extent to which one existed) that preceded the introduction of bubonic plague in western Europe and how Europeans responded. One of the first scholars to challenge the strictly Malthusian interpretation of famine and plague in the fourteenth century was David Herlihy (1930–1991). His combination of attention to detail and the ability to analyze these details to make sense of trends allowed him to counter the strict Malthusians in his study of the medieval Italian town of Pistoia. By examining marriage and fertility rates, Herlihy was able to demonstrate that even before the fourteenth century population growth had begun to slow. There was no Malthusian crisis in the first half of the fourteenth century. The population had already begun, sometimes subtly, to shift in response to available resources. Europe on the eve of the plague may already have begun righting the imbalance between population and resources. In this context, the Black Death was a catastrophic jolt, but not a necessary one that solved a Malthusian dilemma. The passage from his work excerpted here looks at three explanatory models for a preplague crisis and points us toward a greater understanding of the complexity of the balance between population and resources before the plague.

Edward Miller and John Hatcher approach the question of crisis somewhat differently, seeking to understand how the rural English economy began to adapt to the changes wrought by famine. Closely

---

[1]It is important to note that Malthus used his treatise in part as a diatribe against the behavior of the poor of the eighteenth century, whose unchecked sexuality, he argued, contributed to their own misery, because it led to having too many children. Thus, he contended, it would do no good to pay them more because they would just have even more children.

examining the primary participants in the rural economy—peasants and landlords—they elucidate how each group managed the land in attempts to maximize gain and profit. Fundamental to providing these answers is their analysis of rents, wages, and prices. The amount of land that landlords could cultivate, for example, was determined by the number of peasants they could employ and from whom they could collect rents. The dramatic downturn in the population occasioned by famine altered the landlords' decision-making processes. A diminished labor supply might lead a landlord to retract the amount of land under cultivation. If demand for labor was high—as it sometimes was in the aftermath of population decline—the peasants, for their part, might be able to demand higher wages or lower rents in return for their labor. It is worth noting that the "lessons" learned from the rural English economy's adjustment to the postfamine years will of course also apply to similar postplague adjustments.

William Chester Jordan's study, *The Great Famine: Northern Europe in the Early Fourteenth Century,* is a rigorous and enlightening analysis of the documentary record (notably his study looks at a wide swath of northern Europe, whereas previous studies have been confined primarily to England) informed by modern studies of famine and crisis. Arguing that historians have traditionally depicted peasant communities as helpless and passive in the face of natural disasters, he seeks to evaluate how villagers responded to the famines of this era. To what extent, he wonders, did social and community structures provide support in times of crisis? Exploring issues like charity, credit, and crime, Jordan asks, when and why did the social order break down? Jordan's answers to these questions, of course, also help us to better understand the response of Europeans to the other great crisis of the fourteenth century: the onset of the Black Death.

David Herlihy

The Black Death and the Transformation of the West

In this excerpt from his book, *The Black Death and the Transformation of the West* (published posthumously), David Herlihy analyzes the ways in which historians have tried to explain the balance between population and resources in the first half of the fourteenth century. He discusses the use of both Malthusian and Marxist explanatory models, although he critiques both. He also urges an attentiveness to the feudal mode of production and how that shaped the balance between population and resources. Herlihy's own assessment is that the population was indeed in a "deadlock" before 1348 but that population growth was not relentless and, in fact, population size was holding steady even in the face of famine. The Black Death was a dramatic disruption to this deadlock, but one that forced Europeans to move beyond the equilibrium that they were barely maintaining before 1348.

. . . Why were the medieval populations so vulnerable to these killing diseases? Many historians, dissatisfied with medical explanations, have looked to social factors to explain the catastrophic losses. Two proposed explanations have elicited much lively discussion. One is based on Malthusian principles, the other on Marxist.

In 1798 the English clergyman Thomas Malthus published the first edition of his influential *Essay on the Principle of Population.* In it he concluded that human populations would tend to expand up to and beyond the limits of their food supplies. When they passed those limits, a reckoning was inevitable. The reckoning took the form of famines, epidemics, wars, and the soaring mortality resulting from them. These "positive checks," as he called them, violently reduced the community's numbers to a size that its resources could support.

Source: David Herlihy, *The Black Death and the Transformation of the West* (Cambridge, MA: Harvard University Press, 1997) 31–38.

Several historians maintain that the great population debacle of the fourteenth century was itself a classical Malthusian crisis, triggered by excessive numbers of people. Among the most prominent advocates of such a view have been the late M. M. Postan in England, and Emmanuel Le Roy Ladurie in France. Their conclusion—that Europe was overpopulated on the eve of the Black Death—rests on two types of evidence, direct and indirect. The direct evidence is the sheer size that many European communities had attained by ca. 1300. To cite only one out of many possible examples, the Italian region of Tuscany at its medieval height, according to the estimates of Enrico Fiumi, was inhabited by probably two million people. It would not hold such numbers again until after 1850. With its poorly productive economy and stagnant technology, how could medieval Tuscany have supported so big a population? It could not support it, the argument runs, and famines and wars, and the Black Death itself, were the consequences.

The indirect evidence of overpopulation rests primarily on the history of cereal prices and the occurrences of famine. Basic foodstuffs were costly in the late thirteenth and early fourteenth centuries. One price list from Norfolk, from 1290 and 1348, shows there were nineteen years when wheat prices were so high as to indicate dearth and hunger. In Languedoc between 1302 and 1348, the years of scarcity were twenty, nearly the same as the twenty-seven years of adequate food supplies. More dramatic than price series in measuring population pressures against the food supply were the appearances of true famines. In northern Europe, a major famine, known traditionally as the "great hunger," persisted for three years, from 1314 to 1317. Famine struck also right before the Black Death, in 1346 and 1347, in both north and south. A Florentine, Giovanni Morelli, attributes the high mortality of the Black Death to famine the previous year. Not twenty out of one hundred people, he reports, had bread. The rest lived on herbs and vile plants; grazing like cattle, they filled the countryside. "Think," he explains, "how their bodies were affected." In France, Simon de Couvin affirmed: "The one who was poorly nourished by unsubstantial food fell victim to the merest breath of the disease; the impoverished crowd of common folk died a welcome death, since for them life was death."

Malthusian pressures against the food supply are very apparent in pre-plague Europe, as a huge population struggled to live on scant resources. But was there a Malthusian reckoning? There are grounds for disbelief. European population movements in the thirteenth and fourteenth centuries do not adhere very closely to Malthusian predictions. It is not known when the medieval population peaked; the documents are full of gaps, and regional variations undoubtedly were considerable. It is, however, certain that European population levels were already high, at least from the last decades of the thirteenth century. Hence the Black Death did not strike against a population recklessly adding to its size, but one that had been stable for fifty to a hundred years before 1348. If the Black Death was a response to excessive human numbers, it should have arrived several decades earlier. Moreover, if Europe was overpopulated in 1348, was it still overpopulated later in the century, when the number of people had fallen to half of what it had been? And yet the population continued to fall. It did not stabilize until the opening decades of the fifteenth century, and even then remained stagnant at very low levels for another fifty years. Not until 1460 or 1470 does it again begin to grow. These movements of deep decline, long stability, and slow recovery are inexplicable, on the assumption that resources and their availability alone dominate demographic cycles. A British historian, Bruce M. S. Campbell, who studied the Black Death in an English village, Coltishall, concludes: "The extraordinarily prolonged demographic recession which followed the advent of plague at Coltishall, as elsewhere in the country, defies simple Malthusian . . . logic."

The role of famines in affecting population movements is also problematic. The many famines preceding the Black Death, even the "great hunger" of 1314 to 1317, did not result in any appreciable reduction in population levels. They pale beside plague as a waster of human numbers. Even in modern European history, with the exception of the potato blight in Ireland in 1847, famines seem never to have taken exceptional tolls, and never to have reversed the dominant demographic trend. Nor do there seem to be direct linkages between famine and plague, malnutrition and disease. Under certain conditions, malnutrition can even work as a prophylactic against infection. Bacteria need many of the same nutrients as their human hosts. When those nutrients are lacking, the germs cannot multiply. It has even been claimed, although not convincingly proved, that persons prone to anemia — chiefly menstruating women and growing children — enjoyed a certain immunity against plague. The bacilli found insufficient free iron in the blood to support their own fast multiplication. Campbell is doubtless correct in his further conclusion: "none [of the fourteenth-century plagues] had anything whatever to do with the prevailing economic conditions. Plague is an exogenous variable and as such is neither easily nor happily accommodated within an exclusively Malthusian or Marxist interpretation of events."

There are also conceptual difficulties with the Malthusian argument. When is a community overpopulated? Presumably, when it fails to maintain some known standard of subsistence. But that is necessarily a relative, not an absolute measure, which will vary from community to community and from period to period. A count of the hearths of Tuscany at about 1300 makes the region appear very crowded indeed to a modern observer. But what did this mean in real terms? Many Tuscans went hungry, and many were undoubtedly malnourished. But somehow people managed to survive. Until the arrival of plague, the region held its numbers rather well.

Malthus, in sum, seems mistaken in his conclusion that populations grow relentlessly, and that violent adjustments downward have to occur. The medieval experience shows us not a Malthusian crisis but a stalemate, in the sense that the community was maintaining at stable levels very large numbers over a lengthy period. In Tuscany, under these crowded conditions, many lived in misery, but somehow they coped. Malthusian deadlock, rather than crisis, seems the more appropriate term to describe the demographic state of Europe before the epidemics.

A final weakness of the Malthusian interpretation is its failure to consider divisions within medieval society, especially between rich and poor. Surely rich and poor were not subject to the dearth of resources in the same way. Marxist critics in particular have dwelt upon this omission, even as they propose their own explanation for the crisis of the closing Middle Ages.

Marxism makes the balance of classes and the class struggle the chief motor of historical change. Marxist historiography has been from its origins antagonistic to Malthusianism in any form. Exploitation, not overcrowding, explains human misery, and insurrection, not contraception, is the right response. Among the chief architects and advocates of a Marxist interpretation have been an American, Robert Brenner, and a Frenchman, Guy Bois. In an article published in 1976 in the journal *Past and Present*, rich in theory though not in data, Brenner launched a spirited criticism of the Malthusian thesis. Basically he argued that the plague was common to all Europe, but social and economic changes were very different from one region to another. Malthus was not the master of the game; Marx was. Only social structure can explain the regional evolutions. Plagues came and went, but classes and their tensions remained. Late medieval society carried this mark, not the sign of the plague, upon its body.

Guy Bois, in a study of eastern Normandy in the late Middle Ages, published in 1976 and now translated into English, has developed the most elaborate Marxian model of social and political changes across the late Middle Ages. His data show the same shocking reduction in population with which we are familiar. Between the early fourteenth and the early fifteenth century, the population of eastern Normandy collapsed by 70 or 80 percent. Were plagues responsible? Bois thinks not. They occurred in the middle of the fourteenth century, and the population was still declining afterwards. They also occurred in the early sixteenth century, and the population continued to grow. They did not, in other words, redirect the dominant trends. The real driver in this demographic debacle was a crisis in the social order, what Bois calls the crisis of feudalism.

To understand that crisis it is necessary first to appreciate the "feudal mode of production," its characteristics and its contradictions. The basic unit of production in this feudal mode was the small peasant farm, worked with an essentially stagnant technology. The only growth the system allowed was extensive, that is, the expansion of the cultivated area and the multiplication of farm units. But growth under the feudal mode was subject to the law of diminishing returns. As cultivation extended onto poorer soils, so the returns to the average family farm necessarily diminished. In eastern Normandy, the lords monopolized political power and used it to extract rents from the peasants. But the peasants still controlled actual production and the distribution of the harvests. This was a fundamental flaw, or contradiction, in Marxist terminology, in the system. As peasant income diminished, they paid lower and lower rents; the support of their own families had first claim upon them. Initially, the lords did not suffer from declining per-family rents. The continuing expansion of the cultivated area and the multiplication of rent-paying units at first compensated for the lower rents that each family delivered.

But at a certain moment, which Bois dates to about 1315, the decline in per-family rents overcame the increase coming from the larger number of farms. From that moment on, the lords faced continuous shrinkage in the total revenues they collected. Bois calls this a "crisis of feudal rent," and claims it engendered a crisis of feudalism itself.

The lords had to seek alternate sources of revenue. They took to robbery and pillage—the direct expropriation of peasant wealth. They also hired themselves out as mercenaries. And they pressured their overlords, notably the king, to wage wars against their neighbors. In war they hoped to capture a wealthy opponent, hold him for high ransom, and thus repair their fortunes.

In sum, the crisis of feudalism provoked the interminable wars of the late Middle Ages, many of which were thinly disguised pillaging expeditions. But the waging of wars required that the king enlarge his powers and his fiscal resources. State taxes tended to replace feudal rents as the chief form of peasant expropriation. Military bands ravaged the countryside, and tax collectors took what the pillagers left behind. Little wonder, then, that the population collapsed, but this was the effect and not the cause of the crisis in feudalism.

Sensitive to class divisions, Bois's model offers a complex, subtle, and illuminating analysis of late medieval social trends in eastern Normandy. But it does not seem to be as free of Malthusian influences as the author contends. The balance between population and land determines per-farm productivity and the level of rents. Pressures against the land—must we not call them Malthusian?—lower farm productivity and directly engender the crisis in feudal rent. That crisis might be considered a Malthusian reckoning in another form. Bois even concedes that demographic movements seem to follow "a law of their own," and this seems tantamount to admitting that not even Marxist analysis can control the total picture.

Then, too, the crisis of feudalism might well be regarded as an appropriate model of social change in late medieval eastern Normandy. But what about other regions in Europe, such as Tuscany, which possessed very different economic and social systems? Tuscany, for example, included one of Europe's largest cities, Florence, which lived from international commerce, banking, and manufacture. Even its agriculture was very different from that found in Normandy. Did a crisis of feudalism occur there too? The merchant elites of Italy did not respond to falling agrarian rents by resorting to pillage and to mercenary service; they were in fact reluctant fighters. And yet the population movements in the two regions are very similar. What did the Florentine metropolis and the Norman villages truly share, except the experience of plague?

This then is how several historians have viewed the state of Europe before the plague. To my mind, the best reading of the evidence is the following. European population had grown to extraordinary levels during the central Middle Ages, but the result was not a Malthusian reckoning or crisis, but a deadlock. In spite of frequent famine and widespread hunger, the community in ca. 1300 was successfully holding its numbers.

It is likely that this equilibrium could have been maintained for the indefinite future. It is likely too that the Malthusian stalemate might have paralyzed social movement and improvement. Then the plague struck. It appeared as an exogenous intervention; it owed its power not to social factors but to its still obscure nature. And it devastated Europe. But in spite of the havoc it wrought, it did a service to the West. It broke the Malthusian deadlock that medieval growth had created and which might have impeded further growth in different forms. It guaranteed that in the generations after 1348 Europe would not simply continue the pattern of society and culture of the thirteenth century. It assured that the Middle Ages would be the middle, not the final, phase in Western development.

Edward Miller and John Hatcher

Medieval England: Rural Society and Economic Change, 1086–1348

The closing chapter of Edward Miller and John Hatcher's *Medieval England: Rural Society and Economic Change, 1086–1348* points to the ability of Europeans to adapt to changing demographic and economic circumstances. Hatcher and Edwards explore the consequences of the readjustment of population and resources brought on by famine. They argue that while certainly devastating in the short term, these shifts actually helped to set Europe on a different economic path. In the years following the famines of 1315 to 1317, they argue, landowners became increasingly flexible in their management of their resources, adapting to the markets for land and commodities. Peasants in this period enjoyed rising wages that in turn may have given them improved buying power, thereby stimulating the production of certain goods for the market. Ultimately, they contend, these and other

Source: Edward Miller and John Hatcher, *Medieval England: Rural Society and Economic Change, 1086–1348* (London, NY: Longman, 1978), 240–251.

changes created a more diverse economy by the mid-fourteenth century, one better prepared to meet the challenges that came in the aftermath of the Black Death.

When, after a series of melodramatic events, the young Edward III was put in the place of his father in January 1327, economic as well as political troubles lay in the background of the succession crisis. There had been famines in the previous decade; there had been disastrous attacks of livestock diseases; and landowners, or at least some of them, were restricting the scale of their entrepreneurial activity and the rate of their investment in maintenance and improvements. Nor were troubles confined to the agrarian sector. The wool trade, England's greatest trade, which had reached its highest level in the first decade of the new century, had subsequently suffered extreme vicissitudes mainly through government intervention aimed at political or diplomatic advantage. In towns, too, there were many signs of underemployment and the constitutional crisis of 1326–27 was accompanied and preceded by urban social movements indicating an underlying malaise in various places. One chronicler of the times was filled with despair: "Alas, poor England! You, who once helped other lands from your abundance, now poor and needy are forced to beg."

The long-term significance to be attributed to the tendencies evident as the second quarter of the fourteenth century opened is not easily determined. In a sense what happened in those years, catastrophic as events appeared to contemporaries, was overtaken by later events more catastrophic still, which lingered longer in popular memory and have been correspondingly more influential in shaping the views of historians. Of these the most important by far was the coming of plague in 1348. At the same time even the fullest appreciation of the immediate and longer-term consequences of the Black Death does not necessarily mean that we must discount the effects of circumstances a generation and more earlier. True, there had been famines and harvest failures before 1315–17, and the dearth of 1258 provoked lamentations as eloquent as those of Edward II's biographer from the chroniclers of that time. There had also been earlier outbreaks of disease amongst livestock like the "common mortality" that afflicted the sheep flocks of Holderness in the 1280s. King John, too, had manipulated the wool trade before Edward I did so and the social conflicts in London in 1263–65 had been not dissimilar in intensity to those of 1326–27. None the less, certain basic changes in the English economy do appear to be taking place in the generation around 1300 and to have generated something like a new economic balance in the two or three decades before 1348. These changes and that balance are the proper conclusion of this study of the central Middle Ages.

Land and People

Many influences governed the economic developments of the twelfth and thirteenth centuries, but it has been a central argument of this book that the growth of population occupied a key place in the successive transformations which turned King William's England into the England which faced the famines of the early fourteenth century. No one writing in the midst of the great drought of 1976 will be inclined to underrate the disastrous effects that exceptional and "accidental" weather conditions can have; and in an underdeveloped society those effects were obviously far more severe than in a society equipped with modern resources and techniques, and with access to world markets. There are, however, many indications that the multiplication of people, a constant theme in English history from a time well before 1066 to around 1300, was by the latter date creating basic structural problems. These problems, as we have seen, had numerous manifestations. High (and rising) charges were paid for holdings which were often too small to sustain a family; in many cases cultivation had spread to poor and intractable soils; in some places grain-growing had expanded excessively at the expense of stock-farming; on the whole attempts to increase crop yields had failed and it seems probable that, even on demesnes, they had sometimes declined; and rising prices, sluggish wages and the difficulty of finding work made the rewards of labour low. In the last resort the mortalities that accompanied dearths, and above all the moralities of 1315–17, were the measure of this increasingly unfavourable balance of land and people.

At the same time the consequences which flowed from changes in this balance were sometimes contradictory and sometimes differed at different points in time. If we start at the beginning, King William's England was already dominated by landowning classes relying principally on the rents and labour of the dependent peasantry to provide them with income and produce. For the ensuing three or four generations these landowning classes were able, for the most part, to support or even improve their exalted life by a mainly passive exercise of their rights and powers. They managed their manors indirectly through lessees; they even let some demesne lands go and, with them, some of the labour services that had been needed for their cultivation. They were, in other words, for the most part rentiers in an old style inherited from the Saxon past. It was their good fortune that the apparently steady growth of population and settlement in varying measure expanded their incomes by augmenting the acres of land and numbers of men subjected to their lordship.

The great inflation of the years around 1200 and the subsequent steady, if less rampant, inflationary trend upset this balance. Cash incomes from rents and from leases were held down by custom or contract and, at least in the short run, fell rapidly in real value under the impact of inflation. To escape the erosion of their incomes landowners were pushed into becoming entrepreneurs, making the thirteenth century the great age of direct demesne exploitation. Demesne land relinquished in the twelfth century was taken back into hand and sometimes new land was added to it; and labour on a large scale was mobilized to cultivate the lands of lords. *Famuli* and casual labourers in the employ of landlords also multiplied; at the same time obligations from which villeins had been released were often reimposed and the servile implications of villeinage were more stringently defined.

This "manorial reaction" took place in circumstances in which the tide was running for landlords: against a background of rising producer prices, expanding markets at home and abroad, and a continuing growth of population. About prices enough has been said in an earlier chapter; but for a proper understanding of the thirteenth-century agrarian situation the importance of increased outlets for agricultural products both in growing towns at home and in markets overseas can hardly be overstressed. No reader of manorial account rolls, when they begin to be available to us in that century, can fail to note the large contribution made by grain sales (mainly in home markets) and wool sales (mainly for export) in the structure of seignorial revenues. In this sense commerce was not so much a solvent of manorialism and serfdom in this period as it has sometimes been thought to be: it encouraged an expansion of demesne production and the intensification of servile obligations on which, in part, demesne production depended.

The gains that accrued from commerce, however, are not the only lesson the account rolls teach. The abundant supply of labour, whether that of villeins willing to accept the onerous services incident on their holdings or that of wage workers receiving payments which tended to fall in real terms, is a pointer to a population continuing to grow at a rate which increasingly outstripped the gains of colonization. At the same time the gains of colonization and desperate competition for land pushed up the income lords could expect from rents and other charges. This feature of the landlord's boom of the thirteenth century offered an alternative to the way of entrepreneurship into which the great inflation had pushed so many lords of manors. At the very least they were encouraged to discard less productive demesne land and to cease to cultivate distant manors that were difficult to manage effectively. In the process the peasant's share of the marginal soils that had increasingly been brought into cultivation was probably unduly magnified as worn-out demesne acres were added to marginal peasant assarts.

Increasing mortality in the villages was merely one aspect of the economic problems which reached an acute stage as the thirteenth century closed and the fourteenth century opened. Peasant impoverishment implied a low level of domestic purchasing power, for most Englishmen were peasant villagers; and that, in turn, cramped the continued potentialities for expansion in the urban sectors of the economy. The England of 1300, moreover, had few manufactured exports, and the fact that export outlets were repeatedly interrupted by war and political interference had the effect of further undermining the expanding markets on which the earlier phases of the landlord's boom had depended. In these circumstances landowners were less assured that enterprise would be profitable, with the result that the temptation to surrender to the clamour of would-be tenants became more compelling. Especially on less profitable manors or manors presenting management difficulties some lords by the opening of the fourteenth century were displaying a more and more positive "preference for rents." The attraction of this policy was that, given the intensity of the demand for land, the rental value of land might be high.

Adjustment in the Villages

Such demographic data as exist for the late thirteenth and early fourteenth centuries has not yet been systematically investigated; but from a sample of Winchester manors we have evidence of mortality rates which may perhaps be regarded as symptomatic, though not necessarily as typical. The numbers of heriot payers in the famine years of 1315–17 averaged 142 annually compared with 95 in the three years of above average death rates in the previous decade and 48 in the worst years of the late 1270s. These figures, of course, appear low when set against a death toll of 1,429 in the same manors in 1349, topping 200 at Waltham alone or Wargrave alone and at Taunton exceeding 700; but that does not make the mortality of 1315–17 insignificant. The famines of these years were an episode in an era of high mortality that persisted until the Black Death raised it to heights beyond all precedent. The precise significance of the trends in mortality evident on these Winchester manors can only be judged from indirect indicators, but it seems probable the long upward movement of the national population curve was first checked and then reversed. It looks as though the increased death rate may have reduced, however marginally, the intensity of consumer demand, and done something to damp down both competition for land and competition for employment by stabilizing or thinning the number of competitors. It was by no means the only influence at work, but, in the establishment of a new equilibrium in the thirty years or so before the "great pestilence" came, the modified ratio of men to land was of prime significance.

The response of landlords to the new circumstances were very varied, but in general their watchwords were retrenchment, endeavours at cost cutting and the concentration of demesne enterprise where it would yield the best returns. Those of them who cultivated their demesnes directly faced from the 1320s onwards a tendency for most producer prices to fall and for real wages to rise somewhat above the miserable levels that had prevailed before 1315. On the other hand the demand for land among the peasantry, although less undiscriminating than it had been a generation before, was still keen enough to maintain, nearly maintain or occasionally increase the price at which it could be let. In these circumstances there was every encouragement for the prudent landlord to divest himself of his less productive demesnes, so that the contraction of seignorial enterprise continued and was even speeded up in the second quarter of the fourteenth century. The Bishops of Winchester reduced their demesne acreage by a further 17 per cent in the period 1325–49. By 1349 not far short of 5,000 acres had been shed by the bishop's home farms over a period of some eighty years.

The contraction or abandonment of demesne production mitigated for landlords the effects of rising labour costs; and by concentrating cultivation on the better land or by increasing the acreage under legumes they might also be rewarded by a modest improvement of yields. The principal recourse of landowners in this period, however, may have been a new flexibility, a willingness to shift their responses to circumstances, showing how well they had learned to gauge the market for commodities and the market for land. They not only let land go when its cultivation seemed unprofitable: they switched their options as the probable advantage changed or appeared to change, or sometimes as financial necessity dictated. In 1330 a need for cash forced the Abbot of Ramsey to lease two of his wealthiest manors, but in the 1340s an improvement in the prospect of profits caused land to be drawn back into demesne on some manors and more intensive cultivation to be resumed. On the Titchfield Priory manors, while a reduced arable demesne was kept in good heart by the application of marl, manure and seaweed, the sheep flock was built up again after disastrous losses in 1315–17; and at Langenhoe in Essex Lionel de Bradenham adjusted his grain crops both to the quality of his land and the state of the market. At the same time Lionel increased his income from rents by substituting new leases for old customary contracts: like most lords of manors he was by no means solely an entrepreneur.

Seignorial estates faced many problems in the post-famine decades. By and large the cost of labour and the profits of cultivation had turned somewhat against them; and the charge of rebuilding flocks and herds, to say nothing of plough teams, decimated by disease forced many to discriminate between investment that could be undertaken or that might be postponed. On the other hand, there are signs of a new equilibrium being achieved by the 1330s and 1340s even if, as on the Ramsey estates, "the attraction which agrarian production held for the convent was now restricted to even fewer manors, and to still less demesne land on these manors, than in the first decade of the century." The new balance achieved through retrenchment, however, also depended in a measure on the continued demand of the peasantry for land—both established tenant holdings and relinquished demesne acres—and their willingness to pay for it. This is an area in which there are many seeming contradictions, although here once again there are some signs that a new balance was being struck.

The evidence that some land was lapsing from cultivation altogether, or at least from arable cultivation, has already been discussed, and also the unwillingness of tenants except under compulsion to take up land of poorer quality. These features of the land market, together with the tendency of prices to drift downwards and wages upwards, may reflect a less intense demand from a population reduced, or at the very least stabilized, by rising levels of mortality. At the same time, this summary of the situation and the influences which shaped it are in certain respects inadequate. There are clear signs in some places of a very active peasant land market; and on the whole one gets the impression (and until further research is undertaken it can be little more than an impression) that rent levels were reasonably well maintained, although some other customary charges may have been mitigated. Indeed, as we have seen, the Langenhoe tenants were even willing to accept higher leasehold rents in place of their old customary renders. In some parts of the country, too, continued pressure on resources is suggested by continued assarting.

The seeming contradiction between abandoned tenements and an active peasant market for land can, in the light of our present knowledge, only be resolved by hypothesis. We have already suggested that one explanation may be that the peasantry were now better placed to show discrimination between better and worse land. In some districts, this capacity to choose may have owed something to the readier availability of alternative earnings from textile manufacture, mining and the like. Perhaps, too, the improvement of real agricultural wages made life as a labourer more acceptable to some, thus relieving pressure on the land. Most important of all may have been the not inconsiderable amount of land of which lords divested themselves. Admittedly not all the land discarded by lords was taken up by tenants, but a very large part of it was: for, even if it was not the best land, it might well be acceptable to peasants who were insulated from some of the rising costs (especially for labour) which demesne cultivation entailed. Admittedly, too, the letting out of demesne land was not something new in the second quarter of the fourteenth century; but now it was taking place after the prolonged upward movement of population had been checked or even reversed. For that reason putting demesne land on the market is likely to have represented a net addition to the resources available to the peasantry and to have modified the element of desperation that appears to attend the search for land of the late thirteenth-century peasant.

The process of adaptation to new circumstances, of course, was an imperfect one. Lords did not easily, after so many generations when conditions had been consistently in their favour, take easily to a situation in which they were favourable no longer. On the Winchester estates net profits which had fluctuated between £3,050 and £5,350 in the years 1221–83 were down to the £3,700 to £3,800 bracket in the years 1335–44. The achievement of this much stability of income represented a not unsuccessful adjustment to new conditions, but others may have been less fortunate or less skilful. The religious houses in Bishop Grandisson's diocese of Exeter in 1338, for example, appear almost uniformly beset by difficulties. While landlords found that the days of easy profits were over, the fact that the peasantry were still vulnerable to influences beyond their control is demonstrated by the impact on their fortunes and the viability of some of their holdings of Edward III's measures to finance his war with France. The new equilibrium, moreover, might have proved temporary. The check to population growth might conceivably have been impermanent, like the consequences of the mortality caused by the famine in 1258. In the event this did not happen, so that the long-term growth of population was not resumed; and the influence that would have had on the somewhat more equitable distribution of land that underlay the new equilibrium was never put to the test. Instead, the second quarter of the century closed with the coming of the "great pestilence" involving mortality of a different order to that occasioned by any preceding catastrophe. In its wake there was no question either of preserving intact the economic pattern coming into being after 1325 or of returning to that prevailing before 1315.

Manufacturers and Traders

Adjustment to new circumstances in the decades before the Black Death was not restricted to villages: in some ways the tentative and faltering changes that were taking place in other sectors of the economy were even more significant. These changes have been even less adequately explored than the short-term movements in the rural economy, but in one or two areas their direction appears clear enough. This is most obviously true of the manufacture of textiles. The English industry, and in particular its urban branch, had been progressively undermined during the thirteenth century by Flemish competition both in the foreign markets it had been serving in 1200 and in the English home market itself. By the opening of the fourteenth century, however, the tide was turning and, in East Anglia, the south and south-west, and the West Riding, a mainly country industry was producing relatively cheap kerseys and worsteds and aylshams and mendips on an increasing scale. At the same time the revival did not stop in the villages or villages growing into little country towns. It also touched Norwich and Colchester, Salisbury and Winchester, Beverley and York; and it was in no small measure due to the growth of its cloth industry that Coventry in 1362 was in a position to bear the cost of building its "formidable town wall." By this time, moreover, revival had extended to the manufacture of broadcloths as well as cheaper fabrics; furthermore, imports of foreign textiles were down and English cloth had captured both a large part of the home market and new markets overseas. In the 1350s England imported only about half the 12,000 cloths imported by foreign merchants alone at the beginning of the century (the proportion had been even lower in the late 1330s when war made trading hazardous); and on the eve of the Black Death exports of broadcloths and worsteds combined amounted to the equivalent of 5,000–6,000 cloths a year. Industrial growth since the opening of the century was already significant even if it was not yet spectacular.

The extent to which similar development was present in other fields of industry is harder to determine and more difficult to measure. There are some indications of increased activity in the coal-mining region along the Tyne: for coal was exported to Pontoise in 1325 and to provision Scottish castles in 1338; Tynemouth Priory was opening new collieries at Elswick in 1330 and 1334; and in 1356 the Bishop of Durham leased out five mines at Wickham for £333. 6s8d a year. True this figure is quite unusual: the £2–£5 yearly for leases of the Elswick mines is far more typical; but coal, too, was appearing on the industrial horizon. About tin-mining we are better informed. Production in Cornwall had begun to increase at the opening of the century and had almost reached a million pounds annually by 1323–24. Thereafter there was "a burst of exceptional expansion" and output in 1331–32 reached the unprecedented level of 1,643,000 lb. Once again new opportunities were being grasped in the pre-plague generation.

Whether or not the same was true in the "typical" industries of the time—the handicrafts that served the ordinary and everyday needs of Englishmen—is far more difficult to determine and certainly must await closer study than has yet been undertaken of short-term movements in the prosperity of English towns. The upward trend in the number of freemen admitted at Colchester in the 1330s and 1340s and at York in the period 1307–49 is possibly significant in this connection; but the records of admissions to town franchises were governed by rules that are ill-known and by changes in qualification that make them a dangerous guide. At best the data drawn from them indicate that, at least in some towns, a recovery or modest advance of fortunes is not out of the question.

If the bread-and-butter industries directed towards the domestic market are in large measure unknowable, so for the most part is the course of domestic trade. On the other hand, the customs accounts enable us to follow in somewhat more detail the fortunes of some branches of overseas trade. The clearest indications relate to the wool trade: the total volume of exports fell away (as did the corresponding import of manufactured textiles) from the medieval peak of over 41,000 sacks annually in the years 1304–09 to around 24,000 sacks in the years 1333–42. Secondly, the share of English merchants in this trade, which may already have increased substantially over the previous thirty years, increased from around 55 per cent in the early years of the century to around 65 per cent in the 1330s. It looks as though the export boom with which the century opened was English-led and that, in the subsequent shrinkage of wool exports, English merchants retained a much larger share than foreign interests. Other branches of trade display a certain consistency with these trends. In the new export trade in English cloth English merchants shipped four-fifths or more of the textiles exported; and English gains in the Bordeaux wine trade matched gains in the wool trade. Wine imports appear to have been remarkably stable down to the opening of the Hundred Years War, but at the beginning of the fourteenth century Gascon importers handled at least two-thirds of the 20,000 tuns or so coming in each year. By the mid-1320s, on the other hand, Gascon imports had been halved and the trade was now preponderantly in denizen hands. In 1330 the King's Butler's view was that Englishmen were importing as much in one year as the Gascons did in two.

The new economic equilibrium of the 1330s and 1340s, then, is not something confined to the countryside: there are also signs that a change in the structure of the medieval economy was taking place. In the first place a measure of industrial development both in town and country was diversifying, however modestly, the employment opportunities available. Secondly, in a country in which external commerce had been dominated by the foreign merchant, denizens were assuming the dominant role and, in the process, generating resources of commercial capital of a new magnitude. Indeed, in order to finance the French war in the 1340s, Edward III, after he had ruined his foreign merchant-bankers, turned to Englishmen for banking services for the provision of which the monarchy had relied upon Italians since the time of Edward I. The English wool merchants and others who responded got little joy from their new role, but the economic changes of the previous generation had done much to make it possible for them to assume it.

Conclusion

. . . The overcrowding of villages and even the poverty of villagers may have contributed to new economic developments. The poverty of villagers first created a market for "slump" products like worsteds and other cheaper fabrics, often country-made, the manufacture of which initiated the revival of the textile industry. True, the subsequent expansion of this industry, and of the commercial stake of English merchants in it, may have owed even more to the opening of new export opportunities and a measure of improvement in the purchasing power of which ordinary Englishmen disposed by the second quarter of the fourteenth century; but the growth of cloth manufacture, and of mining and other country crafts, was also largely made possible by the reserves of cheap labour available in so many villages. When, in the generation preceding the Black Death, village populations had ceased to grow the country labourer may even have had a genuine degree of choice in some places between industrial and agricultural employment. If that were so, it would help to explain the tendency for agricultural wages to rise at this time; and the complaint of the bailiffs of the Winchester manors in 1332, for all the reduction of demesne acreages, that reapers, mowers and harvest workers were in short supply seems to suggest that the wheel had come at least part circle.

In this context, one is also bound to ask what the effects may have been of some improvement of the real wages earned by labourers and some shift of productive assets to the peasantry. In this area there is no possibility of measuring or calculating; but in principle the effect must have been to increase the purchasing power available in the rural mass market. The development of rural industry, by diversifying countrymen's sources of earnings, would have the same effect. These influences are likely to have been marginal, and they were probably offset at least in part by Edward III's taxes; but they are a possible explanation of some signs of urban recovery in the decades before 1348, and they may have done something to encourage a growth of manufacture and mining.

. . . In brief, the economy of the later Middle Ages developed on the more diversified foundations which were being established during the pre-plague generation. Those foundations, moreover, were more soundly laid than the bases of the older medieval economy that made its failings manifest in the famines and mortalities at the opening of the fourteenth century.

William Chester Jordan

The Great Famine: Northern Europe in the Early Fourteenth Century

Where the previous two selections have looked at the demographic and economic response to crisis, respectively, the selection from William Chester Jordan's book analyzes the social reaction to the preplague crisis of famine. He analyzes the ability of communities to support their inhabitants during times of social and economic stress. He finds, for example, evidence of charitable giving and institutions designed to meet the dire circumstances brought on by famine. It is revealing that this support came from both lay and religious sources. At the same time, however, there were undeniable fissures in the social fabric. Moneylenders (notably both Christian and Jewish) preyed upon those in need. The evidence of migrant poor in this period also suggests that traditional charitable mechanisms could not meet demand. Finally, crime was on the rise in the period following the famine. Having established this context, Jordan turns to the link between famine, morbidity, and fertility. While the population was weakened by food shortages and "strange diets," the long-term fertility rates were not adversely affected.

Despite measures to contain the effects of the famine, the calamity severely tested social cohesion. Many rural people—chiefly the poor— suffered the worst consequences of deprivation. Of course, the story is not one of unrelieved strife. Cooperation, *communitas*, was a deeply treasured ideal among villagers. The real question is to what extent cooperation and mutual support could avert a fundamental breakdown in social relations or delay the worst effects of the harvest shortfalls—malnutrition, disease, and death. In this chapter we begin with the question of community and its limits, and we conclude with the evidence on rural demography that scholars have collected in attempting at least a partial answer to this question.

Source: William Chester Jordan, *The Great Famine: Northern Europe in the Early Fourteenth Century* (Princeton, NJ: Princeton University Press, 1996), 108–113.

Community and Its Limits

The belief was widespread that churchmen should offer themselves in some sort of expiatory gesture for their communities in the period of dearth. Drawing on centuries of precedents the Benedictine monasteries of Saint-Faron of Meaux and Sainte-Colombe of Sens worked out a spiritual union in the crisis whereby common masses and common prayers were undertaken on behalf of the communities (many of them rural) for which they had a spiritual responsibility. This informal bond was formalized in 1324. The abbey of Saint-Denis-en-Broquerie in Hainaut and its brother house Saint-Ghislain published their formal prayer union slightly earlier, on 23 June 1321. For Saint-Ghislain this was one of a number of such spiritual unions that seemed appropriate in these difficult times.

In Normandy and the Beauce processions of barefoot canons and priests took place on saints' days and Sundays; the clerics implored God, as their counterparts in the cities would do, to reestablish the normal rhythms of weather. In the archidiaconate of Xanten, as early as the summer of 1315, a deeply scarred rural society was turning to the multiple display and parading of relics, with prayers and fasting; the local count, Dietrich of Cleves, added his voice to the clergy's in supporting these efforts, which he acknowledged were for the "common utility of all."

Most historians have been skeptical concerning the translation of the virtue of cooperation into practice, despite evidence like the well-orchestrated and ecclesiastically controlled processions in Normandy and western Germany. Guy Fourquin asserted that it was the lower orders who took action in their own name. "Chiliastic hopes," he wrote, "became extremely strong" during the famine, "and whole processions of penitents sprang up. Prophecies foretelling a blood-bath and the massacre of the clergy and the powerful were rife." These are exaggerations, but they should alert us to the fact that the surviving evidence does at least lend itself to apocalyptical interpretations. Indeed, it takes considerable effort to read any behavior during the crisis as evidence of philanthropy in the wide meaning of that term. Or, put another way, there is very little unequivocal evidence of philanthropy. And yet the situation was neither black nor white.

Consider charitable giving. Some producers, like monasteries, whose ideological justification for existence was their provision of religious and material sustenance to the poor in spirit and the poor in goods, did not benefit from the high prices. Where they did not benefit, they could not (or chose not to) enhance the eleemosynary dimension of their activities. Curiously, their restraint has sometimes been taken by revisionist scholars as evidence against the traditional picture of the famine's severity on the principle that if they did not give much more alms, there were not a great many more people who needed alms. Surely the more appropriate conclusion is that the effects of the famine to some degree cut across class lines. Thus Bolton Priory, which was ultimately bankrupted in the agrarian crisis, actually held alms steady in the first year or so; but it felt compelled to cut its charity by almost 90 percent as the famine endured.

Where the impact on institutions was less severe and perhaps where, as in heavily populated rural districts, the manifestations of distress were particularly visible, the monasteries came through with increased alms. In part, one can suppose, their decision was intended to keep the rural workforce in place. In part, it was an effort to forestall theft and acts of violence. But there is no reason to deny the possibility that theirs was also—as they said it was—a genuine response to suffering. Such charity and reassuring gestures to the needy were said (in part self-servingly, of course) to have drained the treasuries of Cistercian abbeys in France "during the period of hunger and dearth" when "many more persons than in prosperous times flocked to the abbeys of the order for alms and shelter."

Certain monastic houses made available or constructed special facilities to care for the rustic poor, while existing local charitable institutions, like scattered rural almshouses and hospitals, were mobilized for the eleemosynary effort of baking and distributing bread. A giant pot was made in 1315 for Abbot Eylard of the Cistercian abbey of Aduard near Groningen, and in it beans and vegetables were cooked daily for the poor who were suffering from hunger during the famine. The pot became legendary: for centuries it was shown to visitors, who marveled at its size; the *ketel* seems still to have been on display like a quasi-relic at the Holy Ghost Hospital of Groningen as late as the eighteenth century.

Lay lords were not immune from such sentiments or efforts, although it is always possible to give a materialistic or selfish interpretation of their actions as well. The lord of Dry Drayton in Cambridgeshire, the historian of that village writes, "as a matter of grace, to help the tenants in their poverty conceded to his tenants half of his fold-right" in the time of the famine. A more cynical interpretation might make a case for his trying to buy off the possibility of raids on his granaries and herds.

Parallel to charity went credit. I have argued elsewhere that it is sometimes difficult to distinguish the two, even though the received opinion appears to be that the class which provided credit to people in desperate circumstances like the agrarian crisis before us were not likely to be considered charitable by their debtors. No- or low-interest loans had a better chance of being regarded as evidence of decency than the high-interest loans typical of consumption lending in the Middle Ages. Regrettably, we know little about friendly lenders, those "hoping for nothing again" (Luke 6.35).

A subset of creditors, pariah group lenders, always gets a bad press, deservedly or not. Certain secular rulers felt the need to allow Jews to settle (and presumably provide credit to their hard-hit subjects), as Count John of Luxembourg did on 29 June 1316. Certain clergy, meanwhile, took it as their special task to condemn and try to forbid the business dealings of Jews with Christians in the famine, as evidence (dated 13 May 1320) from Aschaffenburg and Babenhausen in the hinterland of Mainz testifies. In France there is also evidence that the crown cracked down on Jewish "usury" in the famine years, but the French case is complicated by a number of factors. Jews had been readmitted to France in 1315, nine years after what was supposed to have been the commencement of their perpetual exile from the kingdom. There was a special provision in the charter of readmission that granted them the privilege of pawnbroking at high interest. Indeed, it was this provision that constituted a significant motivation for their returning at all. The provision proved embarrassing, however, after the famine set in; so the crown took steps to protect people especially hard hit by the harvest and vintage shortfalls from losing their property to Jewish pawnbrokers. It looked very carefully into interest rates in order to see whether the permitted limits were being breached, and it authorized respites of up to a year in loan repayments for some debtors.

In any case, much of what the evidence reveals concerning money lending by Christians or by Jews, skewed as it is toward bad debts and sharp lenders, is not pretty. "At Wakefield and other manors" in England studied by Christopher Dyer, "a flurry of pleas of debt" occurred during the Great Famine, both because the poor needed to borrow to buy food and could not repay and, interestingly, because old debts were being called in by creditors who were themselves in a pinch. A similar flurry has been observed in the records of the manor of Brigstock in Northamptonshire: there the upsurge comes slightly later, in the immediate aftermath of the subsistence crisis, and may be a residual litigation effect of the methods employed by creditors to call in debts during the years of the famine itself. The will of a Lombard lender (a citizen of Asti) who was active in the rural country of Burgundy (Franche-Comté) has come down to us from the year 1317. Remorsefully, the moneylender forgave or restored any number of outstanding debts to individuals. What is more fascinating is that he made restitutions to all the villagers ("omnibus habitatoribus villarum") of "Lure, Magny, Vounans, Abbenans, Melesey, Bouhans, Amblans, Velotte, Molans, Pomoy, Villemefroy, Calemoutier, Lievans, Cere, Autrey, Noroy, Borrey, Openans, Oricour, Eprey, etc." The image of a whole region transformed by the economic crisis into debt peonage to a single man, an outsider, is arresting; the deathbed forgiveness of a whole region's debts—forgiveness arising from the fear of hell most probably—is equally so.

Local charity and credit—benign or with whatever intent—were modestly effective if limited responses to the deepening crisis in 1315 and even in early 1316. But by reporting the great and growing hordes of roving beggars in the latter year and during 1317, chronicler after chronicler unmasks the failure of local charity and credit to contain the misery. Ireland saw small holders, who were at first able to offer charity to those less prosperous, reduced to poverty themselves (war was a contributory factor); and then it saw these same people leave their homes to search the countryside for alms. Swedes, having suffered through two horrible years of natural disasters, 1315 and 1316, were subjected to the vagaries and terrorism of civil war thereafter: a funeral song for the princely victims of the strife laments in passing that the "rustics were impoverished" as a direct consequence.

In Germany there is evidence that the rural indigent were making their presence felt by massing near towns; an example is their (probably menacing) presence at the postern and on the thoroughfares of Magdeburg in 1316. A charter confirming the distribution of loaves and wine in January 1317 in the area near Mainz includes an extra provision (*hoc adiecto*) that foresees an increase in the number of people seeking free food. The charter tells how the same amount of food ought to be distributed, with the portions for each supplicant appropriately (*pro rata*) reduced. Further north, people from western Germany were begging at towns all along the Baltic, such as Lübeck in 1317.

The most intriguing possibility, hinted at before, is that elements of this massive vagabond population kept moving east and eventually became patriated in those eastern and southeastern German and western Polish lands being wrested from Slavic and/or pagan control. The pattern—famine in the west, migration to the east—was already familiar. This in part explains why, whatever level of village and homestead abandonment may have occurred in western Europe during the worst periods of the late medieval economic crisis, the regions beyond the Elbe, with far larger individual holdings, were almost always far less troubled by desertion. Little Poland, the area from Cracow to Warsaw and east, for example, saw the peak in the establishment of new franchises for small settlements in the years immediately after 1315. The granting of these franchises (the number was enormous) recognized the settlement of crowds of migrants who effectively turned villages into towns. What adds plausibility to the argument that it was the increasingly rootless, famine-motivated, and job-hungry immigrants from the west who helped swell these settlements is that the franchises under discussion were granted to vills "on important commercial routes." Insofar as the roving begging populations had a goal (and it is misleading to think of them as lacking in calculation), it was to present themselves at commercial centers either on the coast or, as that proved increasingly fruitless, in the more distant hinterlands of great cities like Magdeburg and Bamberg. Certainly, the memory persisted to the sixteenth century that the age of the Great Famine had seen many ruined householders from central and western Germany make their way "to foreign lands."

Another indicator of the inadequacy of local charity and credit in the countryside was the increase in lawlessness ("the rising tide of crime"), specifically theft, and the sharpening of the determination to pursue its prosecution to the fullest. Certainly German evidence coming from the lower Rhine region points in this direction, according to Günter Piecha. In France the government reluctantly recognized the crescendo of attacks on merchants as a national problem in 1317. In Lincolnshire the Great Famine is said by its most thorough and searching historian to have "led to a wave of petty crime," much of which resulted, not surprisingly, from the "inflated corn prices." The object of a great many of the thefts was grain. Edward Britton has amassed evidence showing that the Broughton (Huntingdonshire) "community [was] unusually sensitive to theft during this period [1315–1317], particularly if it involved food stuffs." Rarely anywhere in England was a jury lenient with thieves, even though their stealing was allegedly prompted or necessitated by hunger.

Of course, some of the theft was arranged by men not for their own consumption but so that they might benefit from the high prices for grain and flour. The granary of the Norman abbey of Cerisy was the target of a conspiracy of three clerics determined to steal its hoard of milled grain in 1316. Although as clerics they would probably not have been suspected in the first instance, suspicions for some reason did not turn to them.

They were arrested and imprisoned in the abbey, and were released only when they found sureties to stand stiff bail for them. Had they been successful and managed, undetected, to market a sizable portion of Cerisy's stock of grain through middlemen, they would have been rich and still respected men. As it was, their reputations were sullied forever.

It is virtually certain that this eruption of criminality was strictly circumscribed by type. The evidence is not good, despite Henry Lucas's assertion, for example, that murder rates went up sharply, for unfortunately he drew his conclusion from inadequate information in the Irish Annals. It is also not surprising that there are few unequivocal references to riots. By and large, riots were an urban, not a rural, form of protest. The two factors that might have laid the foundation for rural riots were the hordes of vagabonds and the presence of well-supplied garrison towns in the midst of rural poverty.

In general, groups of beggars became dangerous when they massed, and this, as we noticed earlier, usually took place near towns. The town administrators offered them a little food in return for their moving on, and ordinarily kept the gates closed. Violence during these encounters can hardly be classified as rural. It is true that there were great waves of rural (and urban) discontent in France in 1320 and 1321, inspired in part by calls for a Crusade and directed in part against Jews and lepers; it would not be irresponsible to see the agrarian crisis as an important preliminary to the initiation of the disturbances. In the end the violence that did erupt as groups of discontented rustics wandered about was vented in towns — and largely, for the malcontents ranged widely, in southern France and Aragon where the forces of the crown in both kingdoms finally suppressed them. We will look more closely at 1320 and 1321 in France in our discussion of urban life and the state, in Part III.

Garrison towns, too, may be better treated under the heading of urban life or the state's initiatives during the agrarian crisis, even though they were so often situated in otherwise remote, rural areas and had little of that autonomy and freedom of commerce we ordinarily associate with medieval towns. The embodiment of princely or lordly power in these garrison towns (English power in Wales, for example; German power in the Oderraum, for another) intimidated the often hostile and equally often ethnically distinct rural populations. We have already seen that to some extent the administrators of these towns went out of their way to maintain the loyal part of the rural workforce, by doles if necessary. With little or nothing to lose, natives who were suffering from the bad times and resented the incursions of English or Germans into their home-lands made war, not riots; "racist" literature calling for a kind of ethnic cleansing by war would achieve a terrifying sharpness on the frontiers of northern Christendom in the wake of famine.

Rural Demography

So far in this chapter and its predecessor we have seen that the ordinary rural population suffered by having to pay unwonted prices, sink beneath an ocean of debt, surrender tenements, and go begging. We have seen, too, strong indications that the allocation of available foodstuffs to the needy was quite limited. The upsurge in rural crime is one sign of this limitation. In part it was precisely because of this failure to protect the weakest and most vulnerable part of the population that a significant number of rustics also fell victim to the cruelest forms of physical distress. The most deeply affected regions in rural society were those which suffered under the combined burdens of dense population, harvest short-falls, murrains, and war—especially war. It is certainly likely that the rural population was already poised near the edge of subsistence. But we must not exaggerate the extent of extreme adversity: in the absence of one or more of the additional burdens listed, rural society in fact came through the crisis with a far less intensive demographic shock than was the case, as we shall later observe, in urban areas.

For rural society the most disturbing and extreme allegations are those contemporary or near contemporary reports about people so hungry that they were reduced to eating corpses. One report describes how people went about the cemeteries digging up the newly dead and cooking the soft flesh in skulls. Ordinarily historians regard such accusations (and the even more extreme ones associated with urban behavior during the famine) as fanciful. This is certainly a possibility. On the other hand, the accusations, when of a rural origin, are not random. They tend to come from areas most deeply traumatized by war: the one cited is from Ireland where in-cessantly vicious combat had impoverished the countryside. Moreover, similar behavior is documentable in recent war-intensified famines.

Even if we assume that this kind of behavior did not take place in rural areas during the Great Famine, there might still be legitimate reasons for observers to report such actions as facts. For example, in the best of times grave robbing occasionally took place. It occurred all the more fre-quently during famines, wars, and periods of high prices when thieves were attracted by the possibility of finding coins, jewelry, or quality cloth and grave clothes that could be pawned. In the morning light the physical evidence of grave robbing would look suspiciously like the desecration of cemeteries for food, especially if dogs or pigs disturbed the remains, as was their custom, after the thieves departed. The Irish report might point to grave robbing, the illumination from the torches used by the robbers as the plundered the corpses being interpreted, from afar, as the light from cooking fires. No great leap of the imagination would be required to identify a skull or two, lying on the freshly disturbed earth of the desecrated graves or near a burned-out torch, as cooking pots or dishes.

It goes without saying that the psychological predisposition of people to make and to believe such reports was closely tied to the severity of the crisis they were enduring. Yet however much the psychological stress that gave rise to these allegations needs to be emphasized, it is the biological stress on the rural population that has left the best evidence. We begin with a point made obvious by the intensity of the cost-of-living crisis described earlier, namely, that there was undoubtedly a precipitous decline in average consumption among the rural population from 1315 on. The worst-off in the countryside—the "many paupers"—are said to have "gnawed, just like dogs, the raw dead bodies of cattle" and to have "grazed like cows on the growing grasses of the fields." The author who vouchsafes this information was troubled at the report. Was it right to bequeath testimony of such degradation to the world?

His account points us in an important direction. Famine involves not only a net loss in the intake of food but also, granting the victims' attempts to make up the difference, the intake of "strange diets." Evidence from current famines attests to the presence in these diets of disagreeable plants, bark, leather, cloth, dirt, diseased animals and others—like grubs and vermin—not ordinarily considered palatable, and, in extreme cases, human cadavers. According to J. P. W. Rivers, the significance for bodily health of the "dietary deviations of famine . . . received surprisingly little scientific attention [until recently] and yet they are most important in dictating the pattern of nutritional disease that occurs." It is even possible to infer strange diets from the sorts of nutritional diseases that typify famines, because, however various these diets, they seem to have in common a short list of nutritional lacunae. Or, at least, the diseases associated with recent famines and the nutrient deficiencies accompanying them duplicate to a large extent the diseases (deduced from the recorded symptoms) in historical famines, thus adding weight to the notion that contemporary observers accurately recorded the adoption of strange diets, even if they laced their tales with picturesque metaphors (men "grazed like cows").

The phrase *strange diets* is a good one in that it captures both the psychological and the biological shock of being obliged to consume otherwise repugnant comestibles. But, to repeat a point made earlier, not all strange diets were equal. The range and opportunity of rustics to gather food only marginally inferior in quality if not in quantity to their normal diet far exceeded what the urban poor in big towns could command. And consequently the stress on the human body from strange diets was normally less severe in rural areas (always excepting those suffering the carnage of war) than in towns.

People in the countryside, therefore, were not in general "starving to death." (It is difficult to starve to death even when food intake is completely stopped, as in hunger strikes; and such complete cessation of eating is not characteristic of famines, when people look hard for something to eat.) A few may have eaten fungus-infested rye grain (the damp conditions encouraged the parasite's growth); those who did so probably suffered painful paroxysms, became manic, and died from ergotism, the disease known in the Middle Ages as sacred fire or Saint Anthony's fire. But the accumulated wisdom of the ages stopped most rural dwellers from utilizing spoiled rye, except in the most desperate circumstances.

Many, many more rustics, however, were *weakened* by the decline in caloric intake, by the diarrhea and dehydration that come from adopting strange diets, and perhaps by the decreased nutritional value of some of their substitute foods. People were to die in significant numbers partly because of the increase in morbidity (susceptibility to disease) that resulted from this weakening. War played its role here—both by bringing alien populations (with their own diseases) into contact with rural people whose resistance was low, and by the sheer acts of killing and burning stores. The lethargy (or weakening), the disease, and, indeed, the fear, in turn, brought diminished productivity among rural workers, reducing overall output and therefore spurring on price rises. Not all rustics suffered equally, of course. It was, rather, those among the rural poor whose food intake was most ruthlessly cut and whose diets were most radically altered for whom disease led to death. Presumably, this section of the population was composed principally of unemployed laborers and their families in the densest areas of rural settlement.

Modern work on the biology of malnutrition has established that the increase in morbidity is substantially more acute among newborns (even when they continue to nurse, for lactation, despite famine, persists in new mothers) and among young children than among adults, probably because of the low birth weight of infants and unintentional nutrient deficiencies in the food supplied to young, non-nursing children. What is adequate for an adult can be inadequate for a (potentially growing) child. By making energy intake so restricted and the dependence on strange diets so great, famine differs from traditional malnutrition in poor societies by extending the increase in morbidity, though not typically to the same high level, to members of additional age cohorts. After children, the next most vulnerable are the aged. Men are more vulnerable than women, who have more body fat and traditionally lighter energy needs. This vulnerability (differentially elevated levels of morbidity) is translated into differentially elevated levels of mortality when social-cultural factors fail to induce the leaders of communities and families to favor the distribution of scarce resources to the most vulnerable. The significance, in terms of our evaluation of the famine's demographic impact, is this. The evidence on morality, such as it is, almost all pertains to adult men. Where that evidence strongly hints at high mortality in *sedentary* populations, we must be prepared to imagine differentially higher, though unrecorded, mortality for newborns and children and perhaps for other groups as well. (High mortality among vagabond beggars, whose population is predominantly male, would not justify an extrapolation of this sort.)

To be sure, although medieval commentators, like modern historians, talk routinely about death by starvation, the former, unlike many of their modern counterparts, were always well aware that the nature of the deaths they were recording differed considerably from person to person. Opportunistic infections were at work, and although the chroniclers often used a simple singular word like plague or pestilence (*plaga, pestis, pestilentia*) to describe the situation in the Great Famine, other remarks make clear their recognition that more than one disease was causing the deaths. . . .

It is highly dubious, however, that the famine had a lingering negative effect on fertility. Recent famines have been followed after a couple of years by a return to normal fertility or even a decisive increase in the number of live births; very little convincing evidence exists showing any long-term impact on fecundity, the capacity for reproduction in the surviving adult population. These observations make the little information suggesting a rural "baby boom" after the ebbing of the Great Famine all the more persuasive. . . .

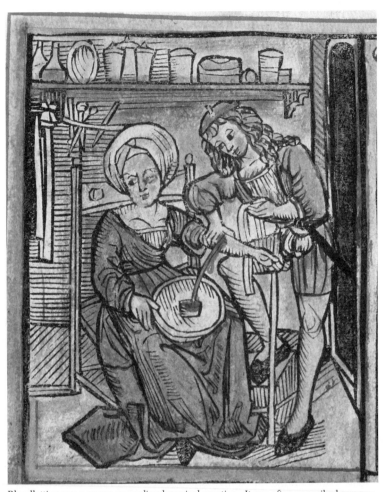

Bloodletting was a common medieval surgical practice. It was often prescribed as a means of restoring the patient's proper humoral balance. (University Library, Prague, Czech Republic/The Art Archive)

PART

II Medicine and Epidemiology

Perhaps the most immediate challenge medieval Europeans faced upon the arrival of bubonic plague was the effort to explain the disease medically and scientifically. University faculty, medical practitioners, and others grappled with a disease marked by alarming symptoms such as swollen lymph nodes and high mortality rates. Thus, there was an urgency to their response, since their contemporaries turned to them for explanations and guidance. Our best knowledge of how these practitioners responded comes from plague tractates or treatises written in the 150 years after the plague's arrival in Europe. The authors of these documents attempted to explain the disease's existence and to provide advice about prevention and cures. Yet, explicating the response of medical and scientific practitioners requires understanding the specific intellectual and conceptual framework that undergirded their investigations of the plague.

While recognizing God's dominion over nature, these writers also upheld a natural order governed by natural causes. They believed that the emergence of plague was due to not only supernatural but natural causes as well. They typically divided these causes into two categories: remote and near. In the case of bubonic plague some authors attributed the disease to the movement and conjunction of

43

the planets. A particularly famous example of this was the position of the University of Paris medical faculty that concluded that the particular conjunction of Mars, Jupiter, and Saturn in the heavens had created "a deadly corruption of the air."[1] These authors often linked near causes to terrestrial factors. Some, for example, attributed the disease to the release of constricted or putrefied air that was trapped in wells or beneath the ground. Others contended that putrid water or corpses left to rot could cause the plague through their ability to alter and thus contaminate the quality of the air.

Thus, many of these writers linked plague to a change in air quality. This is often referred to as the miasma theory. This theory blamed contaminated air for the disease's ability to infect individuals. There was another parallel—and even complementary—explanation for the disease's transmission, a theory of contagion. Although there is disagreement among scholars as to the origins and chronology of contagion theory, medical practitioners of the time also acknowledged the ability of the disease to pass from one individual to another. They believed that an infected individual could spread the disease through breath, perspiration, or even gaze. In this sense, medical authorities believed in transmission through contagion—although their ability to define the precise agent of this contagion was still centuries away from a modern germ theory.

Whatever its cause, source, or means of transmission, the authors recommended avoiding contaminated air and infected individuals whenever possible. If simply fleeing the disease was impossible, the authorities advised a host of preventive measures. In this advice they sought to (1) mitigate exposure to contaminated air and contagion, (2) alter the quality of contaminated air, and (3) improve the individual body's ability to ward off the disease. Limiting exposure to contaminated air could be achieved by avoiding contact with infected individuals and also carefully considering one's natural surroundings. The authors recommended avoiding proximity to standing water and other matter believed to create or harbor contamination. Many of the treatises also included instructions for purifying the air by burning certain herbs.

Finally, these writers offered advice on how to best prepare the body to ward off disease, advising moderation in eating habits, sleep,

[1]Cited in Rosemary Horrox, editor and translator, *The Black Death* (Manchester: Manchester University Press, 1994), 159.

and exercise. Anything indulgent (gluttonous consumption, too much sleep) or excessive (strenuous exercise that might open the pores, thus exposing the body to corrupt vapors) could put the individual at risk. They also practiced Galenic medicine, believing that the ability to ward off disease was particular to the individual. According to Galen (A.D. 129–199), a healthy body was the result of the proper balance of humors or bodily fluids (blood, yellow bile, black bile, phlegm). Each humor corresponded to one of the universe's basic elements and defining characteristics: fire/yellow bile (hot and dry), water/phlegm (cold and wet), earth/black bile (cold and dry), air/blood (hot and wet). The "healthy" balance of these humors could vary from individual to individual and was contingent on factors such as gender and geographical location. In treating sick individuals, medical practitioners sought to restore health by restoring the proper balance of humors. Tellingly, however, the plague treatises devote little space to a discussion of cures, typically concluding that plague usually resulted in death.

The excerpts here from John Henderson's essay, "The Black Death in Florence: Medical and Communal Responses," explore the practical application of these ideas about the plague and its transmission to the needs of a particular city. While medical authorities were often the first called upon to answer to the horrors of plague, many Europeans looked also to another form of authority: their municipal leaders. European cities sometimes had a limited warning of the plague's onset. Reports from neighboring towns and villages about the plague's advancing spread allowed municipalities to react before the plague arrived. Municipal leaders also adapted existing practices to the crisis of plague. Henderson is also interested in the extent to which medical and communal responses overlapped. He argues against the interpretation that medical responses were held back by a belief in corrupt air, whereas lay reactions embraced the concept of contagion and thus battled plague more effectively. Instead he finds that medical writers also recognized the role of contagion in the disease's spread.

It is impossible, however, to separate our understanding of how medieval Europeans responded medically to the onset of plague from modern debates about the identity of the disease itself. In recent years the one certain fact about the Black Death—that the disease that ravaged Europe in 1348 was bubonic plague—has come under scrutiny. Historians and other specialists have argued that the documentary evidence of the fourteenth century does not fit with our modern knowledge of the disease. The well-documented studies of bubonic plague from the late nineteenth and early twentieth centuries—the era in which the plague bacillus and the disease's vector, the rat flea, were first identified—provide a revealing counterpoint to the medieval descriptions of the disease's appearance, symptoms, and spread. To begin with, modern plague does not normally have a high mortality rate. Yet the fourteenth-century plague killed anywhere from one-third to one-half of the population in the areas it reached. The disease that hit Europe in the fourteenth century by all accounts moved swiftly, affecting almost all parts of Europe by the early 1350s (see map on page xxiii). Modern studies of bubonic plague, however, reveal that the spread of the disease is often quite slow. Further, as described in the Introduction, for plague to spread to a human population, its host population, the black rat, would have to experience a rapid dying-off or epizootic. While such epizootics are described in modern accounts of plague, they are absent from medieval descriptions. Such inconsistencies have prompted new hypotheses.

In the 1980s Graham Twigg, a zoologist, was one of the first researchers to comprehensively document the inconsistencies between the medieval and modern behavior of bubonic plague. Reviews of his work were skeptical at best and dismissive at worst. The ideas of Twigg and others have been given new life by the appearance in 2002 of The *Black Death Transformed: Disease and Culture in Early Renaissance Europe.* In this book the prominent medieval and early modern historian Samuel K. Cohn has boldly asserted, "The Black Death in Europe, 1347–1352, and its successive waves to the eighteenth century was any disease other than the rat-based bubonic plague" (1). The passage excerpted here draws on an earlier piece by Cohn that appeared in *The American Historical Review* and provides Cohn's analysis of some of the inconsistencies between modern plague epidemiology and medieval accounts of the disease.

From a different perspective, the article by Michael McCormick also seeks to reconcile modern evidence against its medieval counterpart. McCormick focuses on one of the key players in our understanding of medieval plague: the black rat (*Rattus rattus*). Because a population of black rats would be necessary to explain the presence of bubonic plague in western Europe, McCormick provides a meticulous study of black rats and their patterns of movement and settlement from ancient Roman times through the medieval period. He seeks to understand the arrival of black rats in Europe and how ecology, transportation, and other factors shaped their ability to survive there and possibly contribute to the outbreak of plague in the fourteenth century.

John Henderson

The Black Death in Florence: Medical and Communal Responses

In this passage Henderson describes the overlap between medical understandings of plague and the response of municipal officials. He first examines the belief among the medical community that the plague was the result of corrupt air. Yet, using the Consilia (plague tracts), he also demonstrates that medical practitioners also believed that plague could be transmitted between humans. Some medical writers spoke of "contagion" by which they meant the disease's ability to pass from one person to another—even when there was no physical contact. In linking these ideas to the response of the Italian municipal governments, Henderson finds these authorities basing their actions on the theory of corrupt air *and* contagion by a person's breath. They enacted measures such as denying entry into the city to individuals coming from infected areas, sealing up houses where infected individuals lived, street cleaning, and prohibiting certain trades that polluted the air (treating animal fur, slaughtering animals) within the city walls. All of these actions point to a preoccupation with protecting air quality and limiting contact between the sick and the healthy.

... The aim of the present chapter is to re-examine these sources within the context of medical theory, in order to tease out the relationship between physicians' beliefs about the causes, nature and methods of transmission

Source: John Henderson, "The Black Death in Florence: Medical and Communal Responses," in *Death and Towns: Urban Responses to the Dying and the Dead 100–1600*, ed. Steven Bassett (Leicester, Eng: Leicester University Press, 1992), 136–147.

of plague and the policies adopted by city governments. This may help us to reassess the ideas which underlie many recent studies of plague in late medieval Italy, and in particular the alleged gulf between medical and lay concepts of "pest." It has been suggested that doctors were regarded as blinded by their belief in corrupt air, while the laity were "in advance" because of their recognition of the importance of the role of "contagion" in spreading disease. Although we shall concentrate here on sources of the period around the Black Death, we hope that our discussion of the terminology used by contemporary sources will raise doubts about whether it is possible to make such a neat distinction between theory and practice even by the late fifteenth century when the "contagionist" views of Italian states are deemed to have been well-established.

Medical Theory of Plague

. . . Most plague Consilia conform to a common model: they begin with a section on causes, and go on to discuss methods of prevention and then the remedies. The last two parts were traditional; they followed the model of the *Regimen sanitatis* (Regimen for Health), and outlined ways to adapt the temperature of the atmosphere (by the use of draughts or fires) or of a patient's body (with diet or physical surroundings) so as to render those in "contaminated parts" less susceptible to disease.

From whichever part of Italy the Consilia originated they shared the Hippocratic and Galenic belief that plague or "pestilenzia" was caused by poisonous vapours which emanated from the atmosphere, as in the tractate by the Sienese Mariano di Ser Jacopo, a contemporary of the Black Death. Like many of his contemporaries he prefaced his Consilium with a dedication: "To the egregious Master Giovanni Bandini, a most famous doctor of law, Mariano di Ser Jacopo your citizen of Siena, physician and servant of your health." He then went on to summarize what his Classical authorities, "the oldest doctors of medicine," had to say on the subject:

> And all generally agree . . . that the pestilence derives from corrupt and poisonous air. . . . Do not marvel, therefore, that such air as a poisonous and infected substance should kill so many people in such a short space of time. . . . From this I conclude that the most secure remedy against the pestilence is to flee as early as possibly to a place with healthy air and leave behind the corrupt and infected air. And I have reached this conclusion in the following way. If you give your mouth a poisonous drink, the best and most healthy remedy which one can think of is immediately

Standing water.

to remove and take out of your mouth the drink. In short, to remove the cause is to remove the effect of the original agent.

For Ser Mariano and his contemporaries pestilence was caused by malign vapours emanating from lakes and bogs, though first causes were invoked to explain the appearance of an epidemic at a particular time. The wrath of God at the sins of Mankind often provided the main motor force, followed by the influence of conjunctions of planets, and especially Mars and Saturn; however, this did not dominate discussion of causes, as in the case of the famous contemporary *Compendium de Epidimia* of the Parisian Faculty of Medicine. The corrupt air could also be released from below the earth's surface by earthquakes, together with all manner of vile reptiles such as toads and snakes, reminiscent of the ingredients of the witches' stew in *Macbeth*. Contemporary chroniclers provided fuel for this argument; they recorded that the Middle East and then Italy had suffered from a series of earthquakes over the previous year. The chronicler of nearby Bologna also claimed that in the East in 1347 "it had rained an enormous quantity of snakes and serpents." Finally, the corrupt fumes could be spread to higher ground by wind for, as Tommaso del Garbo says in his tract, "Thus it is from the mutations of the air that many and varied infirmities of our body proceed, as have our authors stated clearly and as we doctors say continuously." In this way healthy places with high altitudes could become infected.

Although these ideas are drawn from plague tracts, they are not specific to plague; they formed the basis for the general theory of disease throughout the later Middle Ages and derive from the Hippocratic and Galenic traditions with the additional influence of Arabic medicine through Avicenna. In Italy this continuity of ideas can be traced from the three extant treatises written in central Italy in the mid-fourteenth century (by Mariano di Ser Jacopo, Tommaso del Garbo and Gentile de Foligno), to late fifteenth-century writers such as Michele Savonarola of Ferrara and the Neoplatonic doctor Marsilio Ficino. Even in the eighteenth and nineteenth centuries, when many believed that disease was spread though contagion, there remained traditionalists who were willing to engage in fierce debate in defence of the superiority of miasmatic theories.

One of the problems when using Consilia to discuss the Black Death is that their authors were not particularly interested in describing diseases. Indeed the terms used by these writers—*epidemia, pestilenzia* or *peste*—refer to general categories of diseases as described in the Corpus of "our authors" of Classical Greece and Rome. It is therefore difficult for us to distinguish between the specific advice for plague and that given for other sicknesses. This stemmed from the nature of a Consilium, which traditionally had been intended to enshrine the recommendations of an authoritative consultant to a patient's physician.

Even by the late fifteenth century, after well over 150 years' experience of plague, such Consilia contained only marginally more information about the nature of pest. For example, Marsilio Ficino's *Consilio contro la pestilenzia* of 1478 lists a collection of symptoms with which pestilence was associated: continuous high fever which worsened as the illness took hold, breathlessness, slow pulse, general heaviness, delirium, bloodshot eyes and torpid urine. Most of these symptoms are no more specific than those associated with any acute illness. The reason for this lack of specificity is that doctors were less interested in the symptoms of a patient than in their own diagnosis and in giving advice on how best to avoid catching the disease.

One of the most significant passages in Tommaso del Garbo's *Consilio contro alla peste* of 1348 related to advice to all those who visited the *ammorbati* (plague victims)—advice which is important because it remained standard for centuries to come:

> Notaries, confessors, relations and doctors who visit the plague victims on entering their houses should open the windows so that the air is renewed (i.e., the corrupt air), and wash their hands with vinegar and rose water and also their faces, especially around their mouth and nostrils. It is also a good idea before entering the room to place in your mouth several cloves and eat two slices of bread soaked in the best wine and then drink the rest of the wine. Then when leaving the room you should douse yourself and your pulses with vinegar and rose water and touch your nose frequently with a sponge soaked in vinegar. Take care not to stay too close to the patient.

By opening the windows, visitors were able to dispel the corrupt vapours which would have collected in the room where the plague victim was sick. The doctor used vinegar to avoid infection since, like rose-water, it had cooling qualities against the heat generated by the corruption of disease. Doctors recommended that anyone who entered the sick-room should carry flaming torches in order to purify the corrupt air in the room.

When considering the influence of the medical world on government policies one is confronted here, as elsewhere, by the problem that many plague tracts were written for individuals rather than for collectivities, as in the case of Ser Mariano di Ser Jacopo's *Consilium* dedicated to

[handwritten margin notes: "Always open windows."; "Alcohol to kill bacteria —"]

Giovanni Bandini, doctor in law. Nevertheless these general ideas had an importance well beyond the visit of the doctor. Their basic philosophy can be detected behind the measures taken by the men who governed the Italian states: they extrapolated from the advice given to the individual in caring for his body to devise counsels about how best to preserve the health of the body politic.

One of the most influential Consilia of this period was that of Tommaso del Garbo, the doctor whom Petrarch claimed to have been so skilled that he could bring back to life the dead, even those whose bodies had turned green after years in the ground. Even so the general form and emphasis of del Garbo's ideas are little different from others. Advice centered around ways of disinfecting homes and the diet recommended to avoid infection. But for del Garbo, as for other contemporary writers on plague, the "principal and most secure remedy is to fly from the place where there is pestilence, and go to the place where the air is healthy." This may have benefited those who could afford to leave, but it did not help either the poor or the skeleton staff who remained behind to administer government.

Tommaso del Garbo also provided more specific advice for the individual, which is important because it summarizes his theory of transmission of plague:

> Each person must guard himself from mixing [conversare] with too many people when the pestilence is in his area. There is always the fear that among the many there are those who have already received the infection and corruption of the air, and who will therefore be able to pass on the corruption to healthy bodies.

Apparently, then, Tommaso del Garbo believed in inter-human transmission of disease through infection. However, we must be careful to define our terms and not confuse the medieval with the modern meaning of "infection." By the later Middle Ages interpretations of the word *infectio* had passed through a number of stages. In Classical Latin texts the meaning was literally discolouration or dyeing, as of cloth or, metaphorically, moral or spiritual corruption. In the Middle Ages, more emphasis came to be placed on physical corruption and in particular the contamination of objects by noxious substances and smells.

Although the later medieval idea of "infection" may sound more akin to twentieth-century definitions, a conceptual gulf separates the two interpretations. Tommaso del Garbo underlined the close link perceived in the later Middle Ages between infection and corruption. It should not be confused with modern germ theory, the transmission of pathogenic agents from the sick to the well.

Even if medical writers emphasized that corrupt air was the most important explanation for causing and transmitting pestilence, by 1348 the word "contagion" had also begun to appear in physicians' discussion of plague. This, too, to twentieth-century ears has a modern ring and could be taken to imply, as it would today, that doctors believed in inter-human transmission of pathogenic material through direct physical contact. However, once again we would be doing violence to a medieval concept. This can best be appreciated when examining how contemporaries employed the term. For example, Gentile da Foligno said that "the communication of the evil disease happens principally from contagious conversation with other people who have been infected." Mariano di Ser Jacopo, on the other hand, stated that "it happens often that men die of plague in healthy air simply through contagion." In the same period the anonymous author of the Montpellier tract of 1349 asserted that "without question the epidemic was thought to be contagious." Further east the very championship of contagionist ideas based on empirical observation later led to the Arab physician Ibn Al-Katib being arraigned for heresy.

While today "contagion" by definition means transmission by touch, in the mid-fourteenth century interpretations were less clear cut: physical contact was of secondary importance. Gentile's "corruption," or the "evil" from which this contagion stems, is the corruption of the air rather than physical matter and is spread from person to person through exhalation. His "contagious conversation" seems to imply "infection" rather than physical contact; talking to the sick was enough to become infected.

"Contagion" in our sources was employed in a variety of ways. Following Classical models, the term was used to describe the negative influence of natural phenomena on man. It was also used as a synonym for sickness, implying corruption and degeneration. However, in common with the sources' Graeco-Roman models there was little discussion of transmission, although at some level the very use of the term "contagion" suggests recognition that physical contact (*tangere*, "to touch") must have played some role, even if secondary, in the spread of disease. The closest recognition of how diseases were transmitted was in Galen's theory of "seeds of disease," which can be found in three of his tracts. According to him these "seeds" are external and corrupt the air. But they can be reactivated within an individual by an unhealthy regimen, which reflects the belief in the relationship between external corruption of the air and the humoral balance of an individual's body. This idea was taken on board by at least one Italian doctor, Tommaso del Garbo, in his commentary on Galen written within three years of the Black Death.

We have now arrived at a less restricted definition of "contagion" than the twentieth-century understanding of the term. It would be more accurate to characterize the medieval concept as what has been called "contingent contagionism," the transmission of a localized corruption of the air from person to person. Plague or pest could now be clearly recognized as one of the diseases listed in Avicenna's *Canon* as transmittable from man to man—not, however, *via* a twentieth-century pathogen but through general factors, the most important of which was the corruption of the air. The general acceptance of this theory goes a long way towards explaining why the authors of plague tracts recommended so many measures to dry the atmosphere: lighting fires, sprinkling strong vinegar and rose-water in houses, and fumigating the rooms with smouldering incense, myrrh and aloe wood.

Lay Perceptions of Plague and Government Policy During the Black Death

. . . Let us now see how far the ideas of either the medical writers or the chroniclers were reflected in the measures taken by governments in Italy. Boccaccio summarizes the basic strategies adopted by the Florentine regime in the mid-fourteenth century:

> And in that [pestilence] no wisdom nor provision was of any use, such as the clearing of the city of much refuse by officials appointed for that purpose, and the prohibition of any sick person from entering [the city] and many counsels [consilia] given for the preservation of health . . . almost at the beginning of Spring of the said year it began to demonstrate its doleful effects in a miraculous manner.

Boccaccio conflates a whole series of measures here. First, he speaks of "the officials appointed for that purpose." Florence, in common with some other northern and central Italian city-states, appointed a magistracy to supervise the necessary measures to deal with the emergency. The size of the commission varied from one city to another, but this reflected administrative customs rather than the size of population. While

Florence appointed an eight-man magistracy, those in Venice and Siena comprised only three.

Second, Boccaccio wrote that the magistrates of Florence had the role of "clearing of the city of much refuse." In Venice, on the other hand, they were charged with the "conservation of the health [of the city] and the elimination of the corruption of the land." Emphasis was placed on cleaning impurities and corruption, which recalls the ideas of the plague tracts. However, just as it is important not to isolate the plague Consilia written during the Black Death from the medical tradition which preceded the appearance of plague, so one must not forget that government measures were based on pre-existing practices within the Italian city-states and in particular on the body of "sanitary legislation" which so many cities had developed over the previous 100–150 years.

In Florence from the late thirteenth century there had been a move to improve hygiene within the city. The 1325 *Statutes* prohibited within the city walls the conduct of trades which produced unpleasant smells, such as the treating of animal fur and the slaughtering of animals in public places. Streets had to be kept clean; every evening the bones which had been thrown down during the course of trading in the Mercato Vecchio were removed, and each Saturday evening there had to be a general cleaning of the whole area. Cesspits could only be emptied at night and all water channels had to be kept clear. In nearby Bologna it was ordained in 1245 that each house should have at least one lavatory, it was forbidden to throw rubbish into the streets, and the inhabitants of each street were required to keep clean the ditch which ran down its centre.

The reasons put forward in this legislation underline how much the measures taken in 1348 were based on precedent and established theory. Thus in a law of 1319 the Priors of Florence had justified their prohibition of the slaughtering of livestock in Borgo SS. Apostoli and Via delle Terme on the grounds that these trades "provoked illness among their inhabitants through their pestiferous exhalations." The rationale behind the law of March 1348—at the outset of the Black Death in Florence—was to avoid the "corruption and infection of the air" which stemmed from the "putrefaction and corruption of things and bodies." The magistracy was authorized "to remove and carry away from the city of Florence and from its suburbs any putrid thing or things and infected persons and similar things, from which could [proceed] corruption of the air and infection." None of these ideas was far from those annunciated by medical treatises.

The most detailed information about measures adopted during the Black Death by any Tuscan city is contained in the regulations drawn up by Pistoia in 1348 for "the conservation of the health of human bodies and the resisting of various and diverse pestilences." They repeat the same laws of other major towns about the banning of animals and butchering from the centre. The Pistoiese were also anxious to restrict the movement of cloth, and declared that "Any cloth brought into the city must be burned in the main square of the city." Once again the reason behind this move was that cloth attracted and retained corrupt vapours.

Other measures adopted by Pistoia were also enacted in Florence. Many appear to have stemmed from the belief that it *was* possible to spread disease through corrupt air. For example, the law of 3 April, enacted at the outset of the plague in the city, denied entry to those coming from infected areas, such as Pisa and Genoa, and forbade the sale or ownership of clothes belonging to any sick person." At Milan, according to the Sienese chronicler Agnolo di Tura, only three families died in the city because the authorities took immediate action by walling up the doors and windows of the houses concerned so that nobody could enter or leave. At the same time one should not exaggerate the extent to which these measures were adopted: governments of some cities such as Orvieto did very little to prevent the spread of plague. Others such as that of Lucca banned from as early as January any Catalan or Romanian from entering the city, presumably because news had arrived that plague was rampant in their countries. Meanwhile the Venetian republic prohibited everybody from coming into the city, but made exceptions for ambassadors.

There was, moreover, little consistency in policy even within the same town. For example, the Priors of Florence who held office in April decided to ban entry to those coming from infected areas, but their successors in June failed to take this notion a step further by preventing citizens from one part of the city from mixing with those from another. The processions ordered for the celebration of the patron saint of the city, St. John the Baptist, in late June 1348 were no doubt widely supported on the grounds that reliance on God's divine power was likely to prove more successful than actions based on a policy devised by any human agency. At this stage there was no conflict, such as occurred in later centuries, between those who advocated an appeal to God and a pragmatic faction anxious to avoid spreading disease. In Perugia, too, crowds of citizens processed through the streets, singing orations and whipping themselves as further proof to God that they were fully penitent of their sins.

In 1348, as in later epidemics, those to suffer the most were the poor because of their sheer numbers, their insanitary living conditions and the breakdown of the normal economic and social networks which provided them with food and employment, and their inability to follow the examples of the protagonists of the *Decameron* by escaping to villas in the country. Governments were aware of these problems, although the sparsity of surviving records makes it difficult to determine the scale of their relief programmes. As we have seen, one response was the clearing up of refuse, which clearly was most plentiful in the poorer areas. To meet the immediate needs of the poor the commune appointed officials to sell bread to the hungry, while nearby Siena allocated 1000 gold florins to be spent on alms for the poor sick. These measures depended less, however, on communal understanding of the nature of the plague than on the customary provision of public and private charity to the poor during emergencies caused by severe food shortages and epidemics.

If the sick poor were an object of concern, an equally severe problem was the disposal of their bodies when they died. Contemporaries leave us in little doubt that, as the heat of the summer of 1348 increased and the pestilence worsened, there was a very grave logistical problem in dealing with corpses. Fears abounded that abandoned bodies would begin to stink, and would thus increase the corruption of the air and in turn the virulence of the plague. The Florentine chronicler, Marchionne di Coppo Stefani, is but one contemporary who has left a vivid description of the scene:

> All the citizens did little else except to carry dead bodies to be buried; many died who did not confess or receive the other sacraments; and many died by themselves and many died of hunger. . . . At every church they dug deep pits down to the water level; and thus those who were poor who died during the night were bundled up quickly and thrown into the pit. In the morning when a large number of bodies were found in the pit, they took some earth and shovelled it down on top of them; and later others were placed on top of them and then another layer of earth, just as one makes lasagne with layers of pasta and cheese.

In this passage Stefani shows that contemporaries conflated the stages which normally followed an individual's death, that is the watching over the dead body, the procession to the church, and the funeral and interment. Other sources confirm this picture. Venice, for example, prohibited the custom of exhibiting bodies of dead people in front of their houses so as to invoke the compassion of their neighbours.

The reasons behind the preoccupation with unburied bodies were not so much the stench as much as the possibility that the dead would generate corrupt vapours. Therefore the Pistoiese authorities ordained that "Dead bodies cannot be taken out of the houses where they died unless they are put in a wooden box bound together with string so that the odours do not escape." Furthermore, in order to avoid the "stink of fetid fumes" each body had to be buried at least 2.5 metres below ground.

Clearly the burial of thousands of bodies a month created an enormous strain on a city which normally might expect no more than one to two thousand deaths a year. The policy adopted was a pragmatic reaction to a desperate situation; even so, there are signs in the legislation that the underlying theories did reflect the basic beliefs of medical writers concerning the role of corrupt air.

Conclusion

There was little sign at the time of the Black Death of the gulf between the medical profession and the laity which is alleged to have grown up in the fifteenth century. The law passed in Florence in April 1348 talked of taking measures to avoid the "corruption and infection of the air" which proceeded from "putrid and corrupt things and bodies." All this suggests that governments and doctors shared the same ideas concerning transmission and infection.

It remains difficult to define the extent to which government measures were based directly on the influence or advice of the medical profession. Many communes since the mid-thirteenth century had employed a *medico condotto* on a regular basis. His main task was to provide free treatment to the poor, but because many of these men were celebrated physicians, they also probably were called upon to give advice to governments. It will be remembered that, for example, Mariano di Ser Jacopo's Consilio was addressed to the lawyer Giovanni Bandini, a member of a prominent Sienese family who may very well have been involved in the Sienese government at the time of the Black Death or else have acted as its representative. Moreover, Gentile da Foligno wrote his longest Consilio for the University of Perugia and at the same time gave advice to the government "for the safety of the men of the city." Other examples can be found elsewhere of governments commissioning such works. In France the best known was the *Compendium de Epidimia* of the medical faculty of the University of Paris, written at the command of Philip IV of France, and in Spain Jacme d'Agramont's tract for the council and people of Lerida.

In Florence the Priors also employed extra medical staff for two specific reasons which throw light on lay attitudes towards physicians. Their first task was to determine the nature of the disease by dissecting the bodies of plague victims, which suggests that the Priors regarded them as the primary experts. Then the physicians were required to give advice to the government on the basis of their findings. Physicians in Perugia were also asked to dissect plague victims; the local *Annals* explain in more detail the reasons for this operation: "A number of doctors conducted an autopsy here; they found that near the heart a gut [*biscica*] had become full of poison; they made it bleed through the vein of the heart." This finding, of course, merely confirmed the physicians in their theories about the real cause of a plague victim's death. It was believed that the pestilential air of plague was drawn into the body, and that it fed upon the moist humors and then poisoned the heart. Death followed rapidly because it was from the heart as primary organ that the lifegiving *spiritus* flowed to the rest of the body. . . .

It is more than probable, then, that although most of the recommendations contained in plague tracts were directed towards the private rather than the public client, not only did governments extrapolate from the particular to the general, but treatises included passages relevant to collective action. At the time of the Black Death Gentile da Foligno, for example, recommended that no sick person should be allowed to enter a city if he came from "contaminated parts," and Mariano di Ser Jacopo of Siena said that one should lock up those houses which had been infected by plague. Both these recommendations were adopted by governments, which suggests a considerable degree of co-operation between administrative and medical personnel.

If at this stage both government and the medical men shared a belief in corrupt air as the source of pestilence, then we may infer not only that the laity had absorbed the theories of the medical men, but that doctors may even have learned from the evidence of their own eyes. The discrepancy, then, which is often posited between the lay contagionist point of view and the medical theory of corrupt air was not present in 1348. . . .

Samuel K. Cohn

The Black Death: End of a Paradigm

Samuel K. Cohn's "The Black Death: End of a Paradigm" is based on his reading of a host of sources. To begin with, he has examined the epidemiological and medical literature of the late nineteenth and early twentieth centuries that identified and elaborated the chief characteristics of bubonic plague and its transmission. He has then juxtaposed this modern medical knowledge against the primary source evidence of the fourteenth century. In the passage excerpted here he argues for the inconsistencies between these two sets of data, looking especially at one of the plague's signature symptoms: the bubo. In so doing, he criticizes the work of various historians, who, he argues, have overlooked or brushed aside these inconsistencies. One major criticism of Cohn's scholarship is likely to be his lack of a candidate for what disease, if not bubonic plague, *did* ravage Europe in the late medieval and early modern periods. Cohn's conclusions will also have to contend with a growing body of scientific evidence that demonstrates the presence of plague in medieval Europe. Recently, for example, archaeologists and microbiologists performed DNA tests on the pulp of teeth found in a fourteenth-century French burial site and found evidence of *Yersinia pestis.*[1]

Throughout the twentieth century, historians and scientists alike have assumed that the "third" pandemic that struck Hong Kong in 1894 and spread across the oceans was the same disease that halved Europe's population in the mid-fourteenth century. Their assumption has rested on the supposed similarity of signs and symptoms between the late medieval and modern pandemics. According to Ann Carmichael, who combines an expertise in medieval history with one in medicine, "Boccaccio leaves

Source: Samuel K. Cohn, "The Black Death: End of a Paradigm," *The American Historical Review* 107, no. 3 (June 2002): 711–717.

[1]Didier Raoutl, Gérard Aboudharam, Eric Crubézy, Georges Larrouy, Bertrand Ludes, and Michel Drancourt, "Molecular Identification of 'Suicide PCR' of *Yersinia pestis* as the Agent of Medieval Black Death," *Proceedings of the National Academy of Science* 97, no. 23 (November 7, 2000): 12800–12803.

no doubt that bubonic Y. *pestis* ravaged Florence in 1348. If the bubo predominated as a sign, we could still be reasonably comfortable after five centuries that there was not much error in the ascription of a death to plague." Nobel laureate and immunologist Sir Macfarlane Burnet has emphasized that diagnosis of diseases in the past must be assessed by epidemiology and not by signs or symptoms alone. But when he came to the Black Death, he forgot his lesson: "The symptoms are characteristic enough to make it easy to recognize the disease from classical or medieval descriptions, and we can be sure that the two greatest European pestilences, the plague of Justinian's reign (A.D. 542) and the Black Death of 1348, were both the result of the spread of the plague bacillus." As health workers in the subtropics are taught, the bubo or swelling in the lymph glands is not unique to bubonic plague. As early as the 1920s, editions of *Manson's Tropical Diseases* insisted that the presence of the bubo was not a sure sign that the malady was bubonic plague and advised doctors to take cultures of the infected area before treating for plague. The sign could equally well signify numerous other diseases: relapsing fever, severe cases of malaria, typhoid, typhus, glandular fever, tularaemia, lymphogranuloma inguinale, and various forms of filariasis.

For some time, scholars have been puzzled by the inconsistencies between what contemporary doctors and chroniclers reported in the fourteenth and fifteenth centuries and what scientists observed on the microscopic and macro-sociological levels in mostly subtropical zones after the discovery of the plague bacillus. One might even argue that the cultural sophistication of doctors at the turn of the century—their knowledge of the late medieval past—was a factor that delayed for a decade or more their acceptance of the complex rat-flea-human vector in the transmission of modern plague. Such a slow and inefficient transmission did not square with the medieval plague, which from contemporary descriptions and the speed it traveled must have been an airborne disease, communicable person to person, and possibly transmitted as well by infested clothing and other objects, as chroniclers reported and governments tried to curb with new plague legislation. Without the assistance of the railway or the steamship, the fourteenth-century disease spread almost as fast per day over land as modern plague does per annum.

Even after repeated observations and experiences of the plague ward as "the safest place" to be in times of plague, early twentieth-century doctors were reluctant to distinguish this disease from the rapidly infectious plague of the Middle Ages or to push aside the lessons they thought they had learned from the past. In India, even though relatives and friends crowded around plague victims, using their hands and clothing to wipe away discharges from the patients' mouths, and practicing "the common custom of receiving the sputa of the sick in their hands," plague wards remained almost completely free of further infection. Yet until around 1907, doctors continued to treat the disease as though it were highly contagious.

Nor does the pneumonic form of plague help solve the riddle, as modern historians continue to assume. First, with modern plague, cases of person-to-person transmission—pneumonic plague or secondary pneumonic complications after the onset of the buboes—have been rare. Secondly, unlike measles or influenza, "droplet" transmission of *Yersinia pestis* in its pulmonary form is extremely ineffective. The worst manifestations of modern pneumonic plague—Northern Manchuria in 1911 and 1921—were limited, the proportions killed under 0.3 percent. With both epidemics, the disease broke out among tarabagan fur hunters crammed in underground inns, 12 by 15 feet, where as many as forty men slept without adequate ventilation to protect themselves against the Siberian cold. Further, in packed railway cars between Harbin and Changchun, the spread and infectivity of this disease remained low. Comparing the Manchurian pneumonic plague and the late medieval pestilence that swept through Europe and Asia, the foremost authority on pneumonic plague, Wu Lien Teh, had doubts about the connection and speculated that the Black Death might have been "a virulent type of influenza such as that encountered in 1918." Such a speculation finds some support in the diagnosis of plague in Kashmir in 1903–1904, where the symptoms of pneumonic plague resembled influenza and occasionally the two accompanied one another. Yet no historian or medical researcher has dared to investigate further these possible connections, and few have suggested other alternatives.

Even if this disease has been intercurrent with other diseases or triggered them, as some have speculated to resolve the discordance between what the sources say and what the epidemiology of modern bubonic plague may demand, the total absence in the documents or from archaeological evidence of any prior or accompanying spread of the disease among rats must be explained. Not only in England and Scotland, where rats existed (even if in insufficient numbers for an epidemic of plague), historians have insisted that this disease was bubonic plague in areas where no evidence of rats appears for the late Middle

Ages, as well as in arctic winters, where the spread of modern bubonic plague in epidemic proportions is impossible.

To resolve the inconsistencies past and present, scholars such as the bacteriologist, J. F. D. Shrewsbury questioned contemporary accounts rather than the disease. He reasoned that England could not have possibly possessed the population densities of people or rats to sustain a bubonic plague with the massive mortality figures claimed by chroniclers or shown by the replacement rates of the clergy. Yet instead of challenging the bubonic plague as the root disease, he dismissed the sources of England's late medieval demographic history. From the biological "laws" of modern plague, he concluded that nowhere did more than 20 percent of the population perish, and for England as a whole, as few as 5 percent died in 1348–1349. Further, he argued, the Black Death, along with subsequent plagues, must have been a disease of towns, despite evidence to the contrary from archaeology and from bishops' and manorial rolls. Some of the highest counts of mortality anywhere come from rural areas such as those around St.-Flour (Auvergne) and in Cambridgeshire, where as much as 76 percent of populations died in the Black Death.

Robert Gottfried questioned the accuracy of Gabriele de Mussis's account of the plague's spread in 1347, when soldiers of the Golden Horde lobbed infected bodies into the besieged Genoese trading port of Caffa on the Black Sea. He rightly pointed out that modern bubonic plague does not spread from dead bodies but requires a rat flea to ingest large concentrations of the bacterium from a diseased rat and afterward to bite a human, regurgitating the bacillus into the human blood stream. But from his knowledge of bubonic plague, Gottfried chose to dismiss the chronicle rather than question what the disease may have been. Finally, Ole Jørgen Benedictow has argued against the general consensus that plague in Nordic countries was pneumonic, by pointing out that even in its airborne form modern plague is not highly contagious. Instead of rejecting or questioning the disease's identity as modern plague, however, he turned to a more unlikely solution, especially for the colder climates of Scandinavia, arguing that it was bubonic plague (even though none of these Nordic sources describe buboes) with secondary pneumonic complications, as though secondary pneumonic plague were more contagious than primary pneumonic plague (which it is not).

Let us return to the supposed "certain" signs of the two plagues—the buboes. Do the two periods of plague match so "unmistakably" as scientists and historians continue to claim? Chroniclers, storytellers, poets, and doctors of the later Middle Ages described swellings as large as onions but also pointed to smaller "carbuncles, rashes, freckles, scabs, and other similar things," which preceded, accompanied, or followed the telltale boils. This additional complication of the late medieval plague is found even in that passage most often cited in support of the Black Death's identity as bubonic plague, that of Giovanni Boccaccio: "From the two areas already mentioned [the groin and the armpit], the aforementioned deadly *gavòcciolo* would begin to spread, and within a short time would appear at random on every part of the body. Afterwards, the illness would change with the appearance of black or blue spots (*macchie nere o livide*) forming on their arms, thighs, and other parts of the body, sometimes large and few in number, at other times tiny and closely spaced."

The largest repository of clinical descriptions of plague after the discovery of the bacillus comes from the first Bombay Report in 1896–1897, conducted by Brigadier-General W. F. Gatacre. Twenty-seven hospitals in and around Bombay City submitted reports, and seven classified their clinical data according to the positions and number of plague boils that formed on their patients. Of 3,752 plague patients admitted to these seven hospitals, 2,883 (or 77 percent) developed plague boils. Of these, less than 6 percent had more than a single boil, and not in a single case did spots, blisters, or rashes spread all over the body. This pattern remained much the same when plague spread to Europe at the beginning of the twentieth century. Of thirty-eight hospitalized cases in Glasgow in 1900, none showed spots spreading over the body, and only two had more than a single boil. Later editions of *Manson's Tropical Diseases* note that the spread of "carbuncles," though rare, has been known to accompany the formation of plague boils; the latest case it cites, however, comes from the London plague of 1665.

Nor should we assume that Boccaccio's description of pustules was poetic invention aimed to heighten the horror of plague. For the second plague in Wales in the 1360s, the Welsh poet Llywelyn Fychan described a similar course: after the "swelling under the armpit, grievous sore lump" came "the shower of peas," "seaweed scales, a grim throng, berries, it is painful that they should be on fair skin." More prosaically, other fourteenth and early fifteenth-century observers—the Franciscan friar of Messina, Michele da Piazza, the Piacentine Giovanni de Mussis, Giovanni of Parma, a canon at Trent, the Saint-Denis chroniclers of Paris, Marcha di Marco Battagli of Rimini, the chroniclers of the Dominicans of Florence (Santa Maria Novella), the Florentine merchant Giovanni Morelli, the compiler of an obituary in Friuli, a chronicler of Split on the Dalmatian coast, a monastic chronicler of Neuberg in southern Austria, and the Englishman Geoffrey le Baker—described the same pustules, *antrachi*, or spots spreading over the bodies of plague victims. When plague arrived at Catania in October 1347, Michele da Piazza distinguished between *antrachi* (pustules) and the "glandule" "as big as goose eggs," both of which spread over the body. Geoffrey le Baker and Giovanni Morelli maintained that, of the two signs, the smaller carbuncles were the more deadly, giving little hope of survival.

In plague tracts, doctors went further in describing and classifying these pustules by size, color, and type. The distinctions were important for their treatments. The famous doctor Giovanni da Santa Sofia, a professor of medicine at the University of Padua, wrote a tract for the town council of Udine in 1367, advising that plague boils be treated with a plaster of pig fat, but for the smaller *antraci* and carbuncles, he recommended a plaster made from pigeon dung (*de stercore columbino*) because of the spots' more "vehement heat." Like the chroniclers, the doctors found the smaller spots the more deadly.

Further discrepancies emerge when comparing the positions of the plague boils. With modern bubonic plague, between 57 and 75 percent of the buboes form in the groin, because fleas, although they can jump a hundred times their own height, usually reach no higher than the shins and most often bite around the ankles. Thus the first glandular node met by the multiplying bacillus is in the groin. Yet not a single late medieval doctor or chronicler privileged the groin as the place where the medieval bubo most often formed, not even Boccaccio and a handful of others who pointed to the groin and the armpits. Nor were these the only sites for the swellings. Doctors, chroniclers, and plague miracle cures often described them in non-glandular areas—on the shins, the back, the face, on arms, and under the breasts. With modern plague, such formations are extraordinarily rare: only fifteen of the plague boils from the 2,886 patients in Bombay in 1896–1897 were located outside the lymph nodes (0.05 percent).

In addition, the late medieval boils' pride of place was in neither the groin nor the armpits, as historians now claim. For the plague of 1361, the chronicler of Parma described them as forming in only one general area—"on the neck, under the ears, that is near the throat." In

counseling where to let blood from plague patients, doctors were especially attentive to the positions of the boils. Almost without exception,
they saw them growing in three glands—the neck, the armpits, and the
groin—and began their prescriptions by turning first to the neck, if they
did not form there, then to the armpits, and lastly to the groin. From
thirty-eight miracle cures between 1348 and 1500 found scattered
through the *Acta Sanctorum* that indicated the place of the plague boils,
more are found in the neck (fifteen cases) than anywhere else. Finally,
the Lucchese doctor Iacopo di Coluccino has left us a rare, if not
unique, source for the care of plague patients before 1450. Slipped in
his diary (*ricordanze*) was a two-page insert (*cedole*) with his clinical notes
on seven plague patients he attended twice daily during the plague of
1373. Three of the seven formed boils; all of them were in the neck or
behind the ears; none were in the armpits or groin. Although small in
number, the cases corroborate the impressions gained from the doctors'
tracts and the miracle cures. . . .

Michael McCormick

Rats, Communications, and Plague

Michael McCormick's article is an example of a historical and ecological
challenge to Cohn's interpretation. McCormick's goal is to demonstrate the
presence of black rats in western Europe in the fourteenth century. Earlier
parts of his essay, not excerpted here, trace the possible means by which the
black rat may have populated Europe during the period of the Roman
Empire. McCormick then examines the ability of these rat populations to
sustain their existence in this region until the fourteenth century. He looks
to a host of factors, like climate and the spatial organization of cities, that

Source: Michael McCormick, "Rats, Communications, and Plague," *Journal of Interdisciplinary History*, XXXIV: 1 (Summer 2003): 14–24.

may have determined the size of Europe's rat population and in turn facilitated the existence of plague in medieval Europe.

Rat colonies extending across the Roman empire are only the first half of the bubonic equation. The second half is their expansion. Big, dense commensal rat populations offer optimal conditions for spreading the disease to human neighbors. A sharply increasing rat population threatens ecological equilibrium and disposes the rodents to disease. Recent mathematical modeling estimates the critical density for that disposition at 3,000 rats per 0.5 sq km. New archeological data challenge the opinion that late medieval Europe had too few rats to have sustained bubonic plague during the Black Death. Judging from 143 rat contexts of the ninth to the fifteenth centuries, medieval Europe's rat colonies were extensive and abundant. In sixty-six cases, excavators estimated the minimum number of individual rats attested. Those contexts yielded a total of 601 rats—that is, they averaged 9.1 rats each (range, 1–167 rats, mode, 1). One-fifth (thirteen) of those contexts displayed ten or more rats, and twelve of those most-infested sites are certainly thirteenth century or later.

Overall, the raw rat counts hint at hugely expanding rat populations around the fourteenth-century plague. In favored cases, which preserve good samples of a rat colony, it may prove possible to refine the raw data of numbers of rats and move toward the question of the colony's population trend. Archaeologists now routinely subject the human populations recovered from ancient and medieval cemeteries to palaeodemographic analysis: They classify the remains by age at death and sex and use various formulas to compensate for underreporting of immature individuals, in order to deduce the size, sex ratio, and age pyramid of the source population. The procedure illuminates the demographic trend—whether the population in question was stagnant, declining, or growing. At least one attempt has been made to assess a medieval rat colony's numbers by age cohort and morality pattern. If such efforts are headed in the right direction, archaeozoologists may be able to apply an appropriately adapted analysis to clarify the dynamics and trend of such rat populations. They could thereby test and check the deductions made about rat population patterns from raw counts of the minimum numbers of individuals and mathematical simulations.

For now, the zoodemographic trend of late antique rats remains more obscure. Whether this lack of hard data is due to insufficient investigation, to greater deterioration of fine rat bones after an additional millennium in the soil, or to lesser expansion of rat populations is unclear. Nevertheless, more than twenty-four of the ancient finds yielded an estimated total of 148 rats, an average of 6.1 rats per context (range, 1–126; mode, 1; one-quarter [6] of the sites had 10 or more rats). The data unearthed so far do not allow anything stronger than a surmise that the extending colonies of rats were also expanding in size, though one carefully scrutinized urban site at Naples yielded successive strata of four, eleven, and fifteen rats.

Extension and expansion of rat colonies need not have been linear processes. Since both have fluctuated substantially in recent centuries, they probably did so in antiquity as well. Black-rat and human populations are linked in demographic terms: Dense human populations foster similar conditions among rats. Even today, despite sophisticated rat-control programs, many large cities are still "literally, rat paradises." The varying demographic trends that are now emerging for different regions of the late Roman empire necessarily have implications for regional rat populations. That the number of humans in the empire's northwest quadrant started to dwindle around the third century should have led to contracting rat populations there, even as seemingly uninterrupted demographic growth ought to have fostered more rats in the southern and eastern Mediterranean regions.

Left to themselves in a conducive ecological setting with unlimited food, rats proliferate famously. The great late Roman cities required massive cereal imports, and rats cannot have been far behind. Given that the Romans transported grain in bulk, and unloaded it by hand, it is fair to assume a substantial loss when Egyptian grain was transferred from Nile boats into state granaries in Alexandria, then put aboard seagoing vessels for shipment to the capitals, and finally loaded onto lighters for the trip up the Tiber or carried up the hill to the great granaries of Constantinople. Similar conditions undoubtedly obtained for shipments to military forces deployed around the empire. That the army relied on interregional grain transport seems to follow from the wide spectrum of ancient grains recovered from Roman military depots. Moving mountains of grain inevitably implies loss, which translated into exceptional resource availability for rats. More food means more rats.

Other factors may have expanded late Roman rat populations, starting with waste treatment. Archaeology shows that garbage often stayed in the towns that generated it but not yet where and how it was treated; according to Roman law, owners or renters were responsible for keeping the street clear in front of their properties. The unsavory sanitation arrangements of the high Roman empire may have worsened in late antiquity. Excavators have observed that, c. 450, some rooms of an apartment block (*insula*), as well as the contiguous city street, began to serve as garbage dumps in downtown Naples. In the very next stratigraphic sequence, c. 500, black rats appear. As the western empire descended into chaos, could dwindling urban administrations, changing social ethos, or simply the failure to enforce the old legal provisions have eroded such sanitation practices as had existed earlier?

Deepening exploration of late antique cityscapes may discern subtle spatial patterns in urban rat colonies that correlate with economic and architectural features. Some will have attracted rat concentrations, others will have discouraged them. In 1950s London, black rats reached beyond the banks of the Thames only in zones characterized by "multistoried, centrally-heated . . . non-residential buildings interspersed with restaurants, cantines, and other sources of food." As Alexandre Yersin, the discoverer of the plague bacillus, observed, the 1894 outbreak at Hong Kong spared resident Europeans almost entirely, even as it devastated the Chinese quarters of the city. Differing building and sanitary conditions appear to foster specific densities of rat infestation and, hence, human infection.

During the plague season in early twentieth-century Egypt, rats avoided crossing broad paved spaces; recent research confirms that wide streets impede rat colonies. Thus, the colonnaded avenues of late antique Constantinople or Ephesus may have discouraged rats from some zones within the city. As street patterns changed in the sixth and seventh centuries, souk-like warrens of shops and squatter structures encroached on those open corridors, foreshadowing the medieval Islamic urban fabric. The new, denser urbanism may have extended rat populations more widely within towns. Roman rats surely flourished along the routes by which the public grain moved from transport ships to granaries and, ultimately, to the public bakeries.

Slaughterhouses also foster abundant rat populations. Witness, for example, modern Alexandria. The waste associated with slaughterhouses excited complaint in medieval London; Elizabethans connected it with outbreaks of plague. The problem of trash removal is crucial to this story. As the analysis of butchered bones clarifies the changing patterns of meat production in Rome and other towns, the mapping of supply networks, meat markets, and slaughterhouses should provide another focus for identifying ancient rat populations.

Finally, block-by-block investigation of the epidemiology of plague in an early modern German town revealed curious islands of resistance among smiths and coopers. The nocturnal habits of the rat go hand in hand with exceptionally sensitive hearing; if the German evidence has been completely understood, rats avoided places where they would have been subjected to the frequent—but irregular—noise of hammering. Roman rats may have behaved similarly.

On a broader scale, warfare brings wide fluctuations in rat populations. Rat numbers jumped repeatedly in the wake of the wars fought on German soil between 1813 and 1945. They would remain high for about two decades before declining. Such surges stem from disrupted supply networks, individuals' makeshift food hoarding, and degraded housing stock. All of these causes sound plausible in a sixth century that saw the Frankish conquest of southern Gaul; persistent banditry on the Egyptian and African borders; Justinian's reconquest of Africa, Italy, and part of Spain; the wars with Persia; and the appearance of central Asian and Slavic marauders in the Balkans.

Another circumstance implicated in a recent plague episode may have also affected late antiquity. The earthquake that hit India in 1993 disrupted food storage and gave rats access to "unlimited energy inputs," that is, food. Rodent populations mounted during the next eight to ten months until they upset population equilibrium. An outbreak of plague ensued in the following year. Severe earthquakes struck the Middle East in the sixth century, and again in 740, on the eve of the final outbreak of the Justinianic pandemic. Constantinople suffered them in 525, 533, 548, 554, 557, and 740; the first and last two seisms were the most destructive. The timing of the earthquake that is known to have struck in December 557 is particularly noteworthy, since it anticipated the plague that is first reported at Constantinople eight months later, in July 558. Granaries must have been damaged, implying temporarily but substantial surges in the food supply available to rodent colonies.

Two further factors drove rodent populations up or down by influencing the overall ecological system. Modern environmental change has been connected with fluctuating vector populations. The long-suspected link between increased precipitation and plague has now been confirmed by a study of the American southwest. At a local level, above-normal precipitation produces increased plague outbreaks; conversely, above-normal dryness diminishes plague. In an arid or semi-arid ecology, precipitation that increases two to six months before rodent breeding peaks launches a "trophic cascade." An explosion of plant and insect growth bolsters the food chain and fosters a surge in the rodent population. In this kind of ecology, increased precipitation succeeded by drought may well be the sequence most favorable to plague transmission: Drought decreases the food supply for the newly swollen rodent colonies, which then disperse in search of food.

. . . Some scholars have wondered whether the centuries-long disappearance of plague after the eighth century might not have been due to the extinction of infected rats. Perhaps rats did in fact disappear from some places. Roman housing may well have been conducive to the spread of rats accustomed to the mild Mediterranean weather, whereas the northern medieval housing and climate *may* have been less attractive for the once-subtropical animal. But the claim that conditions in the north would have discouraged, or even precluded, significant rat populations is overstated. Although black rats in Germany and England today stay close to human habitations, to assume that only human support can sustain rat populations outside a Mediterranean ecology is to underestimate rats' adaptability. Thriving colonies have recently been observed in the cool Atlantic climate of the Hebrides, and, even more surprising, in the subantarctic ecology of Macquarie Island (54° 30' S, 158° 57' E) under conditions that defy the conventional wisdom about their requirements. Besides, the belief that medieval housing and climate were unsuitable for rats is summarily contradicted by their presence on northern sites of the ninth, tenth, and eleventh centuries.

. . . A new twist comes from recent mathematical modeling of the patterns of persistence and recrudescence of plague among rats. In some cases, internal population dynamics of resistant and susceptible rats may have been more important than previously thought. If so, the classic model of bubonic infection — each outbreak requiring the arrival of a new source of infection from outside a rat population — would require modification. The classic model would still hold for smaller rat populations, but the new model suggests that large rat populations, such as those in large cities, could harbor low levels of plague infection for years without causing significant human outbreaks. Without new inputs of infection from the outside, the internal rat infection might reach a threshold high enough to spill over into humans only occasionally, about once every ten years. The mathematical model appears to function for so long as a century. If it should prove well-founded, it will introduce unprecedented complexity into the patterns by which bubonic infection persisted and flared during the late Roman and late medieval pandemics, and lend even greater importance to the detailed history of rat populations. But it still leaves intact the enigma of the disappearance of plague from the Mediterranean world and its hinterlands between the eight and the fourteenth centuries. . . .

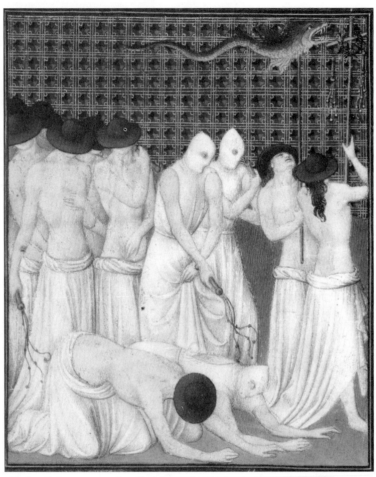

The flagellant movement flourished during the first few years of bubonic plague. The flagellants believed that their bodily mortification was proper penance for the sins of humanity. (Metropolitan Museum of Art, New York, The Cloisters Collection)

PART

 # Religious and Cultural Responses to the Plague

While the previous chapter demonstrated that medieval Europeans sought medical and scientific explanations for the disease's arrival and spread, many of them understood the plague first and foremost through the lens of religious belief. The plague was God's punishment for sinful behavior. It is important to emphasize that Christians typically understood this punishment in a collective sense. Rather than the specific acts of an individual, it was the sinful character of the Christian community that precipitated God's wrath. If plague was indeed God's punishment, medieval Europeans knew that God expected certain penitential and expiatory acts of them. Even before the plague's arrival in a community and, of course, once it was in their midst, citizens tried to ward off or arrest the spread of plague through their repentance. Priests and other ecclesiastical authorities encouraged Christians to demonstrate their contrition through acts of public penance such as religious processions and masses. And certainly, individual Europeans engaged in private devotional practices—prayer, fasting, confession—that they hoped would appease God's anger. The plague also inspired acts of devotional heroism. Many selflessly ministered to the sick and dying, risking their own well-being in the process.

73

While Europeans had recourse to the established belief system of Christianity to help them weather the crisis of the plague, some historians have nonetheless represented their reactions to the plague as superstitious, irrational, and despairing. In the words of Philip Ziegler, "The Black Death descended on a people who were drilled by their theological and their scientific training into a reaction of apathy and fatalistic resignation" (39). While in other parts of his book Ziegler strives to understand the European mentality on its own terms, shirking a presentist interpretation, statements like the one just quoted detract from those efforts. Several of the selections in this section implicitly challenge interpretations like Ziegler's of the fourteenth-century response to the plague, arguing instead for the resiliency and resourcefulness of Europeans in the face of disaster.

Disease and disaster were not new on the medieval landscape, and Christian communities responded accordingly. Yet, at the same time, plague *was* different from previous calamities and required new responses or variations on established responses. While medieval Christians often turned to the saints as their intercessors during times of crisis, for example, the Black Death created specific "plague saints," including St. Sebastian (died c. 300) and St. Roch (c. 1350–c. 1380). Although the reasons for St. Sebastian's veneration as a plague saint are not entirely clear (he was martyred by being shot with arrows, and the plague's transmission and "sting" are sometimes represented as arrows in medieval chronicles and art), he was popularly appealed to in times of plague. By the end of the fourteenth century St. Roch was revered as a plague saint because he had miraculously survived being infected with plague and had equally miraculously cured others of the disease.

The selection in this section by the art historian Louise Marshall explores the use of plague saint imagery as a demonstration of the resourcefulness of Europeans in the face of plague. Rather than embracing despair, they employed their religious beliefs and the artistic representations of those beliefs in deliberate ways to provide reassurance and solace when confronted with disaster. She argues, for example, that the depictions of St. Roch's suffering were meant to demonstrate his acceptance of Christlike suffering. Yet, the knowledge of St. Roch's miraculous cure juxtaposed against his suffering body could be read as a sign of hope by viewers weathering the ravages of plague. Similarly, the image of the Madonna of Mercy warding off the arrows of plague was a reassuring one. In addition, Marshall notes that this iconography was not new to the visual vocabulary of medieval Europe, but rather was shaped to meet the needs of plague suffering.

The excerpt by Laura Smoller takes an approach similar to Marshall's and examines how Europeans "fit" the plague into their existing perceptions about God's judgment and the end of the world. Chroniclers and other writers drew on biblical texts and imagery and linked plague to ominous signs like earthquakes. They mapped plague as a disease spreading westward from the mysterious and wonder-filled East, from pagan lands to the world of Christians. Ultimately, they read the plague as a sign of the apocalypse. In all of these measures, the writers drew on established religious and literary traditions to explain a phenomenon that was like nothing they had experienced previously.

Europeans also modified the notion of collective penance in the time of plague in the use and acceptance of the flagellant movement. The flagellants were penitential brotherhoods that flourished especially in parts of northern and central Europe during the early outbreaks of the plague. They traveled from town to town flagellating themselves as a demonstration of the need to repent before God. The extreme physical suffering that this practice meted out was often compared to Christ's suffering on behalf of humanity. Contemporaries understood it as a privilege to have these groups visit their town or village. If the plague was truly God's punishment, then having such a dramatic manifestation of repentance in your community was certainly desirable. Gradually, however, the flagellants came under the scrutiny of the Church and other authorities. This was in part because they did not answer to any clerical authority, and the Church feared the inability to control and discipline the movement. And, in fact, the movement did become increasingly disorganized, and some within it began preaching anti-Jewish rhetoric and urging violence against the Jews. For all of these reasons, Pope Clement VI banned the movement in late 1349. Richard Kieckhefer's article, "Radical Tendencies in the Flagellant Movement of the Mid-Fourteenth Century," discusses the flagellant movement and the extent to which it was "radical." In so doing, he is able to understand the flagellants as a movement that simultaneously drew on existing elements of Christian belief while adapting those beliefs to the specific circumstances of the plague period.

Hostility toward the Jews of Europe in times of plague was not unique to the flagellants. In some communities residents accused the Jews of spreading the plague by poisoning wells. Such accusations sprang in part from long-standing tensions on the part of Christians toward Jews but certainly achieved a greater virulence during plague outbreaks. The passage from David Nirenberg's book, *Communities of Violence: Persecution of Minorities in the Middle Ages*, challenges historians to recognize the conceptual and methodological challenges of interpreting Christian violence toward Jews in the medieval period. What are the roots of this violence and how do we understand outbursts of violence during times of plague? As Nirenberg demonstrates, hostility between Christians and Jews needs to be understood in its specific historical context. Generalizations about this violence do not further our understanding of its origins or its meaning to contemporaries.

Both this introduction and the other readings in this section explore a wide range of reactions across a spectrum of Christian belief. For the purposes of juxtaposition this section also includes an analysis of Muslim religious reactions to the fourteenth- and fifteenth-century outbreaks of plague. Reactions to the onset of plague in the Islamic world differed from Christian responses but displayed a similar element of adaptation as Muslims sought to make sense of this catastrophe. As Michael Dols's study of plague in the Middle East demonstrates, Muslim writers struggled conceptually with what advice to give in the face of plague. Muslim plague treatises interpreted three major issues. The first was whether to flee a region where plague was spreading. The second was understanding the plague's meaning as a martyrdom and a mercy for believers and a punishment for nonbelievers. Finally, the treatises discussed whether plague was spread by contagion.

Louise Marshall

Manipulating the Sacred: Image and Plague in Renaissance Italy

In her article Louise Marshall looks at images of religious devotion after the outbreak of plague in a new light. She uses these images to argue against historians who have characterized the European reaction to the plague as one of despair and even irrationality. In contrast, she sees in the creation of this devotional art a sense of optimism and empowerment as artists crafted images meant to fortify the faith of the believer. The passage excerpted here deals specifically with the images of St. Sebastian and St. Roch, both of whom were appealed to as "plague saints" in the years following the plague's outbreak. As previously indicated, St. Sebastian's reputation as a plague saint has puzzled scholars for some time. Marshall finds answers to this question in Sebastian's representation as a martyr, interpreting his martyrdom as "the most perfect imitation of Christ." Viewers, she argues, would have seen images of St. Sebastian, frozen at the moment of his martyrdom and shot with the plague's arrows, as a lesson in salvation. Just as St. Sebastian suffered painful martyrdom with the eventual reward of salvation, so, too, would the ordinary European afflicted with plague. Images of St. Roch's "divinely sent" suffering at the hands of plague performed a similar function.

. . . My focus is on images specifically created in response to or in anticipation of the experience of the disease. Such an analysis offers rather different insights into Renaissance responses to the plague than those formulated by Meiss and others. The images to be examined functioned to secure protection from the plague by soliciting the intervention of some powerful heavenly protector. It will be argued that an understanding of the expectations attached to such images and the ways in which they were believed to operate is crucial in evaluating the long-term effects

Source: Louise Marshall, "Manipulating the Sacred: Image and Plague in Renaissance Italy," *Renaissance Quarterly* 47, no. 3 (Autumn 1994): 485–532.

of the plague. In setting up hierarchical relationships of mutual obligation between worshiper and image, those who lived during the pandemic
were not neurotic and helpless, but were taking positive—and in their
eyes effective—steps to regain control over their environment.

Throughout the Renaissance the preeminent saintly defender against
the plague was the fourth-century Roman martyr Sebastain. According
to his fifth-century biography, Sebastian was a valued member of the
Praetorian guard of the Emperors Maximian and Diocletian, who used
his position to visit imprisoned Christians and strengthen them in their
faith. Denounced as a Christian, he refused to apostatize and was sen-
tenced to death. At the Emperors' orders he was taken to a field and, in
the words of the *Passio*, "pierced with arrows like a hedgehog." His executioners left him for dead, but Christians who came secretly at night
to claim his body for burial found him miraculously still alive. Nursed
back to health, Sebastian refused to flee Rome. Instead, he deliberately
sought out the amazed Emperors to accuse them of their crimes against
Christianity. In the saint's own words, "The Lord has resurrected me
that I might come to you and reproach you for your persecution of the
servants of Christ." To no avail of course; once more arrested, Sebastian
was beaten to death and his body thrown into a sewer. Appearing in a
dream to a Christian matron, he revealed the location of his body,
which she duly recovered and buried with all honor.

During the Early Christian period, veneration to Sebastian was a
function of his status as a martyr and was primarily limited to Rome, the
site of his death and the locus of his mortal remains. His cult as a plague
saint was apparently a later development, which cannot be documented
before the late eighth century. In his *History of the Lombards,* Paul the
Deacon (c. 720–c. 797) describes the cessation of an epidemic in the
Lombard capital of Pavia in A.D. 680 after the erection of an altar dedicated to Sebastian. Significantly, in Paul's account the populace of Pavia
did not turn to the Roman martyr spontaneously but had to be directed to
do so by miraculous revelation, suggesting that such a cult was unknown
in Pavia prior to this date. Included in Jacopo da Voragine's retelling of
Sebastian's life and miracles in the *Golden Legend,* the Pavian miracle
was to be a familiar demonstration of Sebastian's protective powers for
Renaissance worshipers.

The origins of Sebastian's cult as a plague saint have long puzzled
scholars. As we have seen, there is nothing in his life or early cult that
would link him to plague. Like other saints, Sebastian is described in

the *Passio* as performing several miracles of healing and exorcism, which served to win converts to Christianity. However, none of these cures involve epidemic disease. Instead, his activities parallel Christ's cures recorded in the Gospels: a mute woman regains her voice, people who have been sick for many years are made whole. Such typical acts of saintly power serve as demonstrative signs of divinely-bestowed grace. In life as in death, the martyr is distinguished by an exemplary conformity to the Christological prototype. The origins of his protective role must therefore be sought elsewhere.

Some scholars, most notably the medical historian Henry Sigerist, have argued that Sebastian's invocation against the plague represents the simple transference of the cult of Apollo as one who both sends and averts the arrows of pestilence. Such an explanation draws on a long tradition of Enlightenment scholarship, which viewed the Christian cult of the saints as a direct continuation of that of the pagan gods. Both cases exemplified the natural propensity of primitive and irrational humanity to lapse into polytheism. Yet, as Peter Brown has so forcefully demonstrated, this is to ignore the profound differences in world view between paganism and Christianity. For late-antique pagans, earth and heaven were immutably fixed, sundered by a chasm to be passed only by the soul after death once the worthless body had been discarded. The gods were distant figures, forever separated from humanity by its curse of mortality: as Artemis tells Hippolytus in Euripides' play, the dying were offensive to divine eyes. By contrast, at the shrines of the martyrs Christianity dramatically breached the ancient barriers and joined together earth and heaven, the living and the dead. The martyrs were fellow human beings who, precisely because of their death, now enjoyed intimacy with God. And through that intimacy came their power to intercede with God on behalf of their devotees.

Alternatively, iconographers have focused on the ancient symbolism of the arrow. In the Old Testament, as a Graeco-Roman myth, the arrow is a potent weapon in God's armory, the instrument of sudden, divinely-inflicted misfortune, disease, and death. So Job recognizes the calamities which have befallen him: "The arrows of the Almighty are in me; my spirit drinks their poison; the terrors of God are arrayed against me" (Job 6: 4); so God promises judgment upon the wicked: "I will render vengeance to mine enemies, and repay them that hate me. I will make my arrows drunk with blood" (Deut. 32: 41–42). The significance of this familiar imagery for Sebastian's cult is undeniable. In this context, the arrows with which he was pierced could be identified with the deadly arrows of the plague hurled at humanity by an angry God. Concrete proof of the currency of such an understanding among Renaissance worshipers is provided by a Perugino panel, where Sebastian addresses God in the words of the psalmist lamenting his afflictions as divine chastisement: "O Lord, rebuke me not in thy anger . . . for thy arrows have struck fast in me . . . there is no health in my flesh because of thy indignation" (Ps. 38: 1–3).

Nevertheless, the symbolism of the arrow is not, it seems to me, in itself sufficient explanation for Sebastian's veneration as a plague saint since it evades any specific understanding of the way in which such symbolism functioned in a Christian context. Instead, the key to Sebastian's cult as a protector against the plague must be sought in the confluence of arrow imagery with the Christian concept of martyrdom as the most perfect imitation of Christ. As indicated in the *Passio*, Sebastian's trial by arrows was understood as a real martyrdom from which he was resurrected by divine power. Thus archbishop Antoninus's observation that Sebastian "through two deaths, possesses two crowns of martyrdom." It is in this context that the Passion-like drama of suffering, death, and resurrection that Sebastian undergoes takes on a salvific charge. In direct analogy with Christ's redemptive death, Sebastian's martyrdom by the arrows of the plague becomes a vicarious sacrifice offered up to God. Christ-like, he takes the sins of humanity upon himself and makes restitution for these sins with his own sufferings. His resurrection demonstrates the acceptability of his sacrifice before the divine judge. Hence the crucial significance of the isolated scene of the martyrdom in Renaissance art. In such images Sebastian places himself as willing victim between his worshipers and a punitive deity, accepting the divinely-sent plague arrows in his own body. To use a graphic metaphor formulated by Leo Steinberg, Sebastian acts as a living "lightning rod," drawing the plague arrows away from humanity and "grounding" them harmlessly in his own flesh.

The expectations invested in Sebastian's cult are most forcibly visualized in a radically new image-type of the saint created during the course of the Quattrocento. The distinguishing feature of this type, which I have called the *martyred* Sebastian, is its lack of narrative action: the archers are either inactive or, more usually, absent. Focus has shifted from the dramatic moment of the martyrdom, when the executioners deliver a volley of arrows and crossbolts into the martyr's flesh, to an isolated representation of the suffering saint. The essential meaning of the images lies in its proferring of Sebastian's pierced *yet living* body before the worshiper's gaze. Logically, it is a somewhat inaccurate scenario, since the archers are said to have left Sebastian for dead. Nevertheless, Renaissance images invariably show him fully conscious and unmistakably alive. In a panel by Botticelli, for example, a serene Sebastian fixes the viewer in his untroubled gaze. Another by Lorenzo Costa sets up an even more dramatic confrontation as the constricting surroundings thrust Sebastian's bleeding but still miraculously living body insistently forward into the actual space of the beholder. In these images historical time is suspended and inverted, transforming the narrative into a devotional image that exists outside of time and place.

As a timeless and ahistorical image, depictions of the martyred Sebastian explicitly evoke representations of Christ as the Man of Sorrows. An enormously popular devotional image, the Man of Sorrows presents the dead and crucified Christ standing upright within his tomb, displaying the wounds of the Passion for the worshiper's sorrowful meditations. In the same way, the mortally wounded Sebastian is shown miraculously alive at the site of his martyrdom. In both it is this supernatural contradiction that spells out the promise of the image for the contemporary viewer. By showing the dead Christ as capable of action and intention, the theme of the Man of Sorrows looks forward to the Resurrection with its promise of salvation. So, too, the image of Sebastian, martyred and yet alive, celebrates his resurrection as proof of his inexhaustible capacity to absorb in his own body the plague arrows destined for his worshipers.

Renaissance creation of a devotional image of Sebastian is highly unusual since this was an image type normally reserved for Christ and the Virgin. Like other aspects of Sebastian's iconography, its existence demonstrates the enormous significance of his cult as a Christ-like redeemer against the plague. By the second half of the Quattrocento the new image had become the standard representational type of Sebastian, far outnumbering both narrative cycles and isolated depictions of the martyrdom proper. Such success is due to the way in which the image allows the worshiper direct access to the promise of salvation from the plague contained in Sebastian's wounded but living body. No narrative detail intrudes upon the intimate relationship between saint and devotee; since Sebastian will draw the arrows, the worshiper rests secure in his presence.

Despite Sebastian's popularity, however, alternative sources of heavenly protection were not neglected. Throughout the pandemic, for many towns the first line of supernatural defense remained the local patron saint. As the heavenly court, the local saint could be relied upon to plead the community's cause with all the vigor and passion of a citizen on an urgent embassy to a foreign dignitary. So a fresco commissioned from Fiorenzo di Lorenzo by the civic authorities of Deruta (Marches) depicts the local saint Romanus on the left, successfully petitioning the divine judge on the city's behalf. Not even the more relevant "expertise" of an actual plague saint, invoked through the presence of Saint Roch, can displace the community's trust in its local patron saint as a specially interested protector: Romanus, and not Roch, serves as the city's primary advocate before God.

With the minor exception of the Augustinian Nicholas of Tolentino, promoted as a plague protector during the fifteenth century with apparently only limited success by his order, Renaissance worshipers recognized only one other universal plague saint. This was the somewhat shadowy figure of Saint Roch, whose life, as it is reported in the anonymous and undated *Acta Breviora*, relies almost entirely on hagiographic topoi. According to this text, Roch was born in Montpelier, in the south of France, at an unspecified date. After a conventionally pious childhood, the youthful saint distributed all his wealth and embarked on a pilgrimage to Rome. Enroute, he passed through several cities in northern and central Italy stricken by plague and effected a series of miraculous cures. Most striking of all, in Piacenza he himself contracted and lived through the disease. Unjustly imprisoned as a spy on his return to France, he spent five years as a model prisoner, unrecognized by his relatives. At his death he was granted the power to save others from the plague by divine fiat. When his body was discovered bathed in a saintly light, a tablet under his head, "written in a divine way in gold letters" proclaimed his status as an intercessor against the plague. The *Acta* ends with an account of Roch's immediate recognition as a saint by the populace and his official canonization by the papacy. Such a triumphant conclusion is hagiographically satisfying but without factual basis. . . .

First documented in Northern Italy in the latter part of the 1460s, Roch's cult as a plague saint gathered momentum during the devastating series of epidemics that swept Italy from 1477 to 1479. Confraternities dedicated to the new saint were founded in Venice and elsewhere. In 1478 the spectacle of Brescia wracked by the plague inspired the city's Venetian governor Francesco Diedo to compose a properly eloquent account of Roch's life. Between 1478 and 1484 Latin and Italian versions of Diedo's text were repeatedly printed in several North Italian cities, beginning with the Milanese editions of 1478/79. Complete with humanist-inspired rhetorical flourishes and lengthy discourses, the Venetian patrician's eminently modern narrative was undoubtedly influential in the further promotion of Roch's cult.

Relying upon the earlier *Acta* for factual information, Diedo's version was distinguished by a more explicitly polemical character, aimed at rectifying what he saw as potentially dangerous neglect of the proper respect and honor due to the saint. He urges his readers to pay close attention to his account of Roch's life, "that you may not offend his majesty in any way." The implied threat would not have been taken lightly; as everyone knew, saints were wielders of power that could easily be turned against those who angered them. As Diedo makes clear, Roch's cult had been divinely guaranteed. Where the *Acta* had been content to summarize the contents of the miraculous tablet recommending Roch's veneration, Diedo provides the exact words: "Those suffering from the plague, fleeing to the protection of Roch, will escape that most violent contagion." To spurn such gifts would be foolish, if not perilous. Directing his comments to his fellow Venetians, Diedo urged the city to rectify its neglect of Roch by immediately erecting a church in his honour: "And when also the foundations of this temple have been laid, then not through the protection of doctors or other men, but by the prayers of Roch and the clemency of God, this city will straight-away be so freed from all epidemic as if it had never been punished by this kind of disease." Diedo's exhortations to his compatriots did not fall on deaf ears. Already in 1481 Roch's name was inserted into the Venetian edition of the Roman missal. His increasing fame culminated in 1485 with the acquisition and triumphant installation of his relics in Venice. From then on, Roch's status as the second major plague saint after Sebastian was firmly established.

As in the Deruta fresco, Roch's characteristic gesture in Renaissance images is the demonstrative display of his plague bubo. Like other late-medieval saints, he welcomed his disease as a divinely sent opportunity to imitate the sufferings of Christ, and Renaissance worshipers understood his patient endurance as a form of martyrdom. Directed outward to contemporaries, the sight of Roch scarred by the plague yet alive and healthy must have been an emotionally charged image of promised cure. Here was literal proof that one could survive the plague, a saint who had triumphed over the disease in his own flesh.

Performed under the divine gaze, Roch's ritualistic presentation of his "wound" secures, indeed compels, divine favor on behalf of his worshipers. This confident trust in the saint's power to wrest clemency from an angry God is dramatically articulated in a panel by Bartolomeo della Gatta, probably from the 1470s. Literally and figuratively the painting presents a confrontation between heaven and earth. Christ's determination to exact punishment from a sinning humanity is met by Roch's insistent petition that his devotees be spared. Divine implacability dissolves in the face of saintly resistance, and Christ countermands his own orders, sending a second pair of angels to intercept and break the plague arrows before they reach the town of Arezzo. Such a startling juxtaposition of apparently contradictory actions vividly illuminates the Renaissance conviction that a saint can force God to have "second thoughts." . . .

Laura A. Smoller

Plague and the Investigation of the Apocalypse

The article by Laura A. Smoller illuminates the use of a different explanatory mechanism in the face of plague. She examines how various authors linked the arrival of plague to existing beliefs about the apocalypse. Their accounts, for example, described omens like earthquakes and fire and toads raining from the sky. These were familiar biblical images drawn from an apocalyptic context. These writers also linked plague to the magical and mysterious land of the East—a region often joined in the popular imagination with natural wonders and monstrosities. Strikingly, Smoller's study demonstrates that not only religious writers but also medical and scientific writers sought to explain the plague by linking it to the apocalypse. In this way, the apocalypse became "naturalized"; it was something that could be explained in natural, not solely supernatural, terms. Such an intellectual construct stood in contrast to the writings of an earlier generation of scholars who believed that you could not subject the description of the end of times

Source: Laura A. Smoller, "Plague and the Investigation of the Apocalypse," in *Last Things: Death and the Apocalypse in the Middle Ages*, eds. Caroline Walker Bynum and Paul Freedman (Philadelphia: University of Pennsylvania Press, 2000), 167–174, 177–184, 187.

to natural explanations. Smoller argues that this "new" way of interpreting plague and its link to the apocalypse allowed these authors to walk a fine line between "dubbing the disease purely apocalyptic or purely natural." Perhaps the onset of plague signaled the end of the world, but perhaps it was just an exceptional natural event.

Plague as Apocalyptic Sign in Fourteenth-Century Texts

So what.

. . . Indeed, earthquakes and other prodigies supported a sometimes open and sometimes implicit apocalyptic discourse in several fourteenth-century chronicles about the plague. By linking the plague and the portents surrounding it with other apocalyptic signs drawn from Revelation or the Gospels, or by quoting key prophecies and passages from Scripture, these chroniclers—usually writing in the immediate wake of the initial outbreak of plague—interpret the appearance of pestilence as one of several signs of the end.

A number of authors associated the plague with known apocalyptic prophecies. For example, the Irish chronicler John Clynn, who apparently perished in the plague himself, inserted in his chronicle the widely circulated Cedar of Lebanon prophecy, now said to have been revealed in a vision to a Cistercian monk in Tripoli in 1347. Along with the now long-past falls of Tripoli and Acre, the prophecy foretold famines, great mortality, and other torments prior to a fifteen-year period of peace and then the final onslaught of Antichrist. Clynn followed up his quotation of the prophecy with the remark, "It is unheard of since the beginning of the world that so many men would have died in such a [short] time on earth, from pestilence, famine, or some other infirmity." And he made specific reference to an earthquake "which extended for thousands of miles, [and] toppled, absorbed, and overthrew cities, villages, and towns" and to the [subsequent?] pestilence that deprived these settlements of any inhabitants. Thus, for Clynn, the earthquake was directly linked to the plague, and both numbered among the apocalyptic torments described in the Cedar of Lebanon prophecy.

Within this context, perhaps, are to be understood other signs and portents Clynn listed in the years prior to 1348. For the year 1337, for example, he described flooding, freezing weather, a sheep and cattle murrain, and the unexpected appearance of roses on willow trees in England during Lent (which were taken to various locations and displayed as a spectacle). And for the year 1335, Clynn related that a large cross was erected in the square of Kilkenny, and many people had themselves branded with the sign of the cross (with a burning iron) as a sign of their pledge to go to the Holy Land. The Cedar of Lebanon prophecy Clynn would quote for 1348 predicted a "general passage by all the faithful" to the Holy Land following the times of tribulation. Looking back in 1348, those pledges too might be seen as a fulfillment of prophecy. The Cedar of Lebanon vision seems to have offered Clynn an overarching explanation for all the various signs he described. In pointing to a period of peace after torments, the prophecy could offer hope and comfort as well as provide meaning to the calamitous events.

Scripture itself provided a key for understanding plague's apocalyptic meaning for other fourteenth-century authors. For example, John of Winterthur, a Swiss Franciscan, remarked upon an earthquake in the Austrian region of Carinthia that preceded the outbreak of the plague, as he traced the disease's progress from "lands overseas" to Christendom (although without describing any marvelous portents such as a rain of fire in the east). "The aforesaid earthquake and pestilence," he wrote, "are the evil harbingers of the final abyss and the tempest, according to the words of the Savior in the gospel: 'There will be earthquakes in various places, and pestilence, and famines,' etc." (Matt. 24: 7; Luke 21: 11). . . .

Heinrich of Herford, one of the authors quoted at the outset of this essay, brought both Scripture and prophecy to bear upon his analysis of plague's role as harbinger of apocalypse. In his chronicle, tracing the world's history up to 1355, he, too, left several pointed indications that the plague and other current happenings were to be understood in apocalyptic terms. First, like John of Winterthur and William Dene, he cited scriptural passages that pointed to the Last Days. Immediately before he described the earthquake and rain of fire, serpents, toads that preceded the plague (in his entry for 1345), Heinrich lamented the sorry state of the world around him, a world full of "dissensions, rebellions, conspiracies, plots, and intrigues . . . among both secular and regular clergy"; "disturbances of young against old, ignoble against noble in many cities, monasteries, and congregations"; simony, to the extent that clerics traded appointments "for money, women, and sometimes for concubines" or gambled for them over dice; and many "disturbances and contests over kingdoms, principalities, archbishoprics, bishoprics, prebends, and other things of that kind." To Heinrich, it looked as if things were turning out "just as the apostle foretold in 2 Timothy 3[: 1–7] and 2 Corinthians 12[: 20]." The references were apocalyptic. In 2 Corinthians 12: 20, Paul had written, "For I fear, lest, when I come, I shall not find you such as I would." Promising that "in the last days perilous times shall come," Paul had detailed in the overtly apocalyptic 2 Timothy 3 the selfishness, disobedience, dissensions, and lawlessness that would reign near the end. Even before he began to discuss the plague and the prodigies surrounding its appearance, Heinrich implied that current events pointed to just those "perilous times" of which the apostle had warned.

Second, Heinrich made oblique reference to other apocalyptic prophecies, namely to the same Cedar of Lebanon prophecy that John Clynn inserted into his chronicle when he described the plague's progress in Ireland. The reference came in Heinrich's one hundredth, and final, chapter, under his entry for the year 1349, in which he described a number of disturbing events: the appearance of a ghost or phantasm, the killing of the Jews for the charge of well-poisoning (a claim Heinrich strongly disputed), the progress of plague, and the appearance of the flagellants. Heinrich condemned the flagellants for their contumacy and disrespect for the clergy, even describing how they had killed two Dominican friars. He opened his discussion of the obstreperous flagellants by saying, "In this year, a race [*gens*] without a head suddenly arose in all parts of Germany, causing universal admiration for the suddenness of their appearance and for their huge numbers." He added that they were called without a head "as if prophetically," both because they literally had no head or leader and because they figuratively had no head or prudence guiding them. The phrase "race without a head" comes from the Cedar of Lebanon prophecy. This prophecy, as mentioned above, described a period of torment, then a fifteen-year period of peace, and finally its end when "there will be heard news of Antichrist." Thus in dubbing the flagellants the "race without a head," Heinrich was inviting his readers to see their appearance as part of the apocalyptic scenario laid out in the Cedar of Lebanon vision. In fact, Heinrich had already specifically connected the flagellants with the "race without a head" and the appearance of Antichrist in the introductory matter to his hundredth chapter. There, in a summary list of the notable events that had occurred around the year 1348, he simply stated, "A race of flagellants, without a head, foretold the advent of Antichrist."

In addition to quoting Scripture and prophecy to link up his own times to end times, Heinrich further implicitly sounded an apocalyptic alarm simply by the sheer number of signs, portents, torments, and *mirabilia* that he described in the final two decades of his chronicle (ca. 1337–55). Beginning in 1337, Heinrich told of a rain of blood, the births of several monsters, a plague of locusts (echoes of Revelation 9: 3?), visions, phantasms, conspiracies, and rebellions, as well as the earthquake, fire from heaven, and rain of toads surrounding the outbreak of plague. In fact, in the introduction to the final chapter of his chronicle, Heinrich pointedly observed that "the beginning of the reign of this Charles [IV of Bohemia, r. 1346–78] seems to be memorable on account of the number of monsters, portents, and other singular happenings that then appeared." He then strung together a list of all the various portents and *mirabilia* that he had already mentioned or would describe in the pages to come. Heinrich did not here specify what we are to make of this clustering of signs, but, given his quotations of Scripture and prophecy, we are perhaps to conclude that, like Matthew Paris in 1250, Heinrich saw the increased number of marvelous phenomena as an indication that the world was nearing its end.

In the final pages of Heinrich's chronicle, however, he interjected that note of caution sounded so frequently in medieval discussions of the end's timing. "And note," he wrote, "that this eighth year of Charles's reign was the 5317th from the beginning of the world, the 3661st from Noah's exit from the ark," and so on, listing counts of years for various other chronological schemes. As Richard Landes has pointed out for the early Middle Ages, such countdowns were inherently eschatological, by either explicitly or implicitly allowing readers to calculate the number of years left until the world's fated 6000th year. Heinrich here followed Bede's calculation of the age of the world, a figure much smaller than other estimates of its age and one that put the end of the sixth (and presumably final) millennium several centuries distant even from Heinrich's time. Further—and here Heinrich showed his realization that this type of countdown could be apocalyptic—Heinrich felt compelled to continue with a discussion of the unknowability of the time of the end. "The time remaining in this sixth age," he reminded his readers, "is known only to God. It is not for men to know the times or moments that the father has reserved to his power" (Acts 1: 7). Indeed, in Augustinian fashion, he stated that the seventh age of repose for the blessed, "its door quietly opened," had begun with the sixth age and ran along concurrently with it. While Heinrich was quite willing to string together contemporary apocalyptic signs and quotations from Scripture, he showed understandable and customary caution in definitely announcing the immediacy of the end.

Although this sort of caution frequently accompanied apocalyptic predictions, the explicit pointers to eschatological texts and prophecies in the chronicles of Heinrich of Herford, John Clynn, John of Winterthur, and William Dene strongly suggest that the constellation of bizarre *mirabilia* described by other chroniclers, such as the earthquakes, hail, and rains of toads and snakes with which I began this essay, were also meant to have apocalyptic echoes. Thunder, hail, and fire falling from heaven figure not simply among the plagues of Egypt (Ex. 9: 23–26), but also in Revelation, in which the first trumpet blast of the seven angels with seven trumpets results in hail and fire mingled with blood (Rev. 8: 7), and the pouring out of the seventh of the vials of God's wrath brings about earthquakes, thunderings, and a plague of enormous hailstones that destroy the city of Babylon (Rev. 16: 21). Indeed, in the letter of Louis Heyligen quoted by the anonymous Flemish chronicler, the reference to "thunder, lightning, and hail of marvelous size," may well be a nod to Revelation 16, in which "every [hail]stone [was] about the weight of a talent" (Rev. 16: 21). The same anonymous chronicler even more ominously described a hailstorm in 1349 in which the egg-sized hailstones had faces, eyes, and tails.

Fire and smoke were other apocalyptic signs featured in fourteenth-century texts about the plague. Stinking smoke attendant on heavenly fire appears in both the Neuberg monastery chronicle and Heyligen's letter among the causes of the outbreak of the plague in the east. The image of fire raining down from the heavens as described in words in these fourteenth-century chronicles could have triggered visual memories of illustrations connected with Revelation. God sends fire from heaven to destroy Satan's army after his final unloosing in Revelation 20: 9. And fetid smoke emerges from the bottomless pit, along with locusts, in Revelation 9: 2–3.

Frogs, too, have scriptural resonances. They number among the plagues of Egypt (the second plague, Exodus 8: 1–15; also Psalms 78 and 105), along with a plague of festering boils (Exodus 9: 8–12). The rain of toads and frogs in fourteenth-century writings about the Black Death also would remind readers of the unclean spirits of Revelation 16: 13, spirits in the form of frogs (*in modo ranarum*) that issue from the mouths of the dragon, the beast, and the false prophet. These frogs, too, are depicted in illustrations of Revelation, and commentators equated the frogs' croaking voices with the blasphemous words issuing from the mouths of the preachers of Antichrist.

Thus, the unusual precipitation of fire, hail, snakes, and toads reported in the chronicles of Heinrich of Herford and the Neuberg monastery and in the letter of Louis Heyligen had an implicitly apocalyptic meaning. The message did not need to be spelled out. With or without quotations from Scripture and prophecy, such chroniclers presented the plague in a decidedly apocalyptic fashion.

Earthquakes, Frogs, Snakes, and Storms as Part of a Natural Explanation of Plague

If the frogs, hail, earthquakes, and other unusual weather surrounding the outbreak of the plague in the east could be read as apocalyptic portents, they nonetheless figure as well in fourteenth-century scientific explanations of the plague. In fact, the whole cluster of bizarre signs associated with the initial outbreak of plague in the chronicles of Heinrich of Herford and others finds its way into medical and scientific treaties as well. These phenomena form part of the natural causes of plague detailed in fourteenth-century scientific writings about the disease. Further, the very chroniclers who insert apocalyptic portents into their treatment of plague sometimes explain these signs using natural philosophy. In scientific writings as well as in monastic chronicles, fourteenth-century authors presented the plague as simultaneously a sign of God's final wrath and a phenomenon capable of receiving a natural explanation.

The best-known scientific discussion of plague from the mid-fourteenth century is the treatise composed by the medical faculty of the University of Paris. As historians frequently note, the Paris physicians blamed the plague on the famous "triple conjunction" of Saturn, Jupiter, and Mars on March 20, 1345. But this conjunction forms only a part of the faculty's analysis of the causes of the plague, which they argue had both a remote cause (the heavens) and a proximal cause (the earth). The conjunction of March 1345 was the remote and universal cause of the plague, and it had the effect, argued the Paris physicians, of drawing up warm, moist vapors from the earth, which were corrupted by Mars (which ignited them and particularly caused corruption because it was retrograde) and Jupiter (whose quartile aspect with Mars [?] caused a bad disposition in the air inimical to human nature). The configuration of the heavens also had the effect of generating many winds, particularly warm, moist southern winds. Thus the triple conjunction served as a universal remote cause of plague.

The Paris doctors also described a more proximal cause of plague, namely air corrupted by bad vapors (also a result of the triple conjunction) and spread about by the south wind. Corrupt air was even more harmful to the body than corrupt food or water, asserted the doctors, because it could more rapidly penetrate to the lungs and heart. Such pestiferous vapors could arise from stagnant water or unburied bodies or could even escape directly from the earth during an earthquake. When they rose and mixed with the air, the whole air would be corrupted, and an epidemic would result. In other words, earthquakes functioned not simply as signs of divine wrath, but in a medical understanding of plague they also were the source of noxious vapors that corrupted the air, causing disease in humans.

Another proximal cause of plague in the Paris medical faculty's opinion was a change in weather. Here, the physicians were following good Hippocratic teaching, which looked to changes in weather as a cause of epidemics. In particular, unusual weather throughout the four seasons could produce a pestilential year, the Paris doctors argued, and they noted that the preceding winter had been warmer and rainier than usual. Further, they feared that the next spring might bring yet another round of pestilence should the winter again prove abnormally warm and wet. While the Paris physicians do not directly mention hail as a feature of plague-generating weather, they nonetheless finger an excess of warm rains (presumably some of which would be accompanied by thunder, lightning, and hail) as culprits in a pestilential year.

Furthermore, the Paris doctors, like the chroniclers with whom I began, added a geographical component to their description of plague's origins. The Paris physicians pointed to the south and east as the ultimate source of plague and the location of the most noteworthy phenomena associated with the corruption of air and outbreak of pestilence. The physicians had stated that the upcoming year might well be another plague year should the winter again be warm and wet. Nonetheless, they asserted that any such plague would be less dangerous in France than in "southern or eastern regions" because the conjunctions and other causes detailed in their treatise would have more effect in those regions. And, they noted, there had been "numerous exhalations and inflammations, such as a *draco* and falling stars." They sky had in fact taken on a distinct yellow and red tone from the scorched vapors, the doctors declared, and there had been frequent lightning, thunderings, and intense winds from the south, carrying great amounts of dust with them. These winds, said the doctors, "are worse than all others, [in] quickly and more completely spreading bodies of putrefaction, especially strong earthquakes, [and] a multitude of fish and dead animals at the seashores, and in many regions trees [have been] covered by dust." Further, the doctors noted that "some say they have seen a multitude of frogs and reptiles which are generated from putrefaction." All of these, the faculty of medicine wrote, "appear to precede great putrefaction in the aid and the earth." "No wonder if we fear that there is a future epidemic coming!" Because the work of the south wind was so crucial in spreading corruption in their explanation, the doctors implied that corruption would arise in the south and east and be dispersed by the winds.

Certainly the faculty of medicine in Paris were no scientific revolutionaries. Their explanation of epidemics arising from corrupted air was completely standard according to Galenic medical theory. And their list of signs and causes of corruption, from unusual weather to earthquakes to frogs and dead fish, again was completely standard. Scholastic science held that frogs, toads, snakes, and worms could be generated from corrupt matter and that such animals were inherently poisonous. In early modern Europe, there would be a strong association between toads and the plague, and persons of all social strata would wear amulets containing various preparations made from toads and arsenic to guard against pestilence.

Nonetheless, the way in which these phenomena cluster together in the Paris medical faculty's treatise is striking. If fifteen lines (of printed text), we move from a reference to southern and eastern regions, to falling stars, to a reddened sky, to thunder and lightning, to dust storms, to earthquakes, to dead fish, to trees overcome by dust, and at last to frogs and other reptiles. One could just as easily be reading the work of Heinrich of Herford as that of the Paris medical faculty. A reader might indeed think these were the "signs in the sun, and in the moon, and in the stars" of Luke 21: 25. And yet they fit entirely within the medical explanation of the plague arising from corruption in the air. . . .

Heinrich of Herford's *Liber de rebus memorabilioribus* is particularly noteworthy for the number of signs and portents the author describes in the final decades of his chronicle, which ends in 1355. As noted above,

Heinrich makes specific mention of a cluster of portents at the start of the reign of the emperor Charles of Bohemia in 1348. Given his citation of apocalyptic texts from 2 Timothy and 2 Corinthians, his use of other apocalyptic language, and his deliberate pointing to the cluster of portents around the time of the plague, it is apparent that Heinrich meant to give his text an apocalyptic slant. And yet, Heinrich also frequently appended to his descriptions of just such marvels explanations drawn from natural philosophy. No longer are these portents seen through the lens of an either/or dichotomy either as natural events or as supernatural apocalyptic signs. In Heinrich's chronicle, the same events are often uncomfortably and unexplainedly both.

For example, for the year 1337, Heinrich described in immediate succession the following prodigies: a rain of blood in Erfurt, a nine-year-old girl bearing a child by her father, and the birth of a baby girl with breasts, pubic hair, and menstrual periods. Then he immediately quoted a passage from Albertus Magnus's *Physica* in which Albert explained just such a monstrous birth. Such monsters, according to Albert, result from an abundance of the material of the first seed and the strength of the heat and virtue forming the infant. "And in my own times," Albert wrote—and Heinrich quoted him—"there was displayed a girl who had been born with breasts and with hair under her arms and in her groin, and her mother asserted that she also suffered from a monthly flow, which without doubt happened on account of the heat that formed and matured [the fetus]." This same principle is at work in the births of children who already have teeth, according to Albert. The sexually precocious girls of 1337 thus could be explained by natural causes. Heinrich did not offer here an explanation—marvelous or scientific—for the rain of blood in Erfurt, although he was careful to note that he himself had seen "its drops captured in a white linen cloth." (The same sort of attention to first-person observation marks the pages of Albert's treatises also.) Several pages later, however, the reader is again inundated with a wave of portents and with a scientific explanation of them.

Under the year 1345, Heinrich opened his discussion of the Black Death, with his quotation of a letter describing the earthquake in Carinthia on the feast of the conversion of St. Paul, a rain of fire in the land of the Turks, and a rain of toads and snakes. Under the same year, he recounted the stories of a number of battles, the appearance of a devil (*dyabolus*) who killed or harassed several men in the household on one Thyderic Sobben, and ghosts (*fantasmata*) who were carousing in a church in Mendene. In the following brief entry for the year 1346, Heinrich noted some important political events: the election of Charles of Bohemia as king of the Romans and the death of King Philip of France. The bulk of his remarks for the year 1346, however, concerned yet another marvelous phenomenon, this time the birth in Westphalia of a lamb with two heads, the lower one a lamb's head and the upper one a bird's head. The monster seemed "both to have been a portent and to be attributed to the virtue of the stars." Heinrich again appended quotations from Albertus Magnus's *Physica* and *De meteoris* offering explications of the birth of monsters. These quotations, however, can apply not simply to the two-headed lamb that Heinrich has just described, but also to the portents in the east in the letter he had quoted with respect to the outbreak of plague.

Following the description of the two-headed lamb, Heinrich quoted three passages from Albertus Magnus. In the first, from the *Physica*, Albert explained monstrous births similar to the two-headed lamb Heinrich described, using as an example the birth of piglets with human faces. In such a case where the offspring had the characteristics of two very different beings, the operation of the heavenly bodies had to be at work, for the seeds of humans and pigs (or, mutates mutandis, sheep and birds) were too different for any progeny to be engendered. Rather, the seeds would mutually corrupt one another. But the planets could induce the pig's seed to take on a form outside of its ordinary capacity, as, for example, when the sun, moon, and some other planets were all in a certain region of Aries and no human could be generated. Presumably, the lamb's bird head was formed in this manner. Next, and with no explanation of why, Heinrich quoted two passages from Albertus Magnus's *De meteoris*. Both dealt with the generation of animals in an unusual manner, but not this time with two-headed sheep, human-headed pigs, or even pig-headed humans. Rather, the two passages Heinrich lined up here describe the generation of animals in the clouds, with resulting rains of small frogs, fish, worms, and, even once, a calf. Heinrich seems to be thinking back to his entry for the previous year about the rain of toads and snakes in the east that preceded the outbreak of plague.

According to the passages Heinrich quoted from Albert, these phenomena, too, were susceptible of natural explanations. As heat causes rainwater to evaporate, Albert had argued, it can draw up a little earthy matter mixed in with the moisture. That mixture, once taken up into the air, begins to harden and to become skin. The continual exposure to heat produces a spirit within that skin, to which the virtue of the stars adds a sensitive soul, so that an animal results. The beings so generated are usually aquatic animals like frogs, fish, and worms because in such rains the watery element prevails over the earthy element. As in the case of the calf that fell from the sky, however, the body of a perfect animal could be formed in the clouds, a fact to be explained by the virtue of the stars. The joint actions of evaporation and the stars, thus—although Heinrich does not explicitly draw this connection—could be responsible for the marvelous rain of toads and serpents that preceded the plague as well.

The same conflation of the natural and the apocalyptic comes in Heinrich's treatment of the flagellants. On the one hand, his most overtly apocalyptic language comes in his description of the flagellants, of whom he wrote, "[the appearance of] a race of flagellants without a head foretold the advent of Antichrist." At the same time, here, too, comes his most blatant scientific explanation of a presumed apocalyptic sign. Heinrich dwelt at length on the flagellants (for more than four pages in the modern edition), whom he condemned as imprudent, defiant, and a corrupting influence. He apparently was drawing on firsthand experience of their rituals, saying that he himself had seen the sharp points at the ends of their whips embedded in their flesh so that they could not easily be pulled out and noting with the empathy of one who had been there that "it would take a heart of stone to watch such behavior without shedding tears." He also quoted at length (perhaps in its entirety) a treatise on the flagellants composed by one Gerhardus de Cosvelde, "rector of the scholars in the city of Münster in Westphalia." This remarkable treatise offered an explanation of the flagellant movement based entirely on astrology.

Gerhardus's analysis of the flagellants rested upon the horoscope he erected for the moment of the sun's entry into Aries on March 12, 1349, the beginning of the astrological year. (The horoscope is also reproduced in Heinrich's chronicle.) For Gerhardus, the key component of this horoscope was the third mundane house, beginning with Aries and containing the planets of the sun, Saturn, Mars, and Mercury. According to Gerhardus, the third mundane house presided over faith, religion, and mutations of religion. The sun was in a position of particular strength in this horoscope (Gerhardus indeed dubs the sun the "lord of the year"), and its position in the mundane house signifying religion meant that it would "multiply a religion and sect." Further, Gerhardus declared that the new sect foretold by the horoscope would have its origins "in the east," since Aries was an eastern sign having significance mainly over Germany, according to Alchabitius, author of a widely used medieval textbook of astrology. Thus the new sect would thrive chiefly in Germany. The fact that Mars and Mercury were in conjunction in the horoscope signified beatings with whips and the effusion of blood. Because the two planets were in Jupiter's *domus*, their influence would lead men to join this sect—and not without hypocrisy (all attributed to Alchabitius).

Every detail of the flagellants' activities finds an astrological explanation in the treatise Heinrich quotes. The flagellants wear a grey hood before their eyes, and thus a saturnine aspect, because in the horoscope Saturn is in the sign of Aries, which has significance for the head. In their rituals, they "fall down to the ground horribly" because the planets signifying the flagellants are in one of the "falling" (*cadens*) mundane houses. The cause of their (partial) nudity is found in the fact that Saturn is both combust (i.e., within a given number of degrees of the sun) and in Aries, the sign of its dejection. Their strange garments arise from the influence of Venus, which is in Saturn's *domus* in the horoscope and is a signifier of women's clothing. The flagellants claim to be inspired by a stone tablet brought down from heaven by an angel. This "fiction" is caused by the falling Saturn (i.e., the planet is in its dejection and in a cadent mundane house), which signifies about heavy things like stones, as well as about oracles and the apparition of secret things. The lying nature of the sect, as well as its instability, result from the baleful appearance of the sign of Scorpio in the midheaven (the tenth mundane house in a horoscope), for Scorpio signifies sorrow, lying, and instability. The fact that Scorpio appears in the tenth mundane house, the *domus* of Jupiter, results in people believing the flagellants' lies and calling them miracles, "on account of Jupiter's faith." In short, Gerhardus concludes, "I say that in my estimation *this sect is purely natural*, and that they are acting under a species of fury called mania. . . . And the sect will not last long, but will end quickly and with confusion and infamy." The apocalyptic "race without a head" is now explained entirely by the stars. If this is not Heinrich's conclusion also, he gives us no sign here, for he moves immediately to a discussion of political events and leaves the flagellants behind.

Even the succeeding passages in Heinrich's text, however, leave the reader poised between marvelous and scientific explanations of events. Under the year 1351, Heinrich described an unusual plague in the town of Hameln. A pit was being dug and cleared out in grounds belonging to one of the town's citizens when one of the workers suddenly fell down and at once expired. A second worker went into the pit to retrieve the body and suffered the same fate. The word quickly spread, but no one knew the cause of the plague. A third worker was sent into the pit, but this time a rope tied around his waist, so that he could quickly be hauled out. Again, the pit proved poisonous, but the worker was able to give a sign as he was becoming stiff and stupefied and was pulled out half-dead. A fourth worker entered the pit and died as the first two had. Opinion was divided, according to Heinrich, on the cause of this singular plague. Some leaned towards a marvelous explanation. They maintained that there must be a basilisk in the pit, able to kill instantly by its breath or even its very glance. Others tended towards a scientific analysis. They held that the earth in the pit had been poisoned by the fact that in the past there had been many latrines in the same place. At length, the pit was filled with a broth-like mixture of boiling water and flour, and the plague was ended, either by the death of the basilisk or by the purging of the poisons from the pit.

This story very closely parallels passages from scientific treatises on earthquakes. In the *De meteoris*, for example, Albertus Magnus claims to have witnessed just such an incident when a long-closed well in Padua was opened up, a happening he attributed not to a basilisk, but to the venomous nature of vapors remaining enclosed within the earth for a long time. There is also a like passage in the anonymous *quaestio* attributing the Black Death to earthquakes. The author of the *quaestio*, like Albert, adduced such a scenario to prove how poisonous were the fumes released by earthquakes. He further remarked that ignorant people attributed death just like those Heinrich here described to the existence of a basilisk in the pit, whereas the explanation was properly to be found in the poisonous vapors enclosed within the earth. Heinrich is clearly aware of both sorts of explanations as he describes the venomous pit of Hameln. Just as he does with the monstrous births and rain of worms and snakes in his chronicle, however, he refuses here to give the nod to either a purely marvelous or a purely scientific explanation. This little "plague" in Hameln, like the universal bubonic plague, is ambiguous in Heinrich's chronicle, capable of multiple interpretations. In the case of the little Hameln plague, Heinrich offers us two competing, and by implication mutually exclusive, explanations. Either there is a basilisk in the pit or the latrines once on this site poisoned the soil. In the case of the universal pestilence, however, the interpretation is not posed in either/or terms. We may understand the earthquakes, fire from heaven, rain of toads, and pestilence *at the same time* as proceeding from God's wrath, as being signs of the approaching end, and as resulting from natural causes.

Multiple Meanings and the Trend to Naturalize the Apocalypse

Why might plague in the minds of fourteenth-century authors bear such a multivalent analysis? Why might one aspect of a description of the plague—frogs, say—carry us effortlessly from biblical imagery (Exodus and Revelation) to natural philosophy? Why does the same cluster of phenomena (earthquakes, frogs, worms, rains of fire) pop up as readily in a natural philosopher's analysis of the disease as in an apocalyptic letter about marvelous prodigies in distant and nearby lands? . . .

It is not surprising that the same cluster of phenomena appear in monastic chronicles and medical discussions of the plague. An event like plague could not be understood entirely apart from God. Once an author began to describe plague with the language of natural philosophy, miasma-generating earthquakes inevitably shaded into apocalyptic earthquakes, and corrupt vapors inside the earth began to look like corrupt enemies within Christendom. Existing eschatology shaped and informed the map on which fourteenth-century Christians plotted the epidemic's course. While mapping can indeed represent the act of possession, of physically and intellectually grasping space, mapping the fourteenth-century Black Death rather inserted it into an orb already freighted with meaning, where earthquakes, plague, frogs, and hail hovered in a polysemic limbo between physical undoing and apocalyptic unveiling.

Second, the ambiguity of the portents in the fourteenth-century plague treatises must be seen additionally as a species of caution in predicting the time of the end, whether reading portents or using astrology or some other branch of natural philosophy to do so. By leaving open the question of whether this plague and these earthquakes were a sign of end times or simply a manifestation of a bad run of weather, fourteenth-century authors could hedge their bets. . . . The Paris doctors mention falling stars, thunder, lightning, earthquakes, and frogs, yet set these apocalyptic emblems within a clearly scientific context. These multivalent signs allowed fourteenth-century authors safely to predict and not predict the end at the same time. . . .

Unwilling definitively to announce that the world was about to end, fourteenth-century authors allowed their presentations to hover between dubbing the disease purely apocalyptic or purely natural. In their indecisive ambiguity, they refused to set the problem in the terms defined at century's beginning, in which the apocalypse was to have nothing whatsoever to do with natural causes. In so doing, they left open the possibility

that events might in fact be seen simultaneously as apocalyptic and resulting from natural causes. . . .Doubtless these authors were terrified
and sought to understand the overwhelming disaster around them in
any and every way possible, even in ways deemed to be incompatible. In
their very human reactions to plague, these writers reopened the door to
naturalizing the apocalypse.

Richard Kieckhefer

Radical Tendencies in the Flagellant Movement of the Mid-Fourteenth Century

Richard Kieckhefer's article tackles one of the most dramatic examples of
penitence as a reaction to the plague. His examination of the flagellant movement seeks to understand how the movement changed over time. In the eyes
of contemporaries and even modern historians it became more "radical" in
the brief years before the papacy officially condemned it. He acknowledges,
however, the inherent difficulty of interpreting the actions of the flagellants,
since they lacked ideological and geographical coherence. Ultimately, he
finds the best explanation for the flagellants' change in message and behavior
when he tracks such changes against the course and movement of the plague.
He argues that "the anticipation of disaster provoked more volatile emotions
than the disaster itself."

I

When the Black Death spread across northern Europe between 1348 and
1350, it inspired a penitential movement designed to ward off God's wrath
and arrest the progress of the disease. The chroniclers speak of thousands

Source: Richard Kieckhefer, "Radical Tendencies in the Flagellant Movement of the Mid-
Fourteenth Century," *Journal of Medieval and Renaissance Studies* 4 (1974): 157–158, 160–165.

of men who joined in processions and went from town to town, flagellating themselves in public. Their purpose was unquestionably salutary, and the practice of flagellation had long been accepted by the Church as a mode of penance. Yet virtually everywhere they went, the flagellants met some degree of resistance. By autumn of 1349 the matter had given rise to concern on more than a local level. The theological faculty of the University of Paris sent a preacher to give a sermon before Pope Clement VI regarding the penitents. On October 20 the pontiff issued a bull condemning the movement as a form of heresy and calling for its suppression by ecclesiastical and secular authorities. In some places the decree was almost immediately effective, while in others there was need for repeated prohibitions over the next few years. The most serious resistance occurred in and around Thuringia, where the movement apparently went underground and survived, at least marginally heretical, for more than a century.

As Herbert Grundmann remarked, one of the most significant questions about the flagellants is why contemporaries "hereticated" them as they did, within so brief a time. To account for the suppression, historians have usually maintained that the flagellants, while originally devout and orthodox, became radical in the later months of the movement. After an orthodox phase of sincere penitence, the flagellants are supposed to have entered a less highly motivated phase in which members were predominantly from the lower classes, discipline was relaxed, anticlerical sentiment led to confrontations with the clergy, and violence ensued, particularly in the form of attacks on the Jews. This thesis has recently been challenged by the East German historian Martin Erbstösser, who proposes that the differences within the flagellant movement were not chronological, but geographical. It was only in the areas of Thuringia and Franconia, Erbstösser argues, that the flagellants underwent significant radicalization. Why did these particular regions breed exceptionally radical flagellants? According to Erbstösser, when the movement passed through these areas it fell subject to the influence of a heresy especially prevalent there, the doctrine of the Free Spirit; this influence, together with that of popular millenarian beliefs, sufficed to make the movement radically and violently anticlerical.

Erbstösser has performed a valuable service in reopening a question that historians have long considered closed. There are problems, however, that he has left unresolved, and doubts may be raised concerning certain of his suggestions. In any case, there is ample reason to return to the sources and reconsider these essential questions: To what extent, and in what ways, did the flagellants in fact become radical? And what were the sources of their radical inclinations?

II

. . . But four specific claims of this interpretation call for special consideration: (i) that the social composition of the movement changed; (ii) that the flagellants took violent action against the clergy; (iii) that they were responsible for violence against the Jews; and (iv) that they adopted heretical doctrines.

Even if it could be shown that the flagellants underwent some sort of fundamental change, it would be difficult to show that this was caused by a wholesale shift in their social composition. It is true that some of the chroniclers speak of vagabonds, thieves, and other disreputable elements as entering into the movement; others complain that women and even children began flagellating themselves. But more commonly the sources given merely conventional lists of the various participants in the movement: Hugo of Reutlingen, for instance, says that "priest and count, soldier and arms-bearer joined with them, as well as master of the school, monks, burghers, peasants, and scholars," while the *Gesta archiepiscoporum Magdeburgensium* states that the flagellants included "some priests and clergy, some noble laymen, and many others in great numbers." In neither case does the chronicler differentiate between an earlier and a later phase. The *Breve chronicon Flandriae* describes the movement during its last few months, yet it still indicates that "there were, it is said, sons of dukes and prices among them, [and] priests and clerics." To be sure, it would be a mistake to take these accounts entirely at face value, but for most regions they are the best sources we have, and they hardly serve to support the traditional two-phase theory. At most, one might suggest that the social composition of the movement may have altered in certain localities; the evidence does not suggest that this change was thoroughgoing.

Likewise, there is only meager evidence for physical violence against the clergy. To be sure, the movement seems always to have had anti-clerical leanings. It was essentially a lay movement—not only in the sense that its members were mostly lay, but in the more important sense that it was outside clerical supervision. Even in the Low Countries, where the flagellants received support from the clergy, they do not seem to have relinquished their principle of lay leadership. Hence, churchmen clearly recognized the movement as a challenge to their authority in religious matters, and chroniclers frequently protested that the movement was formed without proper authority. Matters were bad enough when the flagellants contented themselves with their penitential devotions. The flames of conflict were fanned all the higher, however, when they assumed authority to preach and hear each other's confessions, when they attempted to perform miracles, and when they vaunted their superiority to the clergy. It was perhaps inevitable that the repudiation of clerical control led to confrontations with the clergy, and that these confrontations in turn produced bitter sentiments. What is surprising, though, is how seldom these confrontations led to violence. As Erbstösser rightly points out, the reports of such action derive mainly from the region around Thuringia. And even in this area, the sources generally speak only in vague terms of violence that the flagellants planned to carry out, such as stoning the clergy to death. We have reliable testimony to only one concrete incident, in which one Dominican was killed, while another fled from his assailants.

The flagellants have also been charged with responsibility for the persecution of the Jews in 1349, but the role they played in these pogroms is difficult to discern. Contemporary chroniclers seldom link them with these incidents; one verse chronicle from Brabant states that flagellants killed the Jews, though it gives no specific details. A chronicle written in Lübeck speaks of the flagellants in Cologne as slaying the Jews, though the records from Cologne make no such suggestion. A fifteenth-century chronicle indicated that the flagellants at Frankfurt took part in a pogrom there, but the claim is not borne out in contemporary sources. In the last-mentioned case, the fifteenth-century chronicler evidently made a common error: reading in an earlier source that the flagellants appeared in 1349 and that the Jews were attacked in the same year, he presupposed a connection between the events. What seems to have been the case is that the flagellants, by arousing fear of the plague, stirred the people in various communities to mob action against the Jews. There are some indications that the Jews were apprehensive of the flagellants' arrival, and in one town the Jews seem to have taken the offensive against the flagellants. One can only conjecture, however, whether these Jews feared the flagellants as the cause of potential conflict or merely as its occasion. On the other hand, when the preacher from Paris went to Avignon, he attributed direct responsibility for the pogroms to the flagellants, presumably in an attempt to appeal to Pope Clement's well-known sympathy for the Jews. This preacher was probably not an eye-witness to the violence and did not cite any specific instances in which he knew of flagellants' participation. Again, we are left with no sure way of deciding how much credence to place in his report. Even if we assume that the flagellants did at times take violent measures against the Jews, one might question whether this evidence for radicalization of degeneration of the movement. For after all, pogroms had been carried out on other occasions by otherwise respectable townsmen, and the rumor that Jews had poisoned the wells had resulted in violence in 1348, even before the flagellant movement got under way.

The charge that the flagellants became heretical will occupy us at length in the next section of this article; for now, a few general comments may suffice. Chroniclers commonly referred to the flagellants as a "sect" or as "heretical," and when Clement VI condemned the movement he referred to it as a "sect," but the specific meaning of these terms remains obscure. With only a few exceptions (discussed below), the flagellants' critics failed to indicate specific doctrines attributable to the penitents. Perhaps they knew of such teachings, but did not care to relate them. Yet this negligence would be peculiar, especially in those sources that went to great pains to discredit the movement. When the preacher from Paris delivered his sermon at Avignon, he showed in great detail the dangers of the movement, but said nothing about specific doctrinal errors.

Certain practices of the flagellants might be interpreted as implying heretical belief. Particularly upsetting to the clergy, for instance, was the flagellants' practice of absolving one another from sin. Lay confession was not defined as heretical in the Middle Ages, though its sacramental character was a question of dispute. The regular exercise of such confession, however, was clearly incompatible with respect for the clergy, and relations between the flagellants and the ecclesiastical establishment no doubt suffered greatly because of this usurpation of sacerdotal function. It is difficult to ascertain how extensively the practice occurred; there is no reason to think that it arose merely during a later period of supposed radicalization. Most important, there is no evidence that the flagellants concerned themselves with the subtleties of ecclesiology. Their challenge was not so much doctrinal as practical; the mere fact that they conducted their devotions without clerical supervision was enough for clerics to brand them as "heretical," in the loose sense of that term which became common in the late Middle Ages. Likewise, certain chroniclers branded as "heretical" the flagellants' refusal to pay tokens of respect when a priest elevated the host or read the gospel. But once again, it would be rash to conclude that the penitents held explicit Donatist principles. Many members of the movement were no doubt bitterly anticlerical, but there is no reason to envision them as tampering with doctrine.

Perhaps the cardinal error of the two-phase theory is its supposition that the flagellant movement was cohesive and could succumb uniformly to radical influences. Given the loose organization of the movement, the autonomy of each band of penitents, and the lack of routine communication among the various processions, such a supposition seems wholly unwarranted. From the evidence at our disposal we may perhaps conclude that flagellants in some communities were responsible for violence, and that in some locations the social composition of the processions was altered. But to generalize from such instances would be hazardous, and to superimpose such generalizations on a simple chronological schema would be dangerous in the extreme. It is entirely possible that the social level represented by the movement was rising in one place at the same time that it was declining elsewhere. The potential diversity within such a movement cannot be overemphasized. Unfortunately we have all too little specific information, but the information we do have runs counter to the notion of a simple shift from sincere penitence to radical action. . . .

IV

We are still confronted with the fact that the flagellants of central Germany were distinctively radical. Can we account for this development without subscribing to Erbstösser's thesis? Perhaps the question should rather be why we need to account for it at all. As Herbert Grundmann has made clear in his study of other religious movements, the attitude of the clergy was largely instrumental in determining whether a lay movement would become radical or whether it would enter under clerical supervision and become serviceable to the Church; if the clergy had not "hereticated" the Waldensians, for instance, they might not have become in fact heretical. The same principle applies to the flagellants. We need not hypothesize either corruption by lower-class and criminal elements or influence of preexisting ideologies. The possibilities for radicalization were inherent in the movement from its start. If the flagellants of Austria were not as vehemently anticlerical as those in Thuringia (and owing to the nature of the sources it would be difficult to substantiate this point), the relative tameness of the Austrian groups may derive from their relatively small numbers. Central Germany was the first place in which large numbers of flagellants seem to have gathered, without any form of discipline or supervision. The threat to the Church's authority was obvious; confrontations were perhaps inevitable. The anomaly would seem to be the moderation of the movement when it spread from central Germany to the Southwest. Without coming under ecclesiastical or governmental control, the flagellants there are said to have imposed rigid discipline on themselves. To be sure, this self-control was not wholly effective in preventing friction between the penitents and the clergy, but so far as we know there was no radicalization such as developed in the central territories. One would like to know something about how this discipline was instigated and enforced, but on these matters the sources are silent. It is tempting, for example, to speculate that there may have been a split in the movement in Thuringia; that the radical members remained there and in the latter part of the century formed a sect, whereas the moderates moved south and west, developing their rigid discipline as a reaction against the radical outgrowth they left behind. In any case, the absence of radical developments among the flagellants in the Southwest is more of a mystery than the occurrence of such developments elsewhere.

One may perhaps shed a few rays of light on the matter by investigating the relationship between the flagellant movement and the plague. The course of the plague can be traced with a fair degree of confidence: coming from southern Europe, it spread in a generally northward and northeastward direction. The spread of the flagellant movement, on the other hand, is more difficult to discern and has given rise to disagreement, though if we abstract from minor splinter groups we amy trace the spread of the movement with reasonable certainty: beginning in Austria and perhaps Hungary, the main current of the movement moved north and northwest into Thuringia, then down into Franconia, to the Upper Rhine, and then northward to the Low Countries. Roughly speaking, then, the course was that of a sideways S. Thus, from autumn of 1348 to spring of 1349, when the flagellants moved from Austria to Thuringia and down into Franconia, they were several months in advance of the plague. Sometime in late spring or early summer 1349 the flagellants in their southwestern progression (from Thuringia toward the Southwest) met with the plague in its northeastern movement. From this point on, as the processions spread they entered territories that had already succumbed to the plague. For example, the penitents entered Magdeburg and Erfurt at least six months before the plague reached these cities, but in Strassburg, Cologne, and the Low Countries the movement arrived only after the onset of the plague.

It is perhaps not coincidental that the movement became overtly radical in regions where it preceded the plague, and took on moderate form in precisely those areas where the plague preceded it. Prior to the convergence of the movement and the disease, the flagellants had gone about as precursors of the plague, encouraging people to do penance so that God would spare them the disease. Subsequent to the meeting, though, the movement changed its fundamental purpose; the most it could expect was deliverance from a disease which had already arrived, or protection for the individual flagellant. It is perhaps not unreasonable to conjecture that this change in purpose brought about a change in character. It seems entirely plausible that the anticipation of disaster provoked more volatile emotions than the disaster itself. Before the convergence with the plague, the flagellants' movement served to excite anxieties regarding the plague, but because the tensions were based (for the majority of townsmen) only on imagination of the disease, and not on experience of it, they lacked all sense of realism. During the early months, when people had heard about the plague but had not witnessed it, there was no practical action that they could take and no need for the practical functions of attending to the sick and burying the dead. The only outlet for tension, and the sole means for acting on imagined fears, was perhaps violent action; before the plague actually arrived, this action could easily be diverted against victims who had no real connection with the plague, such as the clergy and the Jews. (It is worth noting in this connection that most of the pogroms of 1348–49 took place before the onset of the plague in each particular community.) Under these circumstances, one might expect that the flagellants' inherent radical tendencies would be fostered and intensified. But when the flagellants entered a town where the plague had already arrived, one might expect that the penitential purpose of the movement would be stressed more clearly, and that radical developments would be less common.

Granted, this speculative explanation probably does not suffice by itself to account for the radicalization of the movement, but it may serve as a partial explanation. The essential point is that the inclination toward radical anticlericalism was an inherent tendency within the movement. The potential for radical developments was always present, and required only a favorable context to become manifest. Thus, one need not postulate that external forces, such as lower-class membership or preexisting heresies, brought about this radicalization; this supposition is unnecessary, and is not borne out by the sources.

David Nirenberg

Communities of Violence: Persecution of Minorities in the Middle Ages

In some parts of Europe the onset of plague led to the disturbing reaction of violence against the Jews. Sometimes these attacks were linked to accusations of well-poisoning. In this excerpt, however, David Nirenberg objects to the tendency of some scholars to look at violence against the Jews during the plague collectively across the European continent. Instead, he argues, events such as these can only be understood in their specific historical and geographical contexts—characterizing them as a nonspecific, irrational, and general phenomenon does little to further our understanding of the tense relations between Jews and Christians in medieval Europe. Thus, his is a study of violence against the Jews in the medieval Spanish kingdom of Aragon in the years surrounding the plague's arrival in that region. Following his close reading of these events, he concludes that Christian attacks on Jews were not simply knee-jerk "scapegoating" reactions but rather responses deeply rooted in the tenuous *convivencia*, or coexistence, of Jews and Christians in medieval Spain. Violence lay just beneath the surface of *convivenica's* customary, everyday interactions.

. . . More than any other event, the coming of the plague occupies a central space in premodern histories and periodizations of persecution. To Carlo Ginzburg, it represents the moment in which "obsession with

Source: David Nirenberg, *Communities of Violence: Persecution of Minorities in the Middle Ages* (Princeton, NJ: Princeton University Press, 1996), 231–233, 236–245.

conspiracy[,] . . . a thick sediment in the popular mentality," breaks to the surface, a critical point in the 1,500-year-long evolution of stereotypes that ends with the witches' Sabbath. To others the sharp outbreaks of violence caused by the plague represent an end point of sorts, the logical consequence of centuries of accreted calumnies, fantasies, and stereotypes about the Jews. It is this centrality that makes 1348 a fitting end to a discussion of violence against minorities, even if, as should be clear, the tragic events of that year are neither genesis nor telos of my narrative. . . .

The appearance of the plague triggered attacks against groups as diverse as Jews, clerics, foreigners, beggars, pilgrims, and Muslims, in cities and towns throughout Europe. The phenomenon is almost universally treated as a general one. The sites of violence, from Cracow to Barcelona, are cataloged and subsumed into a single explanatory mechanism. We are told that the moment was one of "collective panic," a panic expressed in aggression toward the "other," particularly toward Jews. The aggression itself is usually explained sparely, by allusion to psychosocial phenomena: "irrational," "fantasy," "unconscious," "projection." These are important concepts, but they could acquire explanatory sense only in the context of a medieval psychology that is never provided. The genealogy of the fantasies themselves, however, is the focus of a great deal of attention. Some historians have traced the "fantastic" stereotypes and accusations with which the violence was legitimated back to antiquity, and have described their elaboration in the intervening centuries, while others have argued at length over the proportional roles of "learned" and "popular" cultures in the crafting of these ideologies of persecution. I will take a more local approach, emphasizing the particularity of the Catalano-Aragonese experience, rather than focusing on pan-European characteristics.

The bubonic plague reached Barcelona and Girona in May of 1348, Valencia in June, and spread to other cities in the Crown of Aragon. It did not come unannounced. King Peter IV, the Ceremonious, had already received a letter dated the 10th of April from the governor of Roussillon and Cerdanya, who had been informed by the *sénéchal* of Carcassonne and the vicar of Narbonne (both in France) about the pestilence raging there. The pestilence, wrote the governor, was spread by confessed poisoners and had killed a third of the people of Carcassonne, a "great infinity" of those in Narbonne, and half in certain towns of Roussillon. The poisoners, it was said, traveled in the guise of pilgrims. . . .

Very few statements linking Jews or Muslims in any way to the plague survive from the Crown of Aragon, although historians continue to accept the existence of poisoning accusations as a given. There is in fact no textual evidence I know of indicating that Christians in the Crown accused religious minorities of spreading the plague through poison. This argument from silence is stronger than it may seem, because other types of accusations were indeed recorded. Peter the Ceremonious had been told by the governor of Roussillon and Cerdanya across the Pyrenees that the plague was spread by poison put in water and food, and sprinkled on "the benches on which men sit and put up their feet," and he took these accusations seriously enough to write the governor of the kingdom of Mallorca directing him to protect that kingdom from such poisoners. He wrote as well to the caretakers of his children, warning them of the poisoners and ordering them to move the princesses from Tarragona to Montblanc for greater safety. But the king never connected religious minorities with his suspicions, and the issue of poisoning seems to have quickly vanished from the bureaucratic horizon.

Jews and Muslims are equally absent from nonroyal types of documentation, even as accusations against other groups survive. The governor's warning that the poisoners went about clad in the garb of pilgrims and religious, for example, is echoed in the experience of two clerics traveling through Barcelona in May of 1348 on their way to the general chapter of their order. They were told that it was unsafe for them to travel because clerics were being seized on the suspicion "that men dressed as religious poisoned the waters and put potions in them." The clerics' story is preserved in a deposition presenting their excuses for their absence from the chapter. . . .

Nevertheless, Jews were attacked in Barcelona, Cervera, Lleida, Tàrrega, and perhaps in Girona, all in Catalonia. Some of these attacks—Lleida, for example—were so slight as to leave barely a trace in the documentation. Others, like that of a Tàrrega, in which three hundred Jews were killed, can only be described as massacres.

Details are scarce on the riots themselves, nearly nonexistent on the days preceding them. In Barcelona, commercial relations between Christians and Jews appear relatively stable from the advent of the plague in early May until the riot some two weeks later. Loan activity, for example, seems to have been normal in the first two weeks of May but ceased after Thursday, May 15, not to resume until the 26th and then at a very reduced place. It was on Saturday, the 17th, that the riot occurred. On that day, a funeral cortege was escorting a body through the plaza of St. James when some thatch fell from the walls of the Jewish *call*. Those in the funeral party abandoned the body and began to incite the populace. They attacked the *call*, burned debt documents, and killed some twenty Jews.

Similarly (though recorded with even less detail) in Cervera, where, according to Ha-Kohen, the rioters killed eighteen Jews and sacked houses. In Tàrrega, on the "tenth day of the month of Av," mobs yelling, "Death to the traitors" attacked the Jewish quarter. According to Ha-Kohen they killed three hundred people. In all these cases, as with so many acts of violence mediated through bureaucratic documents, we know much more about the administrative reaction than about the events themselves. Nevertheless, it is worth asking the question, why were the Jews attacked, if they were not accused of being poisoners?

Contemporary Jews themselves asked this question in the years immediately following 1348, and the answer they arrived at merits serious consideration: "Without any reason they injure, harass, stone, and even kill the Jews living in the said kingdoms and lands [i.e., the Crown of Aragon], the said Christians declaring that because of the sins of the Jews there come mortalities and famines, and committing the said harms against the Jews so that the said pestilences might cease." Jews were attacked not because they were poisoners, but because their sin precipitated the plague. There were a variety of mechanisms by which this could occur, not all of which implied criticism of the Jews as a group. Sin, even the sin of one individual, was thought to be enough to bring "divine punishment" in the form of plague. For this reason crimes were punished most severely when plague was felt to threaten. In 1379 the sworn men of Valencia wrote to a man who had committed "enormous crimes" that "it was publicly said that [the people] wondered if some great plague would not follow in the land, because of the injustice and impunity of this sin and others." By extension, a number of immoral acts could bring down discipline upon the communities in which they were committed. Royal officials in Mallorca had this in mind when they attempted to forestall the pestilence of 1348 by banning gambling, swearing, working on Sundays, fishing for profit on holidays, and dressing ostentatiously. In this context the sins of Muslims and Jews mattered, especially when they were compounded through commission with Christians. Thus in 1351 the bishop of Valencia wrote to the city council about the many sins committed in the Muslim and Jewish quarters of the city, since he feared lest "by their sins, our lord God all-powerful might wish to send pestilences about the land." The bishop's complaint, that Christians were living in the Muslim and Jewish quarters, along

with his suggestion that they be evicted, had repeatedly (and ineffec-
tually) been made over the previous century. Now it took a new, though
not necessarily more successful, form. Note, however, that these fairly
common concerns about sin were not claims about Jews (or Muslims)
as a group. They did not call for the destruction of a "nation." . . .

With this detailed narrative of events in hand, we can begin to ask
the question of why the Jews were attacked in 1348 at a more general
level. The general answer most commonly given is that the violence
was a stereotypical medieval act of "scapegoating." This type of claim
has been most clearly articulated recently by René Girard. In primitive
societies, he writes, "contagious disease is not clearly distinguished from
acute internal discord." In such societies plague is combated through a
redefinition of the group. A scapegoat is identified, differentiated from
the group, and attacked so that "insiders feel united as they never did
before. They form a new and tighter inside. The alien threat displaces
everything else; internal quarrels are forgotten. A new unity and com-
radeship prevails among those who, feeling attacked as a group, also feel
they must defend themselves as a group."

This common paradigm, whose best-known antecedents are in Freud
and Durkheim, is useful in its insistence that violence has functional
aspects which need to be incorporated into our understanding of social
order. It is not, however, concerned with the processes by which difference is identified and maintained, nor does it ask how these processes
are affected by the cultural and material structures of a particular place
and time. These questions have been left to those historians who, like
R. I. Moore, have adapted the paradigm. Following Mary Douglas, Moore
sees the fear of pollution accreting along social boundaries as a result of
anxiety about disparities of status and power, anxieties that focus on "those
whole functions or value in a society give them much greater importance
than is reflected in their status or influence." In medieval Europe, "the
same anxieties are also easily identified in the fears projected against . . .
groups which are clearly defined by race or caste as occupying an inferior
position while performing essential functions. Such people present the
danger that by asserting their real power they may subvert a social structure which is founded on the premise of their impotence." Moore is interested in historicizing the structural conditions within which specific
groups become the focus of anxiety about social purity and hence the
target of rhetorics of pollution and persecution. He argues that the Jews,
a despised minority, gain increasing economic and political power in the

emerging states of the High Middle Ages. They therefore become the targets of pollution anxiety and are attacked by Christians in an effort to reinforce the social structure. It is here, he suggests, that we may find the transformation of a tolerant to an intolerant Middle Ages, and the origins of the persecuting society in which we still dwell.

Historicized or not, these models are of limited utility in explaining the workings of a multiethnic society like that of the Crown of Aragon because their end point is the obliteration of difference. Even independent of a progressive historical narrative, the scapegoating paradigm identifies difference only in order to destroy it in the quest for ultimate unity. The inherent teleology here is heightened in a historicized version like Moore's, where scapegoating is married to an eschatological account of intolerance that terminates in exterminations medieval and modern. Such a model is impoverishing in some obvious ways. First, with difference reduced to a transient stage on the way to identity, it becomes impossible to understand its importance in a (profoundly corporatist) society like that of the Crown of Aragon. Second, the model can recognize as significant only violence that seeks to destroy difference. It tells us little about everyday violence, about the limited and episodic nature of most attacks, or about the role of violence in the maintenance of minority-majority relations. Its explanatory potential is equally limited with respect to those cataclysmic events that it does recognize as significant, since it removes them from the contexts of more routine violences in which they are embedded and reads them in the light of linear narratives of extermination.

A great many aspects of the massacres that accompanied the plague make sense only if we reconnect them to the sublunary world of context, contingency, and functionality so resolutely ignored by the sorts of models described above. Consider that even in the first shock of 1348, the heightened fears of pollution elicited by the plague functioned within structures far more local than those addressed by traditional narratives, and followed lines of (quite transient) political loyalties. When the plague struck, the Crown of Aragon was embroiled in a bitter civil war, perhaps the most highly pitched moment in a long dispute among nobility, king, and municipalities. (The plague may even be said to have saved the king, for the *Unión* of Valencia that held him prisoner permitted his flight when the epidemic began.) Within this polarized geography of loyalty and rebellion, it is striking that the plague provoked violence against Jews only in the region most loyal to the Crown: in the promonarchical towns of Catalonia. Wherever antiroyalist forces had the upper hand, no Jews were attacked. Context affected violence at even more local levels, in factors intrinsic to particular towns. In Cervera, the physical boundaries of the *call* had been disputed since the time of James II, and many Jews lived outside the Jewish quarter, among Christians. Tàrrega, on the other hand, was a town split by faction. The bailiff of Tàrrega himself, as head of one faction, seems to have led the attack on the Jews. The attack and the inquest that followed mired the town in feud and vendetta for the next two years, with the faction of accusers and their witnesses opposing the accused.

Consider, too, that far from severing cataclysm from stability, contemporaries (especially Jewish ones) spent a good deal of time discussing the ties that bound plague massacre to more traditional forms of violence like Holy Week riots. Some feared that the heightened violence of "sacrifice" during time of plague might spill over to its more ritualized Holy Week mode. At the request of the Jews, the king wrote to officials in Barcelona shortly before Holy Week 1349 that they should be especially vigilant that year, in light of the recent riots. Indeed, initially these attacks may have been more violent than before the plague. In Jaca during Holy Week 1350, for example, a Christian guarding the Jewish quarter was killed by rioters. In Valencia the same year a *sagione* of the criminal justice was injured by a stone. This assimilation of the two types of violence, cataclysmic and annual, to each other is implicit in the formulation chosen by the Jewish aljama of Teruel in its appeal of July 20, 1348, for enclosure and fortification. The aljama did not mention plague-related violence in its request. It stressed instead the danger from "injuries, violences, and offenses" aimed at Jews each Holy Week. Similarly, the accord of 1354 followed its complaint that the Jews were stoned at every outbreak of plague with a criticism of "those more violent among the populace and their followers who think they are doing good work when they build towers and platforms around [the Jews] for Easter" in order to stone them.

Such testimony serves to remind us that, even in cataclysm, we have not left the world of Holy Week riots. In that world the fears of pollution and the expiatory sacrifices ritually expressed in those more moderate events had been constrained and latent alternatives to a normative working equilibrium of coexistence. Now sacrifice (not excision) became a matter of urgent necessity for the survival of a social order beset by plague. The ritualized gestures of Holy Week riots needed to be heightened in the "sacrificial crisis" of 1348. This was not the first time in Christian history that disease was cured by sacrifice. In the previous chapter we saw how the destruction of Jerusalem—the sacrificial crisis at the foundation of Jewish-Christian relations in the diaspora—was triggered by the leprosy God had inflicted upon the emperor Vespasian. Vespasian regained his health by avenging Christ's death. Some thirteen centuries later the coming of the plague as a divine punishment for the toleration of Christ's killers in Christian society was thought to demand a similar expiation: an expiation achieved by transforming the controlled mimesis of Holy Week stonings into the mimetic hysteria of the 1348 massacres. But although they differed in stridency and despair, Holy Week riots and plague massacres were alike in that they were both part of the same violent mechanisms by which the Christian majority articulated the terms of coexistence and made it possible. Both partook of the double register of violence identified in the previous chapters; both were meant as much to reinforce the social order to this multireligious community as to shatter it. In the fourteenth-century Crown of Aragon, the violent definition and demarcation of difference reinforced the unity of various groups within the society at the same time that it maintained that society's potential for heterogeneity.

Even in times of plague and massacre, violence was a central and systemic aspect of the coexistence of majority and minorities. *Convivencia* was predicated upon violence; it was not its peaceful antithesis. Violence drew its meaning from coexistence, not in opposition to it. To call plague massacres (or Holy Week riots, miscegenation accusations, and the like) "intolerant" is therefore fundamentally to misconstrue the terms in which coexistence was articulated in medieval Iberia. Similarly, attempts to periodize through violence, to divide the medieval world into opposing categories of tolerance and intolerance, mutual interest versus mutual hostility, open society or closed, is to miss the dependence of the one upon the other. . . .

Michael Dols

The Black Death in the Middle East

The last reading in this section examines the Muslim reaction to outbreaks of plague in the fourteenth and fifteenth centuries. As Michael Dols
emphasizes, Islamic writings about the disease and the proper behavior of
devout Muslims were fraught with tension. Many teachings instructed, for
example, that a Muslim should not flee from a region where the disease
was present. Such a tenet was unlikely to be universally observed when a
community faced the horror of the plague. Dols illuminates Muslim teachings about the plague through a case study of a plague treatise written by
Ibn Ḥajar al-ʿAsqalānī who had direct experience with the plague and whose
tract demonstrates well some of the key differences between Christian and
Muslim interpretations of plague. His tract exemplifies, for example, key
facets of the Muslim response to plague, including the belief that plague
was a martyrdom for devout believers and a punishment against the infidel.
It also draws attention to the Muslim belief in the role of forces like the jinn
(supernatural spirits that could influence the outcome of events on earth)
in spreading plague.

Along with the naturalistic views of plague, a consensus of orthodox
Muslim belief may be extracted from the plague treatises. It must be
borne in mind that the religio-legal conceptualization of the disease imposed itself on the imagination of all those who dealt with the problem
of plague epidemics. Thus, the religious interpretation should not be
understood as distinct from the naturalistic point of view—no matter
how incongruous—nor should the religious explanation be considered
a wholly static one.

The religious attitudes toward plague changed and provoked continual controversy until modern times. The debated points of interpretation,

Source: Michael Dols, *The Black Death in the Middle East*, (Princeton, NJ: Princeton
University Press, 1977), 109–121.

which have already been discussed, were the following three major tenets:

1. A Muslim should not enter or flee from a plague-stricken land.
2. The plague is a martyrdom and a mercy from God for a Muslim and a punishment for an infidel.
3. There is no infection (contagion).

These principles were operative in Muslim society from an early time, as we have seen, when plague appeared in the newly established Muslim empire in the Middle East. This is particularly clear in the case of the plague of 'Amwās, which itself affected later interpretations of plague.

Despite the difficulty of the first *ḥadīth* or tradition for later generations, who were naturally anxious to avoid plague, the prohibition against flight appears to be a pragmatic medical principle, rather than a strictly theological one. It may argue historically for the recognition of contagion-infection in the plague epidemics that afflicted the early Muslims and the desire to limit the spread of epidemics. Theologically, the principle is consistent with the belief that God sent his mercy and martyrdom in the form of plague, which was not considered to be infectious, to a specifically favored community.

The principle that there was no contagion-infection among men should be interpreted from a theological point of view: only God can cause plague or other diseases. This belief, however, impinged on the presentation of the physicians' clinical observations of plague that demonstrated its contagious nature. We have seen how Ibn Khātimah felt constrained to accept this tenet as established by the *Sharī'ah* or Muslim Law in opposition to his empirical perception of the Black Death, while his colleague, Ibn al-Khaṭīb, stood foursquare against the religious establishment by arguing in favor of contagion. In all three tenets, there is a tension between what the traditions prescribed and what may have been actually observed and felt by a Muslim community subjected to a plague epidemic.

Perhaps the best manner of grasping the predominantly religio-legal interpretations of the Muslim plague treatises, which deal with these principles and their ramifications, is to describe fully one of them as a representative type.

Ibn Ḥajar al-'Asqalānī's plague treatise, *Badhl al-māʿūn fī faḍl aṭ-ṭāʿūn*, is a good example of this literature because it presents the fullest explanation of the relevant tenets of orthodox Islam on plague, based on the

collation of the early *hadīth* literature, as well as the consideration of contemporary medical and theological views evolved during the Black
Death. The author classified his treatise as a work of *furū'* or "applied
ethics" (consisting of the systematic elaboration of canonical law in
Islam). The treatise was written as a direct result of plague's reappear-
ance during the author's lifetime. He tells us that he had drafted a work
on the plague epidemic of 819/1416 but rewrote it much later. We know
that Ibn Ḥajar himself was struck by plague when it occurred in Egypt in
848/1444. On the night of Sunday, 5 Ṣafar/24 May, he felt a pain under
his right arm, where a boil grew as large as a peach. It disappeared completely by the tenth of the same month. Since the latest date of the work
is 848/1444, the final revision may be dated within the four years before
his death in 852/1449. The plague treatise is divided into five chapters
and an epilogue. The epilogue is an historical account of the occurrences
of plague in Islamic history and is a common feature of the plague treatises in the Middle East. A detailed examination of this work furnishes, in
varying degrees, the normative conceptualization of plague and helps to
explain, in part, the Muslim social response to the disease.

The first chapter discusses the early history of plague. The disease
is considered a punishment by God on mankind before the advent of
Islam. The author draws on traditions derived from the Old Testament
prophets to show God's heavy punishment on the form of plagues, particularly on the people of Israel. For example, David's numbering of his
people offended God, and in retribution for his presumption, David
was given the choice of enduring seven years of famine, three months
of flight before his enemies, or three days of pestilence. He chose the
pestilence, and seven thousand people died. The story is also related of
God's punishment of the Pharaoh for not giving Moses and Aaron freedom to leave Egypt. And finally, Ibn Ḥajar gives an account of God's
chastisement of the Israelites by plague for their whoredom with the
daughters of Moab.

On the other hand, plague is considered a mercy and a martyrdom
for the people of Muḥammad and a punishment for the infidel. A number of pious traditions are cited to substantiate this claim, which is the
major theological invention of the Muslim theologians and is, to my
knowledge, unique in Semitic religions. It avoids the difficulty of explaining an evil incompatible with God's nature. The primary emphasis, as the
third chapter of the treatise makes clear, is the desirability of this martyrdom by plague. In the customary list of the five Muslim martyrdoms,

death by plague and by battle are always included; they are equal in God's favor, and the believer is assured of reaching paradise.

It is no accident that the descriptive terminology of plague is closely related to the terms of the actual *jihād* or holy war. The ideology of the *jihād* possibly served as a conscious and useful analogy for the Muslim jurists when they confronted the issue of plague. For example, in the account of 'Umar and the plague of 'Amwās the medieval scholars strongly disagreed with 'Umar's decision to withdraw Abū 'Ubaydah from the plague menace. They related the tradition of 'Ā'ishah, the Prophet's wife, that fleeing from plague was like fleeing from the army, and whoever stayed in the time of plague was like a *murābiṭ*.

The correlation between the holy war and plague is most clearly seen in the important tradition of the Prophet: "The destruction of my nation will be by piercing (*ta'n*) and plague (*tā'ūn*)." That is to say, the end of the Muslim people will be by martyrdom through battle and plague. Another example of this equation is a tradition of the Prophet:

> *The martyrs and those who died in their beds argue with our Lord about those who were killed by the plague. The martyrs say, our brothers died as we died. The deceased on their beds say, our brothers died on their beds as we died. Our Lord said: Consider their wounds which resemble the wounds of the slaughtered, and they are among them. And behold, their wounds had been similar; so they joined the martyrs.*

However, not all of the Muslim scholars considered plague as a mercy and a martyrdom. Ibn al-Wardī laments during the Black Death in Aleppo: "We ask God's forgiveness for our souls' bad inclination; the plague is surely part of His punishment." With an inconsistency which belies the tension between emotion and reason, Ibn al-Wardī claims as well that plague is a martyrdom and a reward for a Muslim despite his sins, while death by plague is a punishment for the disbelievers. Ibn Abī Ḥajalah argues that the ultimate reason for plague is God's punishment of His people for their sins, such as adultery, usury, drinking alcohol, and so forth. This certainly finds support in the historical accounts that relate the renewed enforcement of Muslim laws, particularly against alcohol and moral laxity, during periods of plague epidemics. . . .

This belief in men's suffering and misfortune because of God's anger at their moral offenses is a very old one and was the preeminent medieval Christian interpretation, based on the Bible as well as on Greek and Roman literature.

The second chapter of Ibn Ḥajar's treatise is devoted to the etymology of "plague" (*tā'ūn*) and a description of the symptoms of the various forms of plague. Ibn Ḥajar and other writers generally made a distinction between plague and other communicable diseases; the later were referred to as *waba'*, "an epidemic" or "a pestilence."

Unlike most of the Muslim and Christian writers on plague in the wake of the Black Death, Ibn Ḥajar attributes the immediate cause of plague almost exclusively to the jinn rather than to the corruption of the atmosphere by a miasma; in one form or another, the idea of the miasma was the predominant theory of plague until the late nineteenth century. In this instance, Ibn Abī Ḥajalah's treatise is more representative of the Muslim plague treatises in his presentation of miasma as the chief cause of plague, an ascription he derived from Ibn Sīnā and Ibn an-Nafīs. Although Ibn Ḥajar is aware of the atmospheric theory, he is equally conscious of its defects. He reasonably asks why a plague miasma would appear in a place with a healthful climate; why it strikes one house and not its neighbor, or only one member of a household and not another; and why it attacks different parts of the body, unlike other diseases carried by the air. The inability of the miasmatic theory to account satisfactorily for spatial irregularity in the distribution of plague has always been the greatest weakness of this ancient hypothesis. Ibn Ḥajar believes that there is no contradiction between his explanation and the physicians' miasmatic interpretation, because both held that the disease is caused by a poisonous matter which excited the blood. However, our author asserts that this was the result of the internal piercing of the jinn. This basic tradition for his interpretation is the report of the Prophet:

> The destruction of my people is by the piercing and the plague. It was said: "Oh Prophet of God, this piercing we have known but what is the plague?" He said: "The pricking of your enemies is from the jinn and in everyone it is a martyrdom."

The significance of the jinn as the agents of plague has ancient precedents in the Near East. Demons were accused of generating plagues in ancient Babylonia: Namtar, demon of pestilences, would periodically emerge from hell and roam the streets at night afflicting men. The jinn and their poisonous arrows in Muslim literature—found in pre-Islamic poetry and in the Qur'ān—are paralleled by the angel, in Christian literature and iconography, whose drawn sword is the specific device for striking mankind; its sheathing is the sign of the epidemic's termination.

From ancient to modern times, plague has been portrayed in the West by heavenly angels with swords, arrows, or fuming vessels; the iconography is usually derived from Biblical sources, especially David's vision of an angel with a drawn sword stretching over Jerusalem. In 680, good and evil angels were said to have wandered through the streets of Pavia at night. At the command of the good angel, the evil angel pierced the doors of certain houses with a spear so that the inhabitants would fall ill of plague and die. Similarly, during the siege of Kaffa in 1346, the beleaguered Christians saw the heavenly arrows strike the Mongols and cause the Black Death. . . .

The fourth chapter of Ibn Ḥajar's treatise concerns the prohibition against leaving a land that has been stricken by plague or entering a plague-stricken land. . . . Most of the commentators, however, agreed with Ibn Ḥajar about the prohibition against fleeing; for example, Ibn Abī Ḥajalah states that it was necessary to remain at home, for otherwise the epidemic would only increase in intensity and scope. In contrast to the Muslim interdiction, flight was universally counseled by the European Christian tractators.

Subsequently, Ibn Ḥajar presents the orthodox view that there is no infection. Pestilence must be from God alone. Following one tradition, a bedouin asked the Prophet: "Oh Envoy of God, how do you explain that my camels were as healthy as gazelles, and then a mangy camel comes, mixes with them, and makes them mangy?" Rejecting the implied belief in contagion-infection, the Prophet answered: "Who infected the first camel?" Muḥammad is, furthermore, supposed to have denied the pre-Islamic Arab belief in infection. The orthodox position is summed up by Ibn Ḥajar in the *ḥadīth:* "No contagion, no augury, no ill omen."

The last chapter of the treatise deals with what is prescribed for the Muslim once plague has occurred. Ibn Ḥajar advises prayer and repentance, in groups and individually, for the lifting of the epidemic. All the plague treatises recommend prayer and offer formulae for it, particularly specific verses from the Qur'ān. There is some disagreement among the legal schools about the form of the supplicatory prayers. Ibn Ḥajar did not initially approve of the prayer ritual for the raising of plague based on the ritual for rain (*salāt al-istisqā'*), which consisted of fasting and going out into the desert in procession to pray. He considered it an innovation when the ritual took place at the time of the Black Death in Damascus, without any precedent in *ḥadīth.* Yet during the great plague of 833/1429–1430, Ibn Ḥajar agreed to its legality with the other religious teachers in Egypt. It became a common practice in Egypt in the fourteenth and fifteenth centuries. In addition, Ibn Ḥajar does not approve of the visions of the Prophet and the recommended prayers that were allegedly received by a number of Muslims during the plague epidemics.

Ibn Ḥajar then gives a perfunctory list of medical treatments and a number of prayer formulae for the afflicted (one of which is remarkably similar to the Lord's Prayer). Altogether, he recommends patience, piety, and the visiting of the sick. Furthermore, Muslims are not to curse one another with plague. The prohibition seems to indicate simply that it was not an uncommon curse. In present-day Cairo, one Egyptian may say to another: "kubbah"—"a plague on you," and the other may reply: "kubbatyn"—"two plague boils on you!"

In this final chapter of his treatise, Ibn Ḥajar includes a discussion of Shaykh Walī ad-Dīn ad-Malawī's essay *Ḥall al-ḥibā'*. Al-Malawī questions the utility of beseeching God to raise plague and nicely plays the devil's advocate to much of Ibn Ḥajar's academic interpretation of plague. For, as al-Malawī argues, there is an obvious contradiction in praying for the lifting of plague if it is a martyrdom and a mercy from God. Is such prayer not a fleeing from what has been predestined? Is such prayer not opposed to the Prophet's desire for his nation? Although Ibn Ḥajar answers the questions, they legitimately pull his views back to reality. . . .

Cities like Bruges faced economic upheaval during the plague as quarantines and other attempts to check the spread of plague disrupted trade activity. (Bayerische Staatsbibliothek, Munich, Germany/Bildarchive Preussischer Kulturebesitz)

PART

IV Structures of Order

The two previous sections examined the medical, religious, and cultural responses to the plague. In all of these arenas, Europeans turned to existing structures of knowledge, belief, and expression, adapting them where necessary to the immediate reality of the plague's devastation. In these reactions, medieval Europeans appealed to the authorities around them in their quest to understand and combat the plague. In turning to doctors, university faculty, priests, and municipal leaders for guidance and advice, they were naturally seeking answers from those elements of medieval society that provided structure and order. And yet institutions and structures like the Church and city governments were themselves faced with serious challenges in the wake of the plague. These institutions, for example, faced the terror of the disease and the impact of demographic decline. If a city's leaders or a university's prominent faculty died during the plague, did these institutions suffer as a consequence? In other words, how well did these structures of order weather the disruption and devastation wrought by plague? Did the plague create significant structural and institutional changes in medieval society? Ultimately, plague displayed its ability to strike at the very heart of those institutions that provided stability in medieval society.

The medical and scientific community faced the onset of the plague in distinct ways. We saw in Part I that one of the first major consequences of the plague was the appearance of a large body of plague tractates. Anna Campbell's study of medicine and the plague, *The Black Death and Men of Learning,* is an impressive survey of the plague's impact on Christian and Islamic medical writers in Europe. In addition to analyzing the content of the plague tractates, Campbell has also sought other means of assessing the disease's influence on the medical community. To begin with, while acknowledging the paucity of sources, she is able to demonstrate that medical practitioners also suffered mortally at the hands of plague. She also looks beyond 1348, the plague's demographic impact, and the plague treatises to assess the overall impact of plague on the medical profession in the fourteenth century, finding important developments in the status of surgery and the culture and number of universities.

Existing universities also confronted the disease's impact. The excerpt from the article by William Courtenay challenges, in part, some of Campbell's conclusions about the impact of the disease on universities. Where Campbell extrapolated from the remaining documentary evidence to suggest relatively high mortality among university faculty, Courtenay has studied the records of Oxford University with different results. In fact, he finds lower mortality among the university population when compared to the population at large. Courtenay is also interested in assessing the extent to which the Black Death caused qualitative changes in university education. Rather than basing this assessment on the death of the university's intellectual leaders, however, Courtenay examines other factors. He looks, for example, at how changes in primary and secondary education may have altered the character of university life in the generation following the initial outbreak of the disease.

Beyond the learned fields of medicine and the hallowed halls of the university, other structures of order faced their own challenges. As we saw in Part I in John Henderson's article, municipalities had to respond to the arrival and subsequent spread of plague. And they had to do this while maintaining public order and doing their best to keep trade and markets viable. City residents often disagreed with the policies of municipalities. The imposition of a quarantine (a measure employed in this period as a means of containing the spread of plague), for example, seriously compromised the livelihood of merchants and artisans. Some towns and cities also forbade public processions, which, as we have seen, were often initiated by the Church as a means of collective repentance. In various ways, then, the actions of a town's leaders could conflict with the desires of the populace. Keeping the peace would be no small task.

William Bowsky's article is a case study of the Italian city of Siena in the immediate aftermath of the plague. Governed by a body of nine elite citizens (*Noveschi*), the Council of IX, the city had to contend with a host of problems including declining revenue and discontent in the *contado,* the dependent agricultural communities that surrounded the city. Indirect taxes and forced loans allowed the city to begin its financial recovery. At the same time, however, the ruling elite had to contend with the rise of new social groups that capitalized on some of the economic opportunities that demographic decline had created. These groups began challenging the supremacy of the Council of IX.

Finally, the Church confronted the impact of the plague. The mortality of priests alone was enough to create serious challenges. The sacramental services of the priesthood were in high demand during this period, and surviving clerics struggled to meet this need. In the face of death, for example, Europeans appealed to the established traditions of the *ars moriendi* (art of dying). The *ars moriendi* outlined a code of Christian conduct designed to prepare the individual believer for death. Handbooks of the *ars moriendi* recommended that the believer prepare through contrition and a ready embrace—rather than fear—of death as God's will. If one's soul was in order—properly repentant—then there was nothing to fear from bodily death. The rapidity of the plague's spread and the inability of the clergy (either due to their own mortality or because they had fled—see following) to meet the sacramental demands of so many deaths, threw the comfort of the *ars moriendi* into array. What if one's preparations were put in jeopardy by an absence of priestly authority?

The clergy also suffered at the hands of an increasingly bad reputation. Some members of the clergy fled when the plague began approaching. Although the vast majority remained with their flocks, meeting their pastoral responsibilities (and the mortality experienced among the ranks of the clergy speaks to their diligence in staying their posts), the evidence that some had fled created a poor impression among the laity who felt abandoned by those to whom they turned for spiritual solace and explanation. This behavior on the part of the clergy, in fact, inspired and fed into existing sentiments of anti-clericalism. In some ways, for example, the flagellant movement was an expression of this. By remaining a primarily lay movement with no direct clerical supervision, the flagellants may have been making a statement about their perception of the inefficacy of the clergy in the face of disaster. Finally, some scholars have argued that mortality among the clergy led to declining standards as the Church, desperate to meet staffing needs, accepted "lesser" candidates to priestly office.

In all of these ways, then, the clerical authorities faced a host of challenges. The excerpt from William J. Dohar's book, *The Black Death and Pastoral Leadership,* looks at clerics and their response to the Black Death in the diocese of Hereford. Dohar documents a diocese in crisis, seeking to meet the immediate demands of the plague and subsequent outbreaks. In many ways, religious life went on as before as parishioners made recourse to established rituals and beliefs. At the same time, however, Dohar finds that the clergy in the generation following the plague's initial outbreak did have to adapt. They were spread thinly, willing to pursue creative responses to crisis, and not necessarily as well-qualified as their predecessors had been.

Anna M. Campbell

The Black Death and Men of Learning

Anna Campbell's examination of the medical community at the moment of the plague's onset offers important insights. She demonstrates some of the changes that began to take place in the practice of medicine on the heels of the first outbreak. The first was the elevation of the practice of surgery. Because surgery was a trade that did not require formal education, many university-trained physicians typically held surgeons in low regard. This began

Source: Anna M. Campbell, *The Black Death and Men of Learning* (New York: Columbia University Press, 1931), 109–112, 148–155.

to change in the years following 1348. Surgeons' guilds achieved greater prominence in some areas, and the work of surgeons began to overlap more significantly with that of physicians. Campbell also charts the concerns after 1348 that plague mortalities and associated consequences had brought a decline in intellectual endeavors. This in turn spurred many of Europe's leaders to charter new universities. Thus, by her account, the plague seems to have acted as an intellectual stimulus in Europe.

. . . The fact that the last three of these men were surgeons (two of them, Guy of Chauliac and John Arderne, very distinguished ones), brings to attention a momentous change that occurred in the field of medicine in the fourteenth century, and which may have been accelerated by the Black Death. Till about the end of the thirteenth and the beginning of the fourteenth centuries, surgery had never been held in esteem, nor, except for a period of brilliance in Roman times, had it developed beyond a rudimentary stage. As intellectual activity and curiosity increased in Europe, and the dependence of accurate knowledge upon experimentation became more evident, enterprising spirits began to break through tradition and prejudice. In the thirteenth century the practice of dissection was begun by Mundinus of Bologna; he wrote an *Anatomy* which was the first work of the medieval period devoted entirely to the subject. His pupil and successor was Bertruccius, who, in turn, was instructor of Guy of Chauliac. Others who blazed the trail were John Gaddesden, Lanfranc, Henry of Mondeville, and John Yperman, the last three authors of works on surgery in the early fourteenth century.

But the *Great Surgery* of Guy of Chauliac and the *Practice* of John Arderne show a decided advance over the earlier works of the century, and from the middle of the century a double tendency is increasingly discernible: to break down the barriers between physicians and surgeons, and to standardize the profession of surgery. For instance, in Venice it was against the law for surgeons to practice medicine, and 31 December, 1348, a fine was inflicted upon Andreas of Padua because, in the mortality of 1348, he went out as a physician and cured over a hundred of those smitten with the pestilence; this the Venetian judges attributed to accident rather than to wisdom. Yet in September, 1349, Nicholas of Ferrara was invited to Venice from Padua and praised for his knowledge and experience in surgery: both of the cities in which he had practiced, it is said, had profited by his knowledge of diseases of the lower parts of the body [*crepatorum*], which required a specialist. Guy of Chauliac, though really a surgeon, was physician of Clement VI; and John of Parma, starting in 1348 as papal surgeon, later became physician and surgeon. However the same thing is true of his predecessor, who in 1348 was called physician.

In England an indication of the trend toward raising surgical standards was the formation of surgeons' gilds. The Oxford gild was incorporated by Dr. Northwood, chancellor of the university, in 1348; it included barbers and waferers, but lectures in surgery began to be given about 1350. In 1362 it was decreed that every London surgeon must belong to a gild; further regulations were enacted twice later in the century, and before its close gilds of surgeons had been founded in half a dozen other towns.

The first judicial post-mortem was held in 1302 at the University of Bologna, where Mundinus had earlier inaugurated the practice of anatomical dissection; postmortems occurred also in other universities, Gentile of Foligno holding one publicly in 1341 at Padua. But the first recorded instances of public officials, other than educational authorities, decreeing autopsies seem to occur during the Black Death. In a letter written from Avignon by a cleric of the Netherlands, the statement is made that "anatomical dissections have been performed by physicians in many states of Italy, and also in Avignon, by order and command of the pope, that the origin of this disease might be known, and many bodies of the dead have been opened and dissected." One city in Italy which took such a step was Florence, for in a list of public expenditures dated 30 June, 1348, there is an item "for giving more corpses to physicians who requested them, in order to be able to learn more clearly the diseases of the bodies." Public dissections were decreed by several other cities during the century. In 1376 the duke of Anjou, governor of Languedoc, issued an ordinance to the officers of justice in that province: they were to suppress in their districts the illegal practice of medicine, and to send every year to the medical faculty of Montpellier for dissection the corpse of an executed criminal. The purpose of both decrees is set forth: it is an attempt to save what mortality, epidemics, and war have left of the population; dissection is desirable, since experience is mistress of affairs, and darts foreseen usually cause less damage, and visible dangers can more easily be avoided, than the hidden and the unknown. The last part of the fourteenth and the early fifteenth centuries were a period of renown for the medical faculty of Montpellier, for it then combined the knowledge of surgery with that of medicine. But Pansier calls attention to the fact that after this it again neglected the former science, with the result that it rapidly lost the brilliance which had resulted from the union of the two. . . .

In the establishment of universities, and in the privileges and decrees concerning them, we find a few direct statements of the effects of the pestilence, beginning before it ceased and extending through the succeeding twenty years or more. In 1348 the canny Florentines determined to make their *studium* a *studium generale*, setting their plans afoot, according to Villani, as soon as the plague relaxed, with the intention of attracting people to the city, of increasing it in fame and honor, and of fostering learning and virtue among the citizens. Carabellese considers this a pretext, the real object being to remedy the depopulation of the city consequent upon the pestilence, and to reap material advantage. If such was the case, the results were disappointing, for in 1357 Villani notes that the governors of Florence complained that the expense of their university was far in excess of the profits. In 1364 Charles IV granted it an imperial diploma, but the years immediately following the Black Death were not favorable to institutions of learning, and the difficulties of Florence continued in spite of the emperor's favor.

The decline of learning consequent upon the pestilence was a matter of deep concern to Charles, himself formerly a student at Paris, and is reiterated in the introductions of five charters which he gave to as many different universities between the years 1355 and 1369. The prefaces of the imperial diplomas are much alike, each declaring that the precious knowledge, which the mad rage of pestilential death has stifled throughout the wide realms of the world, is calling upon the emperor to raise her from her prostrate condition. Though the similarity in wording causes Father Denifle to refer to this as the emperor's stereotyped introduction, and though, as he points out, portions of the description of knowledge and her fallen estate are taken from Manfred's references to philosophy in his thirteenth-century charter to the University of Naples, these repeated assertions of the disastrous effects of the pestilence upon formerly flourishing sciences and universities show what an impression had been made upon the mind of the emperor. Nor was this proem employed in all the imperial diplomas whereby Charles sought to revive stricken universities, as is evident in his privileges to Arezzo in 1355, and to Florence in 1364.

A strong statement of the dire consequences of plague, as well as another illustration of the impression made upon the rulers of the people by its ravages, is found in the mandate of the duke of Anjou, governor of Languedoc, in 1376, ordering that the Montpellier faculty of medicine be given every year for dissection the corpse of an executed criminal:

> *Since from the weakness of human nature and the bad mode of living of individuals it often happens that fevers, infirmities, imposthumes, and various other kinds of illness result, from these, unless suitable remedies be supplied through masters, doctors of physical science or of medicine, many persons suffering those infirmities, and almost the greater part, incur the danger of death. And thus the population, which is scantly enough owing to moralities and epidemics that have flourished in these parts, and also to wars wherein many have perished, may be diminished to the greatest possible extent, and the world brought to nothing, . . .*

In documents relating to the three colleges of Cambridge and the two of Oxford whose origin may be traced to the plague, allusions are made to the depletion of the learned classes and to the fact that learning is beginning to fail. In January, 1350, Trinity Hall, at Cambridge, was founded by Bishop Bateman of Norwich, whose brother had died of the Black Death; and in a deed of 6 February, 1350, giving certain revenues to the new college, he indicates that his object in establishing it was to renew the supply of clergy, which had been so greatly decreased by the pestilence. A year or two later this same Bishop Bateman completed the foundation of Gonville Hall, begun by Edmund Gonville in 1348, but unfinished at the time of his death in 1351.

The College of Corpus Christi was established in 1352, under rather unusual circumstances. The increase in fees for celebrating mass that was the result of the mortality among the clergy told heavily on the gilds, and two of those at Cambridge, Corpus Christi and the Blessed Virgin, which had recently been united, conceived the idea of endowing a college whose students would be required to say masses for departed members of the two gilds. Letters patent were obtained from the king in 1352 by the duke of Lancaster, alderman of Corpus Christi, and the college was founded with one master and two fellows. However, according to Cooper, it received five other benefactions in the course of the fourteenth century.

Grief for the sad state of learning and the loss of learned men in consequence of the pestilence, and a desire to assist in trying to find a remedy, are the reasons given for her efforts in behalf of University Hall at Cambridge by a granddaughter of Edward I, Elizabeth de Burgh, Countess of Clare. In her will of 1355 she left bequests to the college, to which she had for some years been making gifts, and its name was changed to Clare Hall in conformity with a desire expressed by her in statutes she gave it in 1359. In the preamble of these statutes she declares that a knowledge of letters is of no small advantage in every walk of life, and that, though it may be acquired in various ways, it is best obtained in a university, which then sends forth trained men for the service of God and the state. This kind of knowledge is beginning lamentably to fail, in consequence of a great number of men having been taken away by the fangs of pestilence, and the countess wishes to do what she can to restore it by increasing the resources of the college.

While these three colleges at Cambridge received their endowments within ten years of the Black Death, it was not till 1362 that the former of the two at Oxford that owe their existence to the plague was established. It was then that Simon Islip, archbishop of Canterbury, who twice made charges of unbridled avarice and neglect of duty against the clergy who survived the pestilence, taking practical steps to remedy the situation, received from Edward III permission to found Canterbury College at Oxford. In the royal license the king expresses his desire for a wholesome increase of clergy by means of the spread of sound teaching, which now through the present epidemic is known to have very greatly failed. The archbishop's own feelings on the subject appear in a document of the following year in which, in confirming a gift made the new college by William de Islip, he writes:

> Since through wisdom, thus not acquired without sweat and labor, kingdoms are ruled and the church militant develops in accordance with justice and spreads her tents; we Simon, &c., frequently pondering upon these matters lying close to our heart, and considering that especially those truly learned and skilled in every branch of knowledge have failed to a very great extent in the epidemics, and that on account of lack of opportunity very few are pressing forward at present for the study of letters. . . .

More than a decade later William of Wykeham founded New College at Oxford, for the purpose, according to the statutes, of increasing the supply of clergy, thinned by "pestilence, wars, and other miseries of the world."

Declarations of the damage done to learning by the pestilence occur not only in privileges and statutes conferred upon the universities by lords spiritual and temporal, but in utterances of the universities themselves. About the year 1350 the chancellor and scholars of Oxford University made petition to the king, "showing that the university is ruined and enfeebled by the pestilence and other causes, so that their estate can hardly be maintained or protected." Mute witnesses of the same facts were books and other pledges given there by the students before the pestilence; these, in 1411, were declared to be so injured by the passage of time that unless they were soon sold they would be entirely worthless. Papal aid in recovering their books, which had been similarly pawned, was one of the objects sought by the students of Avignon in a roll of 1361 addressed to Pope Innocent VI, beginning:

> *Most holy Father, at a time when the university body of your* studium *at Avignon is deprived of all lectures, since the whole number has been left desolate by the death from pestilence of doctors, licentiates, bachelors, and students, some also of the survivors of the same* studium, *who have spent many sleepless nights in the acquisition of holy canonical knowledge, are unable because of the ravages of wars, as is also the case with some of them and of the others because they are weighed down by contests over benefices due them and by the burden of poverty, to be of service to themselves and others, to recover their books, or to be promoted to the degrees which they deserve.*

Complaints, without such specific enumeration of causes, of the decline of learning, of decrease of students and men of learning and of poverty and abuses in the universities are frequent in the two decades following the Black Death. They were made by the universities, by outside authorities in documents relating to universities, and in writings of prominent men of the time. Where French universities were concerned, the Hundred Years' War must be borne in mind as an important cause of decline, especially in complaints like those of Toulouse and Orleans. But even in these two instances pestilence must have been a contributory factor, while it was perhaps of greater importance than the war when the difficulties were attributed to abuses within the universities. . . .

William J. Courtenay

The Effect of the Black Death on English Higher Education

This selection from William J. Courtenay's article "The Effect of the Black Death on English Higher Education" looks at the quantitative and qualitative effects of the Black Death on university life in England. In an earlier section of this article Courtenay seeks to understand *why* the mortality at Oxford University might have been lower than that of the general population. The selection here challenges an older interpretation—held by Campbell and others—that the quality of the intellectual community of the university declined in the years following the Black Death. Particularly notable is his attention to long-term trends. Rather than viewing university education as a static structure, he examines how changes in primary and secondary education in the wake of the Black Death altered university life in later generations. Courtenay also explores the increasing enrollments in theology at Oxford University after the Black Death. He attributes this increase to the staffing needs of the Church but also to the aspirations of families who may have been able to afford university education after the plague.

The Issue of Qualitative Decline

. . . Despite a low mortality rate and the ability of the University of Oxford to maintain its enrollment levels in the face of the Black Death, it is still possible that the plague could have exercised a negative effect on the quality of education by removing a number of important masters, by hurting parts of the university community that contributed most prominently to its intellectual life, or by a general lowering of the quality of incoming students. Each of these areas needs to be examined.

One often encounters the assertion that the Black Death killed the leading writers and thinkers of the English universities, which in turn

Source: William J. Courtenay, "The Effect of the Black Death on English Higher Education," *Speculum* 55, no. 4 (Oct. 1980): 696–714.

precipitated a qualitative decline. It is true that in the period 1348–49 we know that a number of major intellectuals died: John Baconthorp, William of Ockham, Robert Holcot, Thomas Bradwardine, John of Rodington, Richard Rolle, and probably John Dumbleton and John Went. But none of these was at Oxford at the time (their teaching careers having been completed earlier), and Ockham had been living outside England since 1324. Had they all survived the Black Death, it is difficult to see how the quality of education at Oxford after the Black Death would have been any different. One must contrast that group with those who we know survived the Black Death, some of whom were living at Oxford at the time and who continued to teach there. To this surviving group belong Richard Fitzralph, Adam Wodeham, Thomas Buckingham, William Heytisbury, Richard Swineshead, Nicholas Aston, Osbert Pickingham, Richard Billingham, Ralph Strode, and John Wyclif. If the Black Death was a factor here, it was not in removing the great minds of that generation but in removing those who might have been the great minds of the next generation.

The possible failure to replenish one's ranks with equal talent may have been a factor for certain colleges such as Merton and Grey Friars, who together had established much of the intellectual reputation of Oxford in the early fourteenth century. A sharp decline in the general population, if it were to be reflected in the enrollment level of any individual unit within the university, might not appear immediately, but after a period of ten of fifteen years. The Franciscans had a reported increase in the decade immediately after 1349, helped in part by additional scholars from abroad—mostly Italians but also Germans, Czechs, and one Frenchman—but there is a drop in their numbers reported in Emden's *Register* after 1360 until the end of that century. Similar drops can be noted in some of the other mendicant and religious houses. However, the destruction of documents for the religious orders in England has left us only a fraction of the names of mendicant scholars, and one cannot place much credence in the accuracy of the picture formed from these modest statistics.

The evidence from Merton College is more reliable. If one discounts the sharp rise in reported figures in the period 1320–1340 because it includes the presence of abnormally detailed documentation, the reported enrollment levels for Merton are roughly the same throughout the fourteenth century with the exception of the period 1360–1380. Since there is no particular change in the documentation that would explain this decline (from a reported 170 to 136), one can assume that Merton probably experienced a quantitative decline in that period that may have had qualitative implications.

Finally, we must consider the possible effects of the Black Death on the quality of preparation among incoming students. The type of philosophy and theology that was pursued at Oxford in the 1330s was highly sophisticated, requiring very advanced knowledge of Latin, logic, and mathematics. The minds of the Oxford scholars of the 1360s and 1370s may have been capable, but their skills and understanding were only as good as their early training made them, particularly their training in Latin grammar. If we assume the death rate in 1348–49 among masters of grammar in the town schools and the clergy teaching in parish schools was equivalent to that cited earlier for the parish clergy, then the quality of basic education in the decade 1350–1360 would be impaired. We have many references after 1348 to vacancies and the appointment of less qualified candidates. For a period of time primary education would have been less available and in many places less rigorous. We should not assume too gloomy a picture, since throughout the second half of the fourteenth century there remained highly qualified grammarians in some town schools. But, unlike the university, primary education usually depended on one teacher whose presence and training determined the educational future of most boys in that town. It was probably rare for a family to seek out a good teacher in another town; the usual pattern was to be educated locally.

The effects of this situation would not become visible at the university level for some time. The decay of the educational system moved from the bottom upward, and it was a gradual process that took several decades. If significant at all, one would expect to see it in evidence among the arts students in the period 1360–1375 and among the students and masters in the higher faculties in the period 1370–1385. Under these circumstances it is not difficult to imagine students whose skills in Latin and critical thinking were not sufficient for the subtleties of speculative grammar, who found Aristotle opaque, and who ceased to read Ockham, Wodeham, Bradwardine, or Kilvington. No matter how gifted and accomplished the university masters of the 1360s may have been, they could not repair the damage done by a poor elementary and secondary education, and gradually the task of teaching at all levels of the university was fulfilled by those who learned their letters after the Black Death.

The degree to which this last factor affected or altered the quality of learning at Oxford must remain hypothetical. We know that after 1365 the arts faculty moved away from supposition logic to an earlier, more elementary logic. We also know that the theological faculty in the same period moved away from complex metalinguistic concerns to problems of practical theology. There is no question that the philosophical and theological studies at Oxford after 1360 were easier to grasp and did not require as extensive a technical training in logic and mathematics. It is another thing, however, to prove that this change was precipitated by an inability to comprehend the former learning. What may appear to the modern scholar to be a drop in quality may in context be largely a shift in interest. There is little evidence in the university documents that those studying theology after 1350 were any less literate in Latin than their predecessors. The amount of publication by Oxford graduates after 1350 confirms this. Moreover, the University of Paris, which admittedly drew its students from a far larger geographical area, shows few signs of qualitative decline among those whose primary education was subsequent to the Black Death. The achievements of early fourteenth-century Oxford were continued at Paris in the writings of Henry Totting of Oyta, Henry of Langenstein, Marsilius of Inghen, Pierre d'Ailly, Peter of Candia, and John Capreolus. One must assume, therefore, that there were other forces at work beyond any decay in linguistic skills that formed the intellectual milieu of Oxford in the age of Richard II.

A more immediate effect of the Black Death on qualitative change may have come through changes in the "feeder" institutions of the religious orders. The mendicants, who did not have their students prepare philosophy in the arts faculty of the university, maintained their own schools within each province. Many priories and convents provided training in the liberal arts and logic. For the more advanced study of natural philosophy and theology each province maintained several schools (*studia particularia*), usually one for each major subdivision of the province, known in the Franciscan Order as "custodies" and in the Dominican Order as "visitations" or "nations." From these schools mendicant scholars were sent to the *studium generale* at the university for further study in theology and canon law, and to these schools and local convents many of the best graduates returned for a time to teach. In England the mendicant *studia particularia* were often located in large centers of population, such as London, Norwich, and York, and in the crowded, poorer parts of the city, in contrast to the *studia generalia*, which, with the exception of the Carmelites, were located in the smaller university towns of Oxford and Cambridge. If the morality rate in London, Norwich, and York was higher than at Oxford, which it seems to have been, one could expect that the mendicant educational system might have been crippled, although such a fact might be less evident quantitatively in the Oxford data. We know of entire mendicant communities that died, and we can assume that if the quotas for the university convents were filled with a higher percentage of marginal students, the subsequent quality of education when they returned to these schools would be lower. For the Franciscans, on whom much of the intellectual quality of Oxford depended, the presence of a number of great minds in the Oxford and London convents in the first half of the fourteenth century probably created an atmosphere that stimulated others and helped recruit talented young minds. The absence of their equivalent in 1360 may have precipitated a downward spiral that increasingly impoverished Franciscan education. To what extent the Black Death was a major factor here is uncertain. However, the decline in the number of Franciscans significant enough to be noted in contemporary documents (and therefore to be included in Emden's *Register*) is a reflection of an important change.

The University and Society: The Response to the Black Death

The Black Death was an important stage in a steady population decline across the fourteenth century that was accentuated but not begun or fully explained by incidence of plague. By the second quarter of the fifteenth century the English population was only thirty to fifty percent of what it had been in 1300; that is, the decline was possibly as high as seventy percent. And yet, as we have seen, the scholarly community at Oxford did not decline but probably grew in the course of the century. More surprising perhaps, the number of reported theological students in the decade after 1349 increased twenty-eight percent, and it continued to grow throughout the second half of the fourteenth century. If language skills of the average student did not meet the task or if the problems and approaches of earlier scholastic thought were no longer appealing, what magnetic attraction did the university have?

Several studies have shown a growth after 1348 in the number of elementary and secondary schools in England. Most of the growth was in the form of reading and song schools, but some grammar schools were founded as well. Jo Ann Hoeppner Moran has linked this development in the York diocese with an increasing demand after the Black Death for priests and teachers at the local level, although the rise in the number of ordinations lagged behind the rise in the number of schools. One reason for this renewed educational and ecclesiastical commitment was, no doubt, the depletion of the local clergy by plague. Another reason seems to have been the uses to which money was put after the Black Death. With a declining population, money was concentrated in fewer hands, through inheritance and other means. Much of this increased spending power seems to have been devoted to various forms of late medieval piety, in particular the endowment of chantries throughout England.

Guy Lytle has suggested a somewhat different picture at the university level. He sees the period from 1325 to 1430 as one of crisis for the university as a result of the shrinkage of the traditional sources of patronage, and consequently of benefices, income, and job opportunities within the church for university graduates. His assumed decline in university enrollments is, therefore, not simply part of a decline in population but an indication of a growing realization that university study did not necessarily improve one's chances for a comfortable living, and that a young man was better advised after his early education to seek advancement through the crown or some powerful family that could control church positions and other careers. The future lay with the bureaucrat of the royal *familia* or its aristocratic equivalent. This crisis in scholarly patronage was solved only through the development of new forms of patronage. The transition by which Oxford became a university of colleges was part of that solution. While the thesis about a decline in university enrollment in the fourteenth century is questionable, the statistics that Lytle has gathered on the shift in patronage are impressive. They affect both the sources of funding among advanced students at the university and the expectations for a career after the university.

When examining motivations for education in terms of post-university opportunities, one must keep in mind not only the realistic expectations of a position in the parochial clergy or of income from one or more benefices that did not entail the care of souls, but the more distant model of former graduates whose administrative careers, often in royal service, had been rewarded with a bishopric. A crisis in the ability of university graduates to obtain high ecclesiastical office is far less visible, although it may at times have been a factor. No student in theology or canon law was so naive as to hope for appointment to an episcopal see on the grounds of a distinguished academic career. The examples were too few. But the university connection was thought to be an advantage. In the thirteenth century several major scholastic thinkers had occupied important sees: Robert Grosseteste at Lincoln and Stephen Langton, Robert Kilwardby, and John Pecham at Canterbury. The zeal among some leaders in the English church toward the end of the thirteenth century to increase the proportion of candidates with notable academic careers was part of a wider movement in that period toward a learned episcopate and a learned church, paralleled at the parish level by the papal constitution *Cum ex eo*. In addition to those scholar-bishops who were known through their scholastic writings, there were also a number, for example, Robert Winchesley at Canterbury, Simon of Ghent as Salisbury, and John Dalderby at Lincoln, whose high reputations at the university were based more on personality and service than an outstanding scholastic achievement.

W. A. Pantin has argued that the relationship of university and episcopate altered in the course of the fourteenth century. Although the proportion of university-trained bishops remained stable throughout the century, roughly two-thirds of the total appointed to episcopal office, distinguished scholars (a category in which Pantin places men of distinguished university service, e.g., chancellors of the university, as well as men of distinguished scholastic writing) "were gradually edged out of the greater sees like Canterbury, and confined to lesser or distant sees like Rochester or Chichester or Armagh." The pattern that Pantin saw was a gradual shift in emphasis from the scholar-bishop at the beginning of the century, to the civil servant at mid-century, to the aristocratic bishop by 1400. These categories, of course, were not mutually exclusive, but they probably do reflect the predominant reason for appointment. "Thus whereas in the reign of Edward III bishoprics had been given as administrative salaries or rewards, in the reign of Richard II we find them given as political rewards or retainers."

This, of course, is how it looks from our modern perspective. When it is a question of career goals and models, however, the issue is whether and to what extent these shifts were apparent in the period, how they were perceived, and what effect those perceptions might have had on university careers.

Under Edward II there is a marked absence of distinguished scholars among appointments to episcopal office, and in the second decade of the century even university-trained men of the stature of Winchelsey and Simon of Ghent were not being appointed. Pantin noted the difficulties of the Canterbury Chapter in attempting to elect the scholar Thomas Cobham, whose candidacy was rejected in favor of Walter Reynolds, a civil servant. But this movement away from the great scholar may not have been viewed as such, since many of the civil servants who were appointed in their place were at least university graduates.

Throughout the first half of the fourteenth century the tie between university and high church office remained in evidence. Although few scholars whose ideas and writings had made them "household" names at the university were given bishoprics, Edward III did appoint Richard Fitzralph to Armagh and Thomas Bradwardine to Canterbury. The fact that the latter died within a few weeks of his investiture in no way negates Edward's willingness to appoint one of the most brilliant scholars of that time to the highest ecclesiastical office in England. Moreover, some of the civil service appointees were strong supporters of the university and scholarship, most of them university graduates as well. This is true of John Grandison at Exeter, Richard de Bury at Durham, William Wykeham at Winchester, and William Courtenay at Canterbury. The change that would have been most visible would have been the increasing prominence of aristocratic background and of legal training in the appointments in the last quarter of the fourteenth century.

What does the Oxford evidence we have been examining suggest about the role of the university in society in the second half of the fourteenth century? We can perceive a leveling off and even a slight decline in enrollment in the theological faculty during the second quarter of the fourteenth century. Although the qualitative work in theology being done at Oxford at that time was outstanding, and Oxford had many figures of international reputation, that reputation depended largely on the Franciscans, whose education was not dependent on outside patronage and for whom church offices were rarely a principal goal, and the Mertonians, whose needs were cared for on a modest level through the endowment of the college. Beneath that elite level the enrollment in theology slipped from its high in the opening years of the fourteenth century and was declining at a time when the general enrollment of the university was still increasing. Some of this decline may have been in response to the shifts in patronage and the worsening picture for career opportunities for theological graduates in the church. Much of it, I suspect, was a result of the shifting pattern of patronage, which had reduced one of the major sources of funding *at the university* for students in the theological program. When viewed against the total enrollments the number of benefices given to students while at the university was small, but within the category of those to whom benefices were given, namely advanced students in theology and canon law who were not in religious orders, these benefices represented a major and necessary part of university finance. In fact, in the second quarter of the fourteenth century we also find enrollments in canon law declining while enrollments in civil law were rising, suggesting the same pattern. In the university's desire to improve sources of income for its graduates, the issue of present funding may have figured as heavily as future expectation.

It would appear that the Black Death altered that trend. The pattern of distributing ecclesiastical livings did not alter, in fact worsened for university graduates, but something happened to cause the theological enrollment among the reported group to increase sharply in the decade after the Black Death. One has to keep in mind here that the university did not suddenly *permit* more students to attend, for there was no enrollment level. The increase must be seen in terms of attracting students rather than taking students. Suddenly theology, or the careers to which it led, became a more attractive possibility for qualified students seeking careers.

One possibility seems obvious. The high death rate among the parish clergy, which in some areas appears to have run as high as forty percent, produced an immediate need for educated clergy at all levels and, viewed less altruistically, an immediate opportunity for the qualified to receive important positions with handsome incomes. Considering the large number of vacant livings and the small number of university graduates, it is no wonder that the majority of these positions were filled with non-university men. But in the quest for fatter livings many may have felt that a few years at the university might well produce greater rewards in the future. In this crisis the theological program at Oxford may have accepted those less qualified than in earlier years, but they also were now probably able to attract other qualified students who, in the face of a long program with limited financial aid and limited career possibilities, might not have been as attracted before. The slow but steady growth in elementary and secondary schools from the mid-fourteenth century on, at a time of population decline, is further evidence of the growing respect for and uses of education.

A second factor that may explain this shift lies in the chantry endowments, the masses for the dead, and the annual obits that grew rapidly in England in the wake of the Black Death, a reflection of the inherited wealth that could be spent in non-productive activity (viewed from the economic perspective) but grim testimony to the societal need for prayers for the souls of family members whom death may have caught in less than a state of grace. Chantries provided jobs, and many of these went to priests with university backgrounds.

Finally, we cannot ignore the possibility that a university training, particularly in theology, lived on in the social aspirations of many families who before 1348 could not afford the luxury of higher education. It may well be that sudden and unexpected inheritance provided a means of realizing a long cherished dream, quite apart from the issue of whether in the long run the university was the best or most direct route to royal service or a comfortable ecclesiastical living. Either through the attraction of available positions or through the sudden realization of financial support, the enrollments in the theological faculty in the second half of the fourteenth century continued to climb—despite no apparent change in the pattern of ecclesiastical patronage in favor of the university.

To the degree that Emden's *Register* is an adequate reflection of what is going on at Oxford in the fourteenth century, the Black Death did not have the effect on higher education in England often ascribed to it. The mortality rate was not particularly high, either of the brilliant or of marginal scholars and masters. The enrollment levels across the next few decades do not seem to have been seriously affected. It did coincide with a change in interests and possibly a change in quality—certainly within the areas of philosophy, science, and theology on which the reputation of the university had depended. If the Black Death helped catalyze this change, it was by initially impairing the quality of primary education, and only subsequently higher education.

William M. Bowsky

The Impact of the Black Death upon Sienese Government and Society

As William M. Bowsky's article ably illustrates, the city fathers of Siena faced monumental challenges in the wake of the plague's first outbreak. They struggled to maintain agricultural productivity in the farmlands surrounding the city (*contado*) while still ensuring civic peace and public services. One of the most interesting socioeconomic trends that Bowsky's examination of Siena offers is the growing social mobility of certain groups. By the fall of 1349 the city possessed a class of *nouveaux riches* that began threatening the supremacy and political order administered by the Council of IX as the *nouveaux riches* sought to translate its economic power into political might. The city also faced newcomers to the city who arrived in search of economic prosperity. These newcomers also challenged the rule of the Council, since they had not always lived under its dictates. Overall, then, Bowsky argues, the socioeconomic flux of the plague's aftermath may have undermined the city's traditional political structures.

. . . Siena did not try to strengthen itself at the expense of the *contado*. The annual *contado* assessment remained at the low £36,000 set in 1347. This was only 50% more than the original assessment of 1291 even though expenditures had risen more than 200%.

Nor could the *contado* support heavy impositions. Almost all work ceased during the summer of 1348. Fields were neglected and animals left untended, as men were scarcely able to care for their own ill. Mills closed down and most were still inoperative as late as February 1349.

The death toll was high, but varied greatly from one community to the next. In 1353 the Maremma commune of Sassoforte numbered fifty men. Before the plague it had sheltered one hundred sixty men and

Source: William M. Bowsky, "The Impact of the Black Death upon Sienese Government and Society," *Speculum* 39, no. 1 (January 1964): 1–34.

their families. Neighboring Montemassi, immortalized by Simone Martini's fresco in the Sienese communal palace, was reduced to less than fifty men, from a pre-plague population of two hundred and twenty. 19 April of the same year the commune of Cofreno was joined to that of Monte Santa Maria because it only contained four men and three *massarizie*.

Migration as well as plague deaths accounted for these losses. Throughout the period that we are considering, and long after, many *contado* lands lay sterile, unworked because of the shortage of farm labor. From 1354 on the incursions of mercenary companies increased the crime and disorder that followed the plague.

As early as September 1348 communities throughout the *contado* barraged Siena with requests for financial assistance, particularly in the form of remission of rentals and fees owed the commune. The honesty of these petitions is attested by the fact that they were granted despite the loss of income to Siena. Siena was solicitous of the *contado's* troubles. It immediately remitted the one-third of the annual *contado* taxation due in September 1348.

Remissions and even the cancellation of contracts were also conceded to private individuals and groups of men renting communal properties in the *contado*. 14 August 1349 several Sienese Mignanelli who had rented the entire court, district, land, and castle of Marsiliana for eight years beginning 1 January 1348 for £5,950 (at the rate of £850 a year) successfully petitioned for the cancellation of their contract. They alleged that because of the plague they could not hold and use this territory, nor even guard it from Siena's enemies should the need arise. Two of the original renters had died, and, worse yet, it was impossible to find men to serve as either guards or as agricultural laborers. In June 1349 renters at Civitella Ardenghesca received a four-year reduction of one-third in the rentals due from houses and squares in the castle and from olive groves, and a 50% remission of farm rents. But even this aid was insufficient. Six months later all these Civitella contracts were cancelled at the renters' request upon the receipt of small payments.

In 1351 Siena went so far as to aid *contado* communities at the risk of slowing the rate of repopulation of the city itself. Wealthy men of the *contado* who wished to acquire Sienese citizenship were now required to notify the communities on whose tax registers they were enrolled of their intention. This was done so that the communities effected could, if they so desired, protest officially to the City Council. Nor could one obtain Sienese citizenship without first obtaining an official release from his community. This measure passed with almost no opposition, by a vote of 120 to 3.

The Sienese government recognized that *ad hoc* relief to individual communities or renters was not enough. By October 1349 the City Council granted the leading Sienese magistracies authority to combine *contado* communities for the purpose of the taxes and services they owed Siena. This measure was needed because some communities had been completely wiped out and others decimated. The action was taken "since because of the plague that has occurred many *contado* communities are reduced to nothing . . . [it is ordered] from humanity and piety . . . so that they may be kept in the service of the commune of Siena with their customary devotion and faith."

In 1350 it was manifest that a complete new reassessment of the *contado* communities was needed in order that the annual taxation might be imposed in an equitable fashion:

> *Since from the fatality that has occurred all the contado communities generally have decreased in population, but their decrease is unequal. Some have decreased moderately, others immensely, still others have been completely wiped out. Hence there results the great inequality of taxation that exists today. And since whatever is unequal is intolerable the said taxation must be returned to fitting and tolerable equality, and must be made and done anew.*

In accordance with this measure the entire *contado* tax burden was reapportioned in relation to the damage suffered by each community.

The shortage of agricultural labor and the increased demands made by renters, sharecroppers, and farm laborers who survived the epidemic caused Siena to try to attract foreign farm labor into the state. In 1349 such immigrants were promised immunity from taxes and services until 1354 if they would farm specified amounts of land. At the same time those men aged fifteen to seventy who had customarily rented, sharecropped, and worked were heavily taxed unless they farmed the same specified quantities "ad usum boni laboratoris." This law was necessary:

> *Since the workers of the land, and those who customarily worked the lands and orchards, because of their great extortions and the salaries that they receive for their daily labors, totally destroyed the farms of the citizens and inhabitants of the state [districtuales] of Siena and deserted the farms and lands of the aforesaid citizens and districtuales.*

While this measure may have driven some peasants into foreign lands others were probably attracted to Siena itself, augmenting the city's population and labor supply. At least two other measures of 1348 and 1350 were aimed at restricting the mobility of farm laborers and compelling them to adhere to customary contracts, but they were not renewed and were apparently unsuccessful.

Those coming to Siena found a scene of considerable confusion. The epidemic was followed by an increase in the number of crimes of violence and in all forms of abandoned living. As late as 15 September 1350 the City Council lamented the ease with which culprits could evade justice merely by leaving the city.

The Black Death brought about great social and economic dislocation. Severe legislation of 1349 aimed at gaining for Siena the properties, rights, and incomes of those who had died intestate during the epidemic and were not survived by close relatives. By law those legacies pertained to the commune, but many had been forcefully usurped. The new law provided that all who had occupied such estates denounce the fact to communal authorities within two weeks, upon pain of paying double the value of their usurpations. After the two-week grace period anyone could denounce such illegal occupation to the *Podestà* and receive 10% of the fine, while his name would be kept secret.

Other inheritances too were illegally seized, leaving widows and orphans to petition the City Council for redress. So numerous were contested legacies that special courts, judges and commissions were appointed to hear and define such cases. Extant testimony concerning contested dowries proves conclusively that many properties throughout the city, Masse and *contado* were acquired in the wake of the plague without regard to right or legal ownership.

Not all inheritances were worth accepting. Some, burdened by debt, were rapidly repudiated. The forty-one repudiations of paternal legacies approved by the City Council in 1349 are almost double the number for any preceding year.

A major cause for repudiation is found in another area of City Council activity: grants of moratoria, discounts, and remissions of fees to *gabella* farmers and renters of communal properties. The first half of 1349 saw over thirty-five such grants — more than for any previous comparable period.

We need not merely surmise a connection between legacy repudiations and the relief granted distressed tax farmers and communal renters.

For example, in a petition accepted by the City Council 23 October 1349 two sons of a late purchaser of the *gabella* of fish sold in the city stated that they had legally repudiated their paternal inheritance because their father had died burdened by this debt. Unknown to them at the time, however, their mother too had obligated her properties as surety for their father's debt. Hence they had lost both their paternal and maternal inheritances. They requested relief lest because of their present poverty they be forced "to leave the city of Siena and wander about other parts of the world."

So numerous were the pleas for relief that in September 1348 two separate measures were enacted establishing the administrative machinery for granting such aid to renters and *gabella* purchasers damaged by a loss of income caused by the plague.

If post-plague Siena was marked by economic and social fluidity not all were losers. Sumptuary laws were quickly revived because many persons pretended to higher station than that of their birth or occupation. In legislation of 1349 knights, judges, and physicians, and their wives and children under twelve years of age were the sole groups permitted the most lavish and expensive modes of dress.

Much legislation was enacted to protect the rights and properties of the multitude orphaned by the Black Death, but two closely contested measures of 9 April 1350 merit special attention. These hitherto unnoticed acts forbade the orphans of non-nobles, particularly female, from marrying nobles without the prior consent of their *popolani* kinsmen. This was probably an attempt to protect *popolani* legacies from magnates wishing to recoup damaged fortunes or to add to existing riches. The closeness of the votes indicates clearly that not everyone accepted the new economic and social fluidity as a blessing.

Many *Noveschi* and great nobles were plague victims or bankrupted. A notarial act of 7 January 1351, for example, shows three creditors of the bankrupt Francesco di Guiduccio Ruffaldi selling some of his landed properties at Ampugnano for 1,085 gold florins as the result of a compromise arranged by the Consuls of the Merchant Gild.

But all wealth itself did not disappear. Some men enriched themselves with little heed to legal niceties. Others legitimately inherited sizeable fortunes. And *Noveschi* and magnates continued to lead Siena, and to lend to it, as before. Biccherna records do not bear out Agnolo di Tura's contention of 1349 that "all money had fallen into the hands of new people (*gente nuova*)."

By the fall of that year, however, enough *nouveaux riches* had come into existence, or gained sufficient strength, to cause the conservative City Council to enact a revolutionary measure: it ended forever the strict monopoly held by Sienese bankers—the core of *Noveschi* strength—over the right to act as sureties for *gabella* purchasers. Henceforth non-bankers too could participate in this lucrative business, provided that the leading Sienese magistracies approved of their suitability by a two-thirds vote. Nor were all so unlucky as a dyer and a shoemaker who soon languished in prison for backing an insolvent purchaser!

The attack on bankers' privileges was pushed further. By 1355 they were forbidden to hold two key financial offices to which laymen had gained access in 1348 because of a shortage of monks. Like the law protecting *popolani* orphans, this measure originated in the Council of the Military Companies, where lesser gildsmen held greater power than the commanded in the higher echelons of government.

Among those who gained most in social and economic status after the Black Death were the notaries. The few remaining notaries of both the city and *contado* profited from their scarcity. For the first time they assiduously avoided communal offices and vicarships, devoting themselves to profitable private practice and to service in the entourages of those called to high office as *Podestà*, Captain of the People, or War Captain. Notaries ignored both old and new ordinances regulating their fees. They even went so far as to draw up documents that were contrary to the wishes of the contracting parties, and to mock those who employed their services. In October 1352 the commune was forced to abandon its traditional policy of prohibiting clerics from practicing as notaries, even in those causes where the Gild of Judges and Notaries wished to continue the prohibition. This measure was enacted for the explicitly stated reason that notaries were in too short supply. As late as June 1354 the City Council empowered the IX to draft notaries for service in *contado* offices.

Plague survivors with special skills or in very short supply not unnaturally tried to improve their lot by demanding higher wages and prices, beyond what was justified by the increased cost of alimentary products. Stonemasons and others in the building industry were particularly scarce. Like other communes such as Orvieto and Pisa, Siena enacted wage and price regulations. Detailed Sienese ordinances have not survived, but there is proof that on 1 October 1348 the Consuls of the Merchant Gild received authority from the City Council to set both rates and the fines for contravention. The alleged reason for this measure was that artisans and workers were demanding far more than the customary amounts for their wares and labors. Of greater interest, though, is the fact that Siena apparently enacted only three such regulatory measures—two immediately after the plague and a third in March 1350. Even these were not renewed.

If unlike many other European communes and states Siena did not rely heavily upon such controls to restore normalcy, another avenue was open: encouragement of immigration to the city. Possibly on 13 October 1348 the government extended Sienese citizenship to those foreigners who came to Siena with their families and remained for five years. But this is only hinted at in an apostil and in a brief phrase recording a City Council vote—although this is the sole evidence upon which Kovalevsky bases his argument that after the Black Death Siena adopted a liberal citizenship policy, similar to that of Venice. These phrases are not open to so broad an interpretation as that which Kovalevsky gives them. His assumption that the measure applied to those settling in the *contado* as well as in the city is gratuitous, although the inclusion of such persons in similar legislation enacted 18 October 1348 by Orvieto should not pass unnoticed.

If the Sienese government wished to attract new inhabitants to the city this allegedly was not to be at the expense of the *contado* communities, as we have seen from the legislation of 1351 restricting the ease with which wealthy *contadini* could obtain citizenship. Yet the law itself was probably occasioned by *contado* complaints against just such an exodus.

What of actual figures? In point of fact the number of new citizenships granted from September 1348 to April 1355 soared 22.5% over the total number granted during the eighteen years from 1330 to 1348. Enjoyable though it is to deal in percentages, the numbers at stake are a modest eighty and ninety-eight citizenships. After the plague, as before, over half of the new citizens came from the *contado* and most of the remainder from neighboring Tuscan states. Prominent among those whose occupations are known were notaries, merchants, and wool manufacturers.

Any major influx of population after the Black Death came not at this citizen level but from the lower economic and social strata, the strata hardest to trace in extant documents. Substantial indirect evidence points to just such an influx, and to a considerable repopulation of the city perhaps as early as 1351—recalling Kovalevsky's findings for Venice. Such a population increase might explain in part the rapid restoration of Sienese finances. Similarly, the farm labor legislation of May 1349 was conducive to driving agricultural labor off the farms, and, to some extent, towards Siena itself. The legislation of May 1351 assisting *contado* communities to control the exodus of wealthy *contadini* wishing to acquire Sienese citizenship would not have been necessary had there been no such phenomenon. Noteworthy too is Siena's rapid abandonment of wage and price regulations for city artisans and workers, particularly as other communes such as Pisa and Orvieto long continued their use. While as late as February 1350 applicants for Sienese citizenship requested exemption from the statutory requirement that they build new houses in the city or suburbs for the specific reasons that many houses were empty because of the plague and "the city needs inhabitants, not houses," such statements appear in no later applications. Not to be overlooked are the hitherto unnoticed expenditures for several new gates and walls for the city totaling almost £3,000 during the first half of 1352. By March 1353 the Council of the People, reduced one-third after the plague, was restored to its original size. This, coupled with the fact that the *Noveschi*-dominated City Council remained reduced, may indicate the social and economic level of many of the new arrivals.

Returned refugees may account for some of the repopulation. Some immigrants came from the Sienese *contado*, still others from outside the state. But while post-plague Siena housed both *nouveaux riches* and newcomers of modest means these groups were new and unstable elements in the city's political life. And they shared in certain attitudes, if not a clearly formulated program. Neither group accepted with equanimity traditional *Noveschi* methods of government—*nouveaux riches* from a desire for political and social perquisites commensurate with their improved economic status; newcomers to the city because they had not grown up under the rule of the IX.

Their attitudes coincided most closely in hostility to the special privileges and advantages that the *Noveschi* assumed for themselves. Some of these had been criticized occasionally in the past. Now the attacks became so severe that the government took cognizance of the protests and yielded in part. In June 1349 the chief magistrates of the Biccherna were attacked for favoring their friends in the priority of repayments to communal creditors and for allowing speculation in the public debt. It was less than three months later that the bankers lost their monopoly over the right to act as sureties for *gabella* purchasers.

Pressures increased noticeably during the next three years. In the fall of 1350 the IX were ordered to stop receiving and giving gifts. 22 April 1351 the City Council enacted legislation aimed at eliminating suspicions that the tax assessors were favoring members of the IX, the chief magistrates of the Biccherna and the Gabella, the Consuls of the Merchant Gild, and their families. The following 8 July the IX were denied the rights to elect themselves or any other incumbent leading Sienese magistrates to any public office.

So great was the pressure that eleven days later the City Council considered a proposal to enlarge the base from which members of the IX were selected — the fist such proposal to reach the council floor in fifteen years. But the IX were not prepared to admit defeat. Although this measure was sponsored by a leading *Noveschi* it failed by a vote of 82 to 45. This reversal is all the more significant when we recall that the council approved over 99% of the measures that is considered.

The IX continued to see their position threatened. Accused of mismanagement of the public mint, in June 1351 one group of the IX was even deprived of its special immunities against ordinary criminal prosecution. Two months before the fall of the government Sienese bankers were explicitly excluded from two important financial offices.

The Black Death did not directly precipitate the overthrow of the IX. But it was instrumental in creating demographic, social, and economic conditions that greatly increased opposition to the ruling oligarchy. At the next major crisis, the arrival in Siena of the Emperor Charles IV in March 1355, newcomers and new rich were important elements in the revolution that felled a government that had weathered the storms of nearly three-quarters of a century — ending the era of Siena's greatest stability and prosperity.

William J. Dohar

The Black Death and Pastoral Leadership

William J. Dohar examines the plague's ability to alter the character and structure of clerical authority in the diocese of Hereford. To begin with, mortality among clerics was high, creating staffing shortages and other constraints. Dohar also seeks to answer the nagging question of whether clerical standards waned as the number of priests declined. Although he finds evidence in visitation records that parishioners were not satisfied with the behavior and services of their priests, he stresses the need to put these comments in context, rather than attributing solely to the disease's impact. As he notes, parishioners had registered similar complaints before the plague. Also, he argues, "the further one moves from the event of plague itself, the greater the possibility that other forces . . . entered to influence developments in institutions and their management." In addition, he demonstrates the flexibility of local clergy in meeting the crisis generated by the plague. In some instances, for example, they relied more heavily on churchwardens, lay administrators who assisted in running the parish.

Epidemic plague in England did not end with the fourteenth century. In the early years of John Trefnant's successor, the Carmelite Robert Mascall, plague would once again trouble the kingdom and the diocese. In August 1407 Bishop Mascall received a letter from Archbishop Arundel commanding him to oversee masses, prayers, and processions in the cathedral and parish churches of Hereford on account of the many ills that menaced England in those days. Numbered among them was the schism that refused to end and the current civil strife that threatened Henry IV's crown and the peace of England. But of all the trials Arundel recounted, the one that seemed gravest in the letter was the pestilence then threatening the country. The correspondence was all too similar to one shared by Bishop Stratford of London and John Trillek of

Source: William J. Dohar, *The Black Death and Pastoral Leadership* (Philadelphia: University of Pennsylvania Press, 1995), 149–155.

Hereford nearly sixty years before. And just as that first plague moved implacably towards Hereford's borders, so too did this latest.

The mandates *ad orandum pro pestilentia* had acquired a numbing familiarity to Hereford clergy and parishioners over the last decades. The news was always fearsome, but the novelty of special processions and prayers and, perhaps, the hope as well that should have been their fruit, had diminished. Countless families and communities had been touched by death over the long season of mortality, for there had been eleven separate outbreaks of epidemic plague since the Great Pestilence of 1348. So, when Bishop Mascall had the news broadcast through the diocese there were doubtless those who responded anew with fitting expressions of piety while others wondered at the depth of human misery and sin or the unrelenting judgment of God.

More than ritual expressions surrounding sickness and death had changed in the diocese in the last sixty years. Nearly half the diocesan clergy had been struck down in the first plague and subsequent outbreaks continued to erode clerical and lay communities alike. In spite of the activities of the bishops to shore up the diminished numbers of local pastors, it would take another century and a half before the general population and its clerical cohort were restored to something approaching pre-plague levels. Parishioners suffered the deaths of neighbor and kin, and poor parishes struggled to maintain an economic base adequate to support the church and its ministries. And what happened in the parish communities occurred in other places as well. Religious houses diminished in size, some never to recover from the ravages of plague. The number of religious advanced to Holy Orders soared during the plague years, telling of new needs for pastoral care to religious houses. Often struggling to keep their own communities financially secure, some houses were less vigilant in overseeing the pastoral care of the parish churches whose revenues they had appropriated. It was far more difficult for the poorer houses, hospitals, and places of charity.

All these changes in the religious and pastoral dimensions of the church took place within structures and institutions that been greatly tested during and after the Black Death and proved impressively resilient. The fourteenth-century church had inherited a strong institutional framework from the ecclesiastical reforms and the process of centralization that had been among the great legacies of the previous century. Certainly it was not merely the structures that kept the church going, but the individuals and communities who developed them and for whom they made sense. Still, however durable these structures were, the recovery they helped foster in the wake of the plague was only gradually achieved. Social and economic repercussions from the Black Death would continue to be felt long after the event. Even if we credit the foundations and walls of the pastoral edifice with a certain resilience, we have to concede that some aspects of the fabric had changed in significant ways.

The basic features of the parish community remained unchanged after the Black Death: ritual expressions of the faith of the local community went on much as they had before. But provision for prayer and ministry had changed. There were fewer curates to do the pastoral work in Hereford's parishes and those that held cures were stretched between increased responsibilities, either from a certain sense of priestly duty or out of a desire to augment their meager wages. Parishes that had once supported small communities of clergy of varying ranks in orders had to get by with far fewer and sometimes none. The solitude of the parochial cure, especially those churches in the remote and sparsely populated countryside, must have worn on the pastors of the late fourteenth century and accounted, in some measure, for the lapses in clerical celibacy. Local curates found assistance where they could, and this was one incentive for the further development of an office that had begun to appear in parish communities before the Black Death. The *custos* or churchwarden was a parochial administrator, a parishioner who had a mind for business and could provide some aid to the management of the cure by keeping the parish's financial operations and records in order. A further change occurred in patronage with clerical candidates moving increasingly away from traditional, familial sources of support to sponsorship by local religious communities. Schools and educational opportunities underwent changes as well over the course of the fourteenth century. The cathedral school's reputation had been tarnished, traditional if modest stipends for junior clerics in the parish had all but disappeared, and fewer rectors allowed themselves the hope of spending time at a university away from their cures. But here again restriction forced innovation and change: more clergy were acquiring a pastoral education from the growing volume of pastoral manuals, homilaries, and mass-books available in the late fourteenth and early fifteenth centuries.

These changes that took place within the apparently durable structures of church life point to a question with which this study began: was there a decline in the standards of the parish clergy in the decades following the Black Death? Any answer to this question needs to be qualified in two general ways: first, the plague's effects were far from following a single direction of impact and response. In fact, the further one moves from the event of plague itself, the greater the possibility that other forces, perhaps only distantly related to the changes associated with the plagues, entered to influence developments in institutions and their management. Certainly, by the end of the fourteenth century there had been an accumulation of dismal events that had added greater burdens to the church and its pastoral mission. Men of letters would recall the plague as the watershed event between better days and the difficulties of the present. But their perception and others' had been shaded by some of the larger social and economic changes that had gone on in England and the church during the second half of the century. The schism that dominated the higher echelons of ecclesiastical power revealed the weakness that plagued even the greatest authorities in the church. Some priests had earned notorious reputations for leading crowds of peasants in their campaigns against customary obligations and traditional wage scales. Other preachers were drawn to the new and dangerous opinions of John Wycliffe and his followers, and Hereford pulpits became yet another source of dismay and division in some communities. Thus, there can be no easy connection between most plague-events and the status of the clergy by the century's end; yet the idea that the Black Death presented a myriad of problems, institutionally and personally, and required an equally diffused range of responses, cannot be ignored.

Second, the whole question of clerical standards in the late medieval church needs to be weighed carefully. We know from their appearance in the records that medieval clerics were far from uniform in background, their sense of profession, patronage, education, and ecclesiastical status. The large and nondescript categories of "higher" and "lower" clergy reveal very little of the diversity that existed among their ranks, differences among the sons of promise and prosperity, university scholars, wage-earners who were the yeomen of pastoral care, guild chaplains, chantrists, royal clerks, and poor parsons. The pastoral effectiveness of any of these was based upon a few simple principles: that he have the ability to function freely in the exercise of the church's sacraments, that he do so with regularity and dignity and that he build up rather than neglect or tear down his community. There were almost limitless ways in which these things could be done (or not) and every pastoral act was in some sense shaped by the setting in which it occurred. If any one in the fourteenth century knew this, it was the bishop. As the first pastor of the diocese, he was meant to be the guardian of the apostolic tradition and the preserver of unity among his people. But he knew as well, through his ministers and by his own sight, the disparate nature of his diocese. Even in a place as remote and as small as Hereford, the variety of pastoral concerns was great; each community existed with its own spiritual and human needs; each had its own customs, honored or broken; each its measure of support in seasonal dues and offerings; each its curate by institution or appointment. All of this does not suggest that diversity reigned where unity was needed, but that religious life in the fourteenth century was much influenced by concerns which were, in the end, quite local. Though this was beginning to change somewhat by the end of the century, we look in vain for clear standards set out to be met by parish clergy. What standards did exist were tersely described and sometimes generously interpreted by ecclesiastical authorities. The greatest concerns bishops had at ordination were not so much in the decorous qualities of candidates but in their defects. If a man was free from those few impediments which could threaten his effectiveness as a minister, and if he showed promise for prospering in his office, then there was little reason to dismiss him from the ranks of *ordinandi*. The best standard of a man's work in the pastorate was observed in place, a standard in some sense clarified when parishioners answered the inquires of diocesan visitors by saying that all was well in their parish.

Still, the picture of pastoral care in Hereford at the century's end is often not a flattering one. In their depositions at Trefnant's visitation, Hereford parishioners provide us with some glaring cases of misfits at the altar, men who were patently inept at exercising the arts of arts, some on account of ignorance, poor training and spare opportunity for learning, others out of an incompetence that was not adequately challenged by the usual pastoral authorities of rural dean, archdeacon or bishop. But it must also be said that there was little that was new to the clerical follies of the late fourteenth century saving, perhaps, the first signs of the new heresy and the gathering strength of its first adherents. Priests well before the Black Death had been brought to justice as criminous clerks; they had to be reminded of the need for study; they were put back from ordination or delayed in their institution to a living if their learning was shamefully insufficient. Bishops always had trouble overseeing the work of their subordinates, not only the parish clergy themselves, but the rural deans, archdeacons, and cathedral dignitaries that had so much influence on pastoral care.

Thus the question of a decline in the quality of pastoral leadership does not so much revolve around the degree of change in the diocese as much as its resistance to change. Ecclesiastical structures and operations had withstood a great test in the catastrophe of the Black Death, but it was also true that some of these same institutions and approaches to them had become too fixed and brittle. For example, the institutional demands of the diocese remained pretty much the same after the plague as before, but there were far fewer priests to administer them and far fewer innovations provided by visionary leaders of the post-plague church. It could hardly come as a surprise, then, that the evils of pluralism should fall upon the church in such circumstances. There were plenty of grasping clergy who attempted to collect church benefices as other wealthy men collected land, but in Hereford, as elsewhere, curates already taxed by the ministry of their own parishes felt obliged or pressured to labor in more than one vineyard. Church leadership showed a similar institutional conservatism in the matter of clerical salaries. The wages set for stipendiaries even after the scandalous behavior of clerical mercenaries in the hard times following the plague continued to ignore the poverty of most chaplains and the changing economy of the times. This discrepancy only added to the anxieties over class and opportunity that distinguished the fewer beneficed clerics from their more numerous non-beneficed brothers. It was almost inevitable that bishops like John Trefnant should encounter a low morale and slackened discipline among the poorly paid and just as poorly trained stipendiaries in his tour through the diocese.

There were further changes in society that were too great to ignore: the Black Death had provoked new struggles or revived old ones regarding the social and economic identities of common laborers. When local and national markets began to rebound in the years following the plague, and people availed themselves of new opportunities in work and status, the clerical life seemed a less desirous choice to many. As traditional forms of alliance and solidarity had changed in many places, so a greater mobility characterized much of society, including the emerging middle class from which most candidates for the clergy came. Old local loyalties declined, and testimonies for titles were steadily connected with institutions of stability such as religious houses, that offered a reputable or at least a familiar name to men little known in the territory.

Reprimanding the bishops of Hereford for not adjusting to the larger changes from without is perhaps too easy an accusation to make. In many ways it is hard to imagine that they could have done much otherwise. They were bound to act within certain limits established by custom, law, and the authorities to which they themselves were subject. Their conservatism was understandable to the extent that innovation of any kind is always cautiously regarded in times of change. Their efforts by and large were devoted to stabilizing the traditional means of assuring salvation. They naturally relied on the structures which had formed them and served as the basis of authority and order in the diocese. At least for Hereford, things might have been far different had a man of less talent and determination than John Trillek been bishop during the plague years. His own response to the pastoral crisis that gathered quickly with the advance of the plague was to be a pastor and to carry out his duties as best he could. We have little reason, given the evidence available, to conclude otherwise. Though the diocese was rocked by yet another plague only months after Trillek's death in 1360, Lewis Charlton was a man equal to his predecessor's talents and abilities. In many ways the challenges he faced were greater than those confronted by Trillek. Charlton witnessed the continuing decline in clerical recruits while attempting to secure the pastoral life of the diocese in spiritually and economically difficult times. The good fortune the diocese had in the quality of its bishops diminished slightly in the brief pontificate of William Courtenay. It was surely not that the young bishop was inept but rather that he seemed preoccupied with other things. His contributions were small and there is little reason to believe that he left the diocese in greater difficulty than he found it. But had Courtenay delivered there the power of his intellect and force of rule that characterized the man later as archbishop, some of the difficulties the diocese continued to experience during John Gilbert's rule might have been eased. Gilbert, another able man, was too busy with the affairs of state to tend as vigilantly as he might to the local concerns of Hereford parishes and clergy. Indeed, during his years the diocese witnessed the first inroads of heterodox teaching from the followers of John Wycliffe. John Trefnant's arrival came at an auspicious time. Intelligent and self-possessed, he was content to busy himself with the cure of souls and the administration of his beleaguered diocese. Perhaps overly zealous in bringing errant Christians to trial—he was a litigious prelate—Trefnant was more devoted to the concerns at home than his immediate predecessors had been.

In the diocese of Hereford, as elsewhere, changes in institutions and attitudes gradually took on the accepted forms of church life. Though the

Black Death and subsequent epidemics did not alter forever the basic manner of pastoral leadership and care in the diocese, what changes had taken place were far-reaching. They were at first immediate and devastating in the loss of lives occasioned by the plague and the attendant disruptions in society, economy, and religion. Past the crisis of plague, these effects merged with other great forces from within and without that marked this time as an age of adversity: the continued ruin of war, the scandal of the papal schism, and the new ways of thinking and believing that touched the very foundations of the Christian faith. Still, the plague, though one of many factors of change in this period, was the most significant and enigmatic event in the history of the late middle ages. Its origins were enshrouded in mystery and its operations buried in physical realities far beyond the ken of medieval people. Unlike wars and schisms which are the fruit of human folly, the plague was God's judgment on the age and its effects, even when they had disappeared from the superficial structures of church and society, lingered far longer than any military conflict or ecclesiastical argument devised by princes and popes. For generations medieval people would meditate on the violent and random nature of death and impress their musings in poetry, painting, and architecture. Some had turned away in despair from a church that had revealed its human corruptability and inconstancy in the face of trial. But most medieval Christians continued to search for meaning and identity in this calamity as in any other, through the comforts of the community at prayer and the pastoral care of the church.

By the fifteenth century commerce began recovering from the economic and demographic disruption of the plague. (Museo Civico, Bologna, Italy/The Art Archive)

The Socio-Economic Impact of Plague

Part IV began an examination of the longer-term impact of the Black Death. The Church, the university, and secular government all contended with and answered to the challenges posed by epidemic disease. Emphasizing social and economic change, Part V also seeks to understand the effects of the Black Death on medieval Europe. In order to examine these changes it is important first to understand the demographic consequences of the disease. As noted in the Introduction, Europeans probably had no acquired immunities to the plague. As a result, the population loss suffered was catastrophic. Estimates vary from region to region throughout Europe, but on average twenty to thirty percent of the population perished at the hands of the disease.

This dramatic jolt to population levels disrupted the social and economic life of medieval Europe. In most parts of Europe the population did not begin to recover until the late fifteenth century. Thus, for almost a century and a half Europe faced a declining or stagnant population. This state of affairs impacted the economy in a variety of ways. Agricultural prices dropped due to falling demand. At the same time, though, wages rose as a diminished population stimulated a demand for labor. Rents and land prices declined, and there was a marked shift away from farming marginal lands. The availability of (relatively) cheap land opened the land market to a greater segment of the population. High mortality concentrated greater wealth in the hands of survivors, giving them unique opportunities as investors and patrons. Would this dramatic reversal of fortune in the second half of the fourteenth century improve life for those fortunate enough to survive the plague?

In many ways, the postplague economy stood to benefit that segment of society most often disadvantaged: the peasantry. Although somewhat overstated, for example, some scholars have credited the Black Death with being the catalyst for the decline of the feudal system in England. As demand for labor grew, peasants were placed in an advantageous position. Landlords anxious to maintain the productivity of their land agreed to commute or abolish traditional manorial obligations. Lower land prices made it possible for peasant proprietors to acquire more land. The first two readings in this section examine the question of the plague's impact on the peasantry.

The piece excerpted from Paul Freedman's book, *The Origins of Peasant Servitude in Medieval Catalonia,* turns an eye to the peasants of Catalonia, the northeastern region of Spain that includes the port city of Barcelona. These peasants, known as the Remences, struggled under an oppressive seigneurial system. Notably, Freedman finds that the improved conditions brought on by the dramatic decrease in the population after 1348 did little to mitigate the powers of the lords in this region. Peasants continued to suffer under the legally sanctioned mistreatment of their overlords and increases in the cost of redemption—the amount required for a Remença to be released from servitude to a lord.

The selection by John Hatcher looks at the status of agricultural workers in England in this era and finds a set of circumstances different from the ones outlined by Freedman. His overall argument is directed primarily against a body of recent scholarship that has sought to minimize the ability of the Black Death to improve the lot of peasants. These studies have posited that wages did not rise dramatically and that even minimal rises were offset by rising prices. In the excerpts here, Hatcher counters this position in two ways. The first is to examine literary evidence in which authors gave voice to widespread complaints about peasant demands. Second, Hatcher also urges historians to not rely solely on examining wages paid on landed estates in England during this period. Other forms of compensation existed. He hints at the end of the article (a portion not excerpted here) that the improvement of peasant circumstances—and the attempts of landlords to constrain these advances—did much to create the challenge to feudalism embodied in the Peasants' Revolt of 1381.

As Hatcher's conclusions demonstrate, such dramatic changes in the socioeconomic landscape certainly created rising expectations among the peasantry and lower classes. At the same time, however, landlords also adapted to the shifts in the landed economy. Just as peasants sought to capitalize on the demand for their labor, these elites modified their position in the marketplace accordingly. To offset the rising wages that labor demand had created, for example, some landowners diverted their resources away from labor-intensive activity. Instead of turning the land over to the plow—an effort that required a steady supply of agricultural labor—some of them invested in pastoral endeavors. Herding sheep, for example, was a land-intensive enterprise that did not necessitate as many workers.

This clash of peasant expectations and landlord adaptation became a pitched battle in England in 1381 with the outbreak of the Peasants' Revolt. The roots of this conflict can be traced to the socioeconomic upheaval wrought by the plague. Throughout England peasant laborers had successfully demanded higher wages. The government, however, responded vigorously in 1351 with the Statute of Laborers, which returned wages to their preplague levels. Resentment over measures like these was only exacerbated in 1380 when the king levied a highly unpopular poll tax. Resistance to the tax began to take a violent form.

The passage by Christopher Dyer traces the links between socioeconomic change in the postplague period and the outbreak of the English Peasants' Revolt of 1381. He accomplishes this, in part, by examining who participated in the uprising. Overall, well-to-do peasants were among some of the prominent rebels. These peasants were living through a period of improved standards of living and may have agitated for greater prosperity and a lessening of the bonds that tied them to their overlords. Notably, many of the rebels also played a role in the management of the manors on which they lived, holding positions such as bailiff and constable. Thus, Dyer finds part of the explanation for the uprising in the participation of these individuals, who, he argues, occupied an awkward place on these estates and may have ultimately sided with their fellow peasants rather than the landlords.

Another group that stood to benefit from the shifting tides of the agricultural economy was women. Historians have wondered whether women were able to gain a greater foothold in the medieval economy after the plague due to the greater demand for labor. Mavis Mate's book, *Daughters, Wives and Widows after the Black Death, 1350–1535* examines the experiences of women in rural England in the decades following the plague. She finds that the plague changed women's lives in an immediate sense, but overall the plague did not upset traditional ideological structures that hemmed them in. Like their male peasant counterparts just discussed, women did earn higher wages in the postplague period. In addition, high mortality rates did allow some women to inherit property that might otherwise have gone to male siblings. Yet, in these instances the pressure to marry quickly and subsume the property under a husband's authority was even greater, so wealthy heiresses tended to marry younger than their less-well-off counterparts.

So far the readings in this section have examined the rural economy. This is commensurate with the living arrangements of most Europeans in the fourteenth and fifteenth centuries. Europe was overwhelmingly rural and agricultural. At the same time, however, many of these agricultural laborers and their landlords did produce for the marketplace. Demographic devastation, the disruption of measures to combat the plague like quarantines, and a diminished labor supply for the production of finished goods undoubtedly influenced larger market forces. The selection by Harry Miskimin examines how the outbreak of plague affected industrial production and patterns of market consumption. Industrial productivity rested on the complex interaction of capital for tools and technology and the skill level of artisans. Industry could also be shaped by declining demand for certain products that freed resources for other uses. Mills that once ground grain, for example, could be used for fulling cloth. Industry also responded in this period to a much greater demand for various kinds of luxury goods.

Paul Freedman

The Origins of Peasant Servitude in Medieval Catalonia

Paul Freedman's analysis assesses the status of peasant-landlord relations in Catalonia after 1348. Landlords tried to counter the peasants' improving standard of living by exacting high redemption prices and through legally sanctioned forms of mistreatment. In some instances lords were willing to make concessions in order to keep peasants on their land. Overall, however, Freedman argues, the lords had been expanding their powers and privileges well before 1348, and as a consequence the upheaval of the postplague period could do little to alter land tenure arrangements or improve the fate of the peasants. In short, Catalonian peasants did not benefit in the same ways as their English counterparts.

Lordship after the Black Death

. . . General histories and local studies agree that Catalan lords attempted to increase their revenues and tighten their control over tenants after 1348. In particular instances peasants might take advantage of economic market forces, that is to say, the shortage of labor might have strengthened their bargaining power over wages or terms of leases. In large measure, however, lords used their jurisdictional and, ultimately, political authority to defy the market and to increase the scope and effect of powers they already possessed, powers of coercion or of control.

One therefore finds an increase in the price of redemption and a renewed application of seigneurial mistreatment during the late fourteenth century. How quickly the lords could react to offset the deterioration in their income may be problematical. José-Luis Martin says that

Source: Paul H. Freedman, *The Origins of Peasant Servitude in Medieval Catalonia* (New York: Cambridge University Press, 1991), 166–168, 171–178.

the short-term influence of the Black Death allowed peasants who held good land to improve their position, but that for peasants in marginal areas, the possibility of annexing new vacant land did not necessarily tempt them or appear as if it would improve their economic condition. Lords could use a variety of means to wrest more from a smaller tenant population: shorter leases, stricter terms of establishment, and coercion to stay if the lords needed them.

Vicens Vives distinguishes the formalization of seigneurial regulations from a subsequent imposition of their oppressive provisions. After 1348 the right of lords to "seize and mistreat" (*prendre e maltractar*) appeared in customals, while the church council of Tarragona in 1370 forbade *Remences* from entering orders, thus further defining them as serfs. With the shortage of labor, peasants could afford for a time to laugh at such rules, but the fall of prices and onset of economic crisis allowed lords to make these restrictions effective.

As may be seen from the previous chapters, the lords, long before the Black Death, had already set up mechanisms to oppress their tenants. With respect to such practices as redemption, the Black Death seems to have worsened already resented practices. In other instances, as in the application of the right of mistreatment, a largely theoretical right was turned into a lucrative abuse.

What Cuvillier has called a "durcissement féodale" was experienced throughout Old Catalonia in the late fourteenth century. What remains at issue within this general framework is: (1) when this hardening of lordship effectively constrained the peasantry; (2) how much it affected the well-off as opposed to the impoverished peasants; and (3) what specific practices were key to this oppressive process. In terms of chronology one can point to the 1380s as crucial for the organization of peasant resistance. By this time, therefore, the seigneurial reaction was clearly being felt and the first organized resistance is visible. On the question of differential effects on social strata within the peasantry, Cuvillier and Tuñon de Lara discern *both* a seigneurial reaction and increased distinctions between elite and ordinary peasants. It remains to be seen how much the *Remença* agitation was related to this growing internal contradiction. In what follows we shall concentrate on the third of the issues raised above: specific aspects of seigneurial reaction, but we wish to consider these aspects in light of their effects on peasants of different regions and social levels. . . .

Redemption Prices

The price of redemption always varied greatly, as already noted, and depended on particular circumstances. The only fixed price was for young women who married into the jurisdiction of another lord. For them the usual redemption tariff was set at 2 sous, 8 deniers and this remained in effect after 1348. While lords had difficulty in changing rents and other fixed customary obligations, they could increase the tariff for redemption for most of their tenants. As long as they wielded effective police power, or its semblance, they could forestall largescale desertion of holdings and reverse the unfavorabe supply and demand relation that tended to force higher wages or better leases. By demanding a higher redemption payment the lords were attempting to cancel the advantages theoretically afforded by the operation of the economic market.

Some sixty-eight redemption charters issued by the diocesan charitable foundation, the Pia Almoina, of Girona show roughly a doubling of mean redemption prices (expressed in sous of Barcelona) in the period 1348 to 1400 when compared with the period 1300–1348. For the earlier period the average tenant paid 64.6 sous (fifty transactions), while after the Black Death the figure was 132.8 sous (eighteen transactions). This represents a significant increase, although not extreme in view of the rise in wages.

What may also be important is the relative paucity of redemptions after 1348. There is no direct evidence that lords refused liberty to *Remences* willing to pay. Later versions of the *Customs of the Diocese of Girona* required lords to agree to the redemption of tenants who married but allowed them otherwise a right to refuse to accept redemption payments. At the same time, according to Gaspar Feliu, there were few heads of households who were able to redeem themselves so that the lords' paramount interest in keeping tenements occupied was not vitiated by redemption.

Serra Vilaró has found evidence of a similar trend from documents in the archives of Bagà for Pinós and Mataplana tenants. He cites thirty-one documents from 1294 to 1348 whose mean redemption price amounts to 38.2 sous. After 1348 and before 1411 eleven documents (not including one that is undated and another listed perhaps erroneously at 150 pounds!), show an average price of 122.2 sous. The lords of Pinós were willing to move tenants to better lands within their jurisdiction, but discouraged departure from their lands by high redemption prices, agreeing at the same time to guarantee certain individuals future redemption of children or even heads of households provided they left an heir to remain tied to the land.

Application of the *Ius Maletractandi*

A further aspect of hardening lordship after 1348 is the putting into effect of the right of seigneurial mistreatment. This right, enshrined at the Corts of Cervera in 1202, legitimated what had been flagrantly illegal practices and underscored the isolation of servile tenants from the protection of Catalan customary law.

There is little to show how lords exercised this privilege before 1348. The legislation of 1202 allowed lords not only to coerce tenants' bodies but to seize property without explanation or justification. The absence of litigation over seigneurial mistreatment in the thirteenth century (in contrast to the numerous complaints of the twelfth century) may indicate either that the level of seigneurial violence had diminished, or that the *ius maletractandi* was effective in deterring any potential appeal, thus it covered up its own traces.

After 1348, the lords can, at least occasionally, be seen to use the right of mistreatment as proof of their control over tenants and also to deprive tenants of redress. In addition to the fundamental legislation of 1202, a law enacted at the Corts of Girona in 1321 forbade "rustics" (in general) from making appeals against their lords to any public (royal, civic, or ecclesiastical) tribunal. After 1348 this right was exploited. Tenants were compelled explicitly to acknowledge seigneurial rights "whether just or unjust; licit or illicit," to recognize that they might be seized, punished, and mistreated. The *Customs of the Diocese of Girona*, composed in the late fourteenth and early fifteenth centuries, allowed lords to hold their tenants at will in chains, stocks or prison. In a letter of 1402 to her kinsman Pope Benedict XIII, the Queen of Aragon denounced the right of mistreatment as a common abusive practice, along with the bad customs and redemption.

One case most clearly demonstrates what was at stake in the claim to exercise a *ius maletractandi*. It cannot with certainty be dated to the post-plague era, although it occurred either shortly before or after 1348. It does provide evidence for the use of seigneurial mistreatment in the harsher climate of the fourteenth century in general. As an exemplary piece of litigation it would stimulate subsequent legal comment and controversy. A peasant named Pere Ermengol appealed to the king against the lord of Les Pallargues (Segarra), Gilabert de Rajadell, who had imprisoned him and confiscated his holding. Apparently the lord of Rajadell denied the right of the king to intervene or hear the appeal, giving as the reason for this denial the legislation of the Corts of Cervera and Girona. A manuscript at La Seu d'Urgell contains a *consilium* of the lawyer Jaume de Calbet reluctantly supporting the arguments advanced on Gilabert's behalf. Calbet incorporated an earlier discussion that had referred in general terms to the *ius maletractandi*. Calbet disagreed with the conclusion of that earlier *consilium* that such a manifestly unjust law cannot be considered valid. For Calbet the law was odious but valid.

As noted previously, Catalan lawyers found it difficult to justify a law abrogating customary protections. What in earlier works (such as the ordinary gloss to the *Usatges*) appeared as a theoretical question would become urgent as the right of mistreatment became routinely enforced. Thus the *ius maletractandi* figured prominently in the increasingly acrimonious controversies over whether servitude was licit within the context of Catalan law and tradition. It was denounced by Tomàs Mieres (before 1438) and was at the center of peasant demands and seigneurial refutations before and during the civil war.

Changes in Favor of Tenants

Lords faced with the prospect of desertion might respond by offering more favorable conditions of tenure with regard to rent, or by offering communities exemption from servile obligations. The plague does not appear to have produced the same upheaval in land management as it did elsewhere. In European regions with substantial demesne farming the plague forced a wrenching adjustment to falling agricultural prices and higher wages. As demesne farming had never been important in Catalonia, such radical restructuring was unnecessary. The lords were, however, faced with a crisis in their income and the value of their lands. Despite the changes in the labor and land supply that would seem to compel a decline in rent or an amelioration of conditions, there is no indication that after the Black Death the exercise of lordship waned or that peasants became more independent or oriented to the market. There was no weakening of communal bonds in favor of individual enterprise (as has been posited for England), nor did lordship dissolve because of such peasant individual economic activity (as perhaps took place in Germany). The strategies of lords and peasants (to apply a grandiose term to rather localized adaptations), were less in the direction of major changes in the rural economy than in the nature of adjustments in the relationship between lord and peasant that gave either more liberty or less to the peasant in order to preserve the lord's income, but which did not fundamentally change the physical shape of agricultural holdings or the manner in which land was held.

Even before 1348 certain lords had agreed to reduce the proportionate payments in kind (*agraria*) to a more modest amount, or to a fixed payment. In Llambilles (Gironès) proportionate payments on two properties were commuted to a *census* paid in coin. In Roussillon a one-third obligation was converted to 3 *modios* of wheat annually while a one-fourth payment became half an *emina* of barley.

After 1348 favorable changes of this type became more common and they were more obviously reductions rather than commutations. In the Baix Llobregat, for example, the usual proportion of one-fourth plus an additional one-sixteenth was reduced in the late fourteenth century (although this process had already accelerated in the two decades *before* the Plague). In Osona, La Selva and Maresme lay lords and ecclesiastical institutions often reduced or eliminated the *tasca* (one-eleventh) and the *census*. Serra Vilaró has discerned a similar tendency in the Alt Berguedà. On the eve of the Black Death customary rents were one-half of the harvest plus an additional *tasca*. The *tasca* was eliminated from many contracts immediately after 1348, and by 1380 harvest portions had in many cases been reduced to one-third or one-quarter. In order to assure the occupation of otherwise vacant manses the lords of Pinós and Mataplana were forced to accede to certain reductions in obligations and even in the impact of the bad customs. The lord might, for example, trade exemption from the bad customs for the tenant's promise to remain on the land.

Lords may be said to have employed both coercion and favorable terms to maintain the profitable exploitation of their property. They combined tightening their hold on tenants with a measure of concessions with regard to specific obligations. The inconsistency of approach and the peasants' own estimation of the post-plague situation created resentment as the perceived rights and powers of the peasants against the lords came into increasing prominence. The combination of seigneurial reaction and peasant expectations led to the same sort of conditions of social conflict in the Catalan countryside as existed elsewhere in late

fourteenth-century Europe. What differed was the greater length of the
Catalan conflict. From 1380 until 1450 there was no open, generalized
revolt to compare with the English Peasants' Revolt of 1381, nor was
there the achievement of an equilibrium or even of seigneurial hegemony
so that grievances might have disappeared from public view. There was,
rather, a long-standing war of attrition. By 1450 it would have seemed
that a seigneurial reaction had substantially attained its goals in combat-
ting the ability of servile tenants to profit from the change in population
and labor supply. Lords had raised redemption rates, and increased the
scope of expropriation outside of fixed rents, particularly in the application of *mals usos* and the right of arbitrary mistreatment. To be sure
there were parallel movements in the direction of loosening the bonds
of servitude in order to provide a positive inducement to productive cultivation, but by and large the proverbial stick was found more useful
than the proverbial carrot.

Catalonia is the prime example of seigneurial victory, in the short-
and mid-term, over economic forces after the Black Death (although
obviously in the longer run it is the unique example of the defeat of
seigneurial demands by rebellion). In the thesis advanced by Robert
Brenner, Catalonia is singled out for the ability of its lords, at least for a
time, to resist the "market" and demographic forces that logically
should have favored peasant freedom. While in England attempts at
wage control, limits on peasant mobility, and increase in rents had
failed by 1400, in Catalonia (as in parts of Eastern Europe), the plague
was followed by a sharpening of seigneurial control that was effective.
In parts of Eastern Europe this change would be encouraged by the
weakening of state authority and would deepen in the modern centuries. In Catalonia royal power would be challenged but not eclipsed by
the nobility. Everywhere in Europe lords logically tried to respond by a
combination of strategies, tightening control whenever possible while
offering better terms to tenants when that appeared profitable or necessary. The fact that the same demographic cataclysm produced in different regions different effects in the relations between lords and peasants
is used by Brenner to demonstrate the weakness of the Malthusian
model. The variety of effects appears to show the ability of force and the
system of rent to overcome the impersonal pressures of demographic and
consequent economic shifts. In fact, as Brenner argues in an article devoted more particularly to Eastern Europe, the success of extraeconomic
forces of repression was so generalized in early modern Europe that it

is England and the Netherlands that constitute the exception, not the supposedly "backward" lands of the East.

Brenner has been accused of oversimplifying the distinction between his concentration on the seigneurial regime and the emphasis of the "neo-Malthusians" on subsistence and population. The weakest part of Brenner's argument, however, is his desire to place seigneurial reaction in the context of the supposed transition from feudalism to capitalism. This is especially dubious as regards Catalonia. As Jaume Torras has shown, there was no concentration of tenements into large estates in Catalonia after 1486, nor was Catalan agriculture particularly market-oriented, expansive, or capitalistic in the early modern era; certainly not when compared with England. Where Brenner's theories do seem significant is in reemphasizing the ability of lords to exploit advantages of power that already existed prior to the Black Death. Lords could enforce exploitation of the peasantry in defiance of pressures for liberalization attendant upon the decline of population. In reminding observers of the Middle Ages of the central importance of force, Brenner offers a way of understanding Catalonia in the context of late medieval Europe. It is an extreme case, because of the degree of force required for lords to impose a quite oppressive regime, and extreme also by reason of the ultimately sanguinary outcome of this effort. But it is only one of several examples of such efforts throughout Europe, whose degree of success varied in extent and duration.

Underscoring the inherent role of power in the medieval system of land tenure, Brenner also allows one to situate the consequences of 1348 in a larger chronological setting. There was not a sudden, spasmodic seigneurial reaction that overturned an earlier benign condition. Rather there was already before 1348 a theoretical and practical structure in place that articulated servitude by means of symbolic and economically significant pressures. The "bad customs" and the right of mistreatment expressed a licit but ultimately violent authority. These rights could be mobilized to substantial effect after 1348, but they had already been established in a process taking place gradually over centuries *before* 1348. The crucial period in the construction of seigneurial authority in Catalonia was not the era of economic crisis or of civil war but rather before 1348, in an aggressively prosperous and expansionist epoch.

This is not to deny the link between the civil wars of 1462–1486 and late medieval economic and social forces, or that the demands of peasants were not strengthened by reason of the decline of population, the support of the kings, and other factors that started with the Black Death. But in seeking the origins of the agrarian system that was overthrown in the late fifteenth century, the post-plague era should be viewed as accentuating and making more critically important the ability of lords to supplement annual agricultural income by the application of additional rights. These rights were widely acknowledged to be abusive ("bad") customs, but they were of unquestionably long pedigree by 1348. We shall consider in the following chapter the process by which the seigneurial success of the post-plague era was challenged and the immediate origins of the *Remença Wars*. . .

[handwritten annotations: No peasant Revolt, but why? Stable Catalonian Economy due to peasant control.]

John Hatcher

England in the Aftermath of the Black Death

As noted earlier, John Hatcher's article argues against recent scholarship suggesting that peasants did not see improving circumstances after the Black Death. Instead, Hatcher finds that the plague was a decisive turning point in the lives of English peasants. In the selection here, he builds his case first on chronicles and literary sources. While Hatcher acknowledges that both are complicated by prejudices, he nonetheless urges their usefulness in providing insight into the living conditions of peasants. These sources portray peasants with ample leisure time who were beginning to assert the pretensions of their social superiors. Hatcher also finds support for his argument in estate accounts. While wage payments point to only a modest increase in wages (and one that was probably offset by rising prices), Hatcher finds that other payments in cash and kind are also recorded in these records. When these compensations are taken into account, the improving circumstances of the peasantry become clearer.

The place of the Black Death among the most dramatic episodes in history has long been secure. The demise at a single stroke in the mid-fourteenth century of at least a third of the population of the known world

Source: John Hatcher, "England in the Aftermath of the Black Death," *Past and Present*, 144 (August 1994): 3, 9, 11–14, 16–20.

has understandably exercised a perennial fascination for both the popular and the scholarly imagination. Yet the influence historians have attributed to this catastrophe in the shaping of the course of subsequent social and economic development has long since fallen far short of what might have been expected from the scale of the deaths it caused. . . .

. . . The thrust of this article therefore is to question whether the gains of labourers and smallholders before the price falls set in from the late 1370s were in fact as limited as it has long been conventional to believe. Central to this examination will be an investigation of the ability of the data on prices and wages, which have been collected from manorial records, to reflect accurately the movements which took place in real wages and disposable incomes in the three decades after 1350. It will be noted below that when one turns to encompass a broader range of evidence of how employers and employees behaved, and of the rewards which were given and received, it becomes immediately apparent that conventional historical wisdom runs counter not only to a priori reasoning, but to the opinions and beliefs of people who lived through the aftermath of the Black Death.

. . . In direct contradiction to the statistical findings of historians, the chroniclers of the post-plague years wrote repeatedly and bitterly of the high cost of workmen, their arrogance, their over-indulgence in leisure and, of course, their contempt for the labour laws. According to Knighton, after the Ordinance was published the workmen were "so arrogant and obstinate that they did not heed the king's mandate, but if anyone wanted to have them he had to give them what they asked" or lose his crops, while from the time that the statute was passed "they served their masters worse from day to day than they had done previously." John of Reading claimed that the debasement of the coinage in 1351 led to still higher wages, so that labourers worked less and worse. Complaints and parliamentary petitions from employers concerning the impotence of the sanctions which they had at their disposal, including most notably the Statute of Labourers, abound throughout the period under scrutiny, and they provide compelling evidence of a belief in the persistence of the scarcity and high cost of labour. The concerns of commentators and employers, heightened by fears for the very survival of the traditional social hierarchy, are brought into stark relief in the burgeoning literature of the later fourteenth century. The "estates" and "complaint" literature of the period is a well-respected source for the fears and prejudices of élite society, but the numerous portraits it contains of those whose allotted role was to toil in order to provide their superiors with sustenance have been accorded scant weight by historians. Whereas a previous generation of scholars was inclined to neglect observations on the conduct and lifestyles of the lower orders as relatively unimportant for their studies, the present generation has largely chosen to look elsewhere for its evidence, consciously shunning sources which are judged to be vitiated by bias. G. R. Owst in 1933 felt justified, when writing a volume of almost six hundred pages devoted to sermons, in proclaiming that "A page or two will enable us to dismiss the one remaining class of society"; in 1991 D. L. Farmer, who has assiduously addressed the fortunes of the peasants and labourers, explicitly favoured the evidence of manorial accounts over the testimony of "critics of social change and disorder, like the poet John Gower or the monastic chronicler Henry of Knighton."

At first glance it is undeniably tempting to favour business accounts, which seemingly provide a factual record of the payments which were made to employees, over the polemical assertions of writers who dealt bewilderingly by turns with observation, castigation and the road to salvation. Yet does the comfort bestowed by quantification rest upon secure foundations, and is the testimony of contemporaries so riddled with bias that it is rendered worthless to the historian?

A long-term drift in favour of statistical evidence on the part of historians, and the warnings voiced by influential literary critics of the "relativism" and "positivism" which can result from excessive attention to the historical context of texts, have not been conducive to the utilization of literature for information about the age in which it was composed. Yet later fourteenth-century literary texts can be made to yield a wealth of insights for the historian of society. Although much medieval literature has often been correctly diagnosed as presenting a gallery of traditional stereotypes rather than a mirror of contemporary society, the works of a number of later fourteenth-century writers resonate with the social, religious and political realities of this tumultuous age. Although leading writers with scant exception clung to a traditional hierarchical ideology, many were aware that their audiences were widening and deepening, and that in these perilous times it was appropriate for their writings to assume a more direct social function, with description, instruction and exhortation taking precedence over entertainment. Prominent among the images and messages urgently conveyed is the stark contrast evident in the world about them between the lamentable failings of present society and the eternal ideal of a harmonious and prosperous community in which the members of each of the three estates selflessly fulfilled their divinely ordained roles. In keeping with the tone and content of many contemporary sermons, each of the three estates is subjected to fierce criticism for falling far short of the immemorial standards required of it, but nowhere is the immediacy of the reporting more evident than when the failings of servants, labourers and peasants are addressed. Read sensitively, much later fourteenth-century literature can be seen to convey, not merely age-old expressions of the inherent viciousness of oppressed masses seeking to break free from the bonds of perpetual toil, but reports of actual achievements secured in an age of bewildering shifts of fortune and authority.

In fact, the poetry of the period, and especially the wide social worlds created by Gower and Langland, describe patterns of behaviour which have a good measure of economic coherence, and which closely resemble those which we would be disposed to recreate for ourselves if no other evidence existed. Furthermore, in their treatment of the lower orders many literary sources accord closely with the import of governmental, judicial and seigneurial records. The élites whose views are represented in surviving records tell us that those whose allotted role was to toil in order to provide them with sustenance have become selfish and greedy; they are demanding extremely high wages and extravagant fringe benefits, including fine clothes and the best food and drink. They are lazy; they refuse to work unless they are hungry, and when they do accept employment they labour far less assiduously than in past times. Most workmen prefer to be hired by the day, refusing to serve by the year, or indeed by any term of reasonable length. They break their contracts and wander from place to place and from employer to employer. They engage in unbecoming leisure pursuits, including excessive drinking, poaching and hunting, and their enhanced incomes enable them to buy clothes and other commodities which are unbefitting their lowly status.

. . . John Gower, a contemporary of Langland, fills a substantial part of his copious verses with nostalgia for a bygone age when, in stark contrast to the aftermath of the Black Death, not only did the higher estates obey God's prescription, but the third estate also knew its place. In the *Mirour de l'omme*, written before 1378, Gower rebukes the labourers of the present day for their laziness and for receiving wages three times more than their work deserved, and he laments:

> *So goes the world from bad to worse when they who guard the sheep or the herdsmen in their places, demand to be rewarded more for their labour than the master-bailiff used to be. And on the other hand it may*

be seen that whatever the work may be the labourer is so expensive that whoever wants anything done must pay five or six shillings for what formerly cost two.

This sad state of affairs Gower contrasts nostalgically with the good old days, and relates how:

The labourers of olden times were not accustomed to eat wheat bread; their bread was made of beans and of other corn, and their drink was water. Then cheese and milk were as a feast to them; rarely had they any other feast than this. Their clothing was plain grey. Then was the world of such folk well-ordered in its estate.

In the Vox *clamantis* (*c.* 1378) Gower complains that "our happy times of old have been rudely wiped out, for a bitter day afflicts the present," and he seeks to explore where the responsibility lay for the "strange and highly burdensome evils [which] attend us almost daily." Each stratum of society is examined by him in turn, and few within them are absolved from guilt; the prime failing being the pursuit of personal gratification to the neglect of the common good. The vices of peasants, labourers, and servants warrant a lengthy diatribe. Gower, who was a member of the gentry and had held manors in Kent, writes with much firsthand experience of workmen and even at times uses the first person. He finds that sloth rules among those whose duty it was to "enter into the labours of agriculture, which are necessary for obtaining food and drink for the sustenance of the human race," and grieves that "Now, however, scarcely a rustic wishes to do such work; instead he wickedly loafs everywhere":

they are sluggish, they are scarce, and they are grasping. For the very little they do they demand the highest pay . . . one peasant insists upon more than two demanded in days gone by. Yet a short time ago one performed more service than three do now, as those maintain who are well-acquainted with the facts . . . They desire the leisures of great men, but they have nothing to feed themselves with, nor will they be servants . . . everyone owning land complains in his turn about these people; each stands in need of them and none has control over them. The peasants of old did not scorn God with impunity or usurp a noble worldly rank.

Gower then writes of:

yet another group, associated with the peasants, which is widespread and has no discipline. They are those who are unwilling to serve anyone by the year. A man will retain them for scarcely a single month. On the contrary, I hire such men for even a day's pay—now here, now somewhere else, now for myself, now for you . . . Because such a man is hired as a member of your household, he scorns all ordinary food . . . he grumbles . . . and he will not return tomorrow unless you provide something better.

Nor did the effrontery of the labourer stop at demanding leisure and "things for his belly like a lord." According to Gower, "Servants are now masters and masters are servants . . . the peasant pretends to imitate the ways of the freeman, and gives himself the appearance of him in his clothes." What is more, such lowly people now had an appetite for luxuries, including beds and pillows, and the "rich man in the city could hardly procure his modest and proper foods."

The wealth of corroborative material contained in an extensive range of records dating from the 1350s to the 1380s amply supports John Gower's claim that the faults he found within society were not merely a personal opinion but a reflection of the views of all prudent people, which he reports "just like a well-informed messenger." The works of Gower and Langland have been quoted at length because they contain the fullest and most coherent analysis, but they are broadly representative of observations contained in the literature, chronicles and sermons of their age. Moreover, legislation was enacted to curb not only the excessive rewards enjoyed by common people, but the manner in which they spent their ill-gotten gains. A statute in 1363 was directed towards the correction of "the outrageous and excessive apparel of divers people against their estate and degree," and prescribed detailed regulations for the dress of grooms, agricultural workers and those lowly persons who did not have goods to the value of 40s., thereby confirming the exasperation felt by Henry Knighton with "the elation of the inferior people in dress and accoutrements in these days, so that one person cannot be discerned from another, in splendour of dress or belongings." And in 1390, in response to a parliamentary petition complaining that "low persons . . . at times when good Christians on holy days are at church, hearing divine services, go hunting in parks, rabbit-runs and warrens of lords and others," a statute was passed prohibiting "any kind of artificer or labourer" from taking or destroying "beasts of the forest, hares or rabbits, or other sport of gentlefolk."

It is no coincidence, still less a contradiction, that a literary cult of *sancta rusticitas* in which honest and true workmen were idealized, especially in the form of the ploughman, should thrive at a time when contemporary rustics were thought to be so manifestly delinquent. Wyclif's admonition to the labourer to "lyve in mekenesse, and trewly and wylfully do thi labour" was uttered when the battle was in real danger of being lost. Exhortation to spend a life of toil in order to secure eternal bliss in the next world went hand in hand with coercion and the threat of punishment in this. In Chaucer's pilgrim band there are three idealized portraits—the knight, the parson and the ploughman—one from each of the three estates. They differ starkly from the vibrant three-dimensional characters who form the rest of the throng, because unlike the others they were not intended to be representative of the social realities of the later fourteenth century. The qualities ascribed to the knight, parson and ploughman instead are a flat recitation of the traditional virtues appropriate to each of their estates in a divinely ordered society, and as such they were in direct contrast to the selfishness which Chaucer's audience might be expected to perceive all around them. Accordingly, the ploughman:

> *a trewe swynkere and a good was he,*
> *Lyuynge in pees and parfit charitee,*

who loved God, helped his neighbours, paid his tithes, and dressed in a simple tabard.

Sharply declining population was bound to increase the ratio of land to people, but it is likely that the scarcity of labour was further aggravated by the pronounced buoyancy of the post-plague economy. Predictably, employers as a class responded by attempting to negate and circumvent market forces, but although as a body they supported the enactment of labour legislation they lacked the solidarity necessary to ensure its successful enforcement. In default each employer's own best interests were served by securing enough labour to perform the work which he needed to be done, and this involved competing with other employers by offering higher wages and more allowances. As a Commons petition of 1376 complained, servants and labourers "as soon as their masters accuse them of bad service, or wish to pay them for their labour according to the form of the statutes . . . take flight and suddenly leave their employment and district." It also grumbled that:

> *above all and a greater mischief is the receiving of such vagrant labourers*
> *and servants when they have fled from their masters' service; for they are*
> *taken into service immediately in new places, at such dear wages that ex-*
> *ample and encouragement is afforded to all servants to depart into fresh*

> *places, and go from master to master as soon as they are displeased about any matter.*

Most significantly, the petitioners continued, "For fear of such flights, the commons now dare not challenge or offend their servants, but give them whatever they wish to ask, in spite of the statutes and ordinances to the contrary." These precise sentiments must have been shared by the employer who brought an action before the justices when two of his servants, to whom he was giving respectively 2d. per day with food and 7s a year and a quarter of corn every ten weeks, were enticed away from his service by another who offered them each 12d. per day. In the words of Bertha Putnam, "The statutes of labourers must be regarded not as having created a new system or a new set of economic relations, but as affording proof that radical changes had occurred, ushering in a new era." The high prices which farmers could obtain from selling their produce enabled even a sharply rising wage bill to be comfortably absorbed, especially by those employers who were able to call upon labour services from their tenants to satisfy part of the needs of the demesne.

In direct contrast, however, the accounts kept by the great landlords of the income and expenditure of these estates reveal, at first sight at least, scant trace of the inflation of wages and the cascade of blandishments which contemporaries witnessed all about them. Instead the accounts of estates beyond the ambit of London generally record relatively modest increases in basic rates of pay. The composite indices compiled by Farmer, for example, have payments for a range of agricultural tasks increasing by 12–28 per cent comparing the 1340s with the 1350s, and 20–40 per cent comparing the 1340s with the 1360s. Further investigation, however, soon reveals that the wage payments incorporated in these indices are far from comprising the total remuneration which workers received. The construction of adequately representative time series demands data which are not only voluminous and continuous, but amenable to precise quantification. As a consequence those compiling such series have had to ignore a whole range of additional payments in cash as well as in kind which are referred to in the accounts.

Christopher Dyer

The Social and Economic Background to the Rural Revolt of 1381

Direct to argument: Hatcher.

Using the records of over one hundred manors, Christopher Dyer investigates the social and economic roots of the English Peasants' Revolt of 1381. He finds the roots of the uprising in the volatile mix of rising expectations and landlord reactions. The passage excerpted here focuses particularly on the rebels themselves. Dyer strives to identify who participated in and led the revolt. Notably, he finds that individuals who held an administrative position on the manor (acting, for example, as constables) played a critical role in the rebellion.

Was the revolt of 1381 merely a "passing episode" in English history, an irrational aberration, or was it deeply rooted in the economic and social life of the later middle ages? The frustration of historians who despair of finding a social explanation of the rising is understandable, as causes suggested in the past have been shown to be inadequate. There is little evidence to support the theory that labour services increased in the late fourteenth century, and we can no longer accept the view that the revolt was caused by the dissolution of the traditional feudal order by the advance of a money economy. There is now general agreement that the conditions of peasants as well as wage-earners tended to improve after the plague of 1348–9, so that any economic explanation of the revolt must be expressed in terms of rising expectations. Did the actions of landlords frustrate these expectations? Was there a seigneurial reaction in the post-plague decades? In order to consider these problems it is necessary to define more closely the groups who made up the rebel ranks, and to examine their motives and aims. These questions are too numerous to

Source: Christopher Dyer, "The Social and Economic Background to the Rural Revolt of 1381," in *The English Rising of 1381*, eds. R. H. Hilton and T. H. Ashton (New York: Cambridge University Press, 1984), 9–10, 14–19, 41–42.

receive a full answer in a single essay. In concentrating on them here, the political and religious aspects of the revolt, which deserve to be properly considered in any full assessment of the complex events of 1381, will be unavoidably neglected.

Much of the literature on the 1381 rising was published before 1907, when most of the chronicle sources were already in print, and many of the relevant classes of public records were available for research. The main sources for investigating the social and economic background, the manorial records, lay scattered in the muniment rooms of country houses and the offices of local solicitors. This study is based on the mass of this local material which is now more readily available. Such is its bulk that it has been necessary to concentrate on the four counties of Essex, Hertfordshire, Kent and Suffolk. The method of research has been to compile an index of non-urban places affected by the revolt, and then to look for manorial records of those places, or at least for manors in their vicinity. The manorial records were used to compile biographical studies of individual rebels (supplemented by some information from the archives of central government), and to examine the changes in rural society in the forty years before the revolt. The records of more than a hundred manors have been consulted, though many more sources for the four counties are known to exist. . . .

With the exception of the handful of gentry and clergy who participated in the revolt in our four counties, notably in Suffolk, the social status and economic position of the rebels is not easily defined. We know something about their material possessions from the escheators' valuations of the goods and lands of indicted individuals, and the records of the royal courts sometimes give the rebels' occupations. This evidence shows that 100 of 180 rebels from the whole area of rebellion owned goods valued at £1 to £5, and 15 of them were worth more than £5, including the very affluent Thomas Sampson of Suffolk and John Coveshurste from Kent. The poorer rebels, and those with non-agricultural occupations, were especially numerous in Kent. This is sufficient to show that we are dealing primarily with people well below the ranks of the gentry, but who mainly held some land and goods, not the "marginals" recently claimed as playing an important part in the revolt; in other words most of the rebels were peasants and artisans.

By combing manorial and government records for the names of known rebels, it is possible to find out more about their backgrounds. This has been done for eighty-nine rebels, forty-eight from Essex, eighteen from

Hertfordshire, thirteen from Suffolk and ten from Kent. Of them, forty-six are recorded as rebels in central government records, mainly indictments, and forty-three can be identified as rebels from the manorial documents. The Kentish rebels will be discussed separately because of the nature of that county's documents.

Of the remaining seventy-nine, we have information about the landholding of almost fifty of them. Thirty-eight are recorded as holding land by customary tenure; six held both free and customary land, and five are recorded only as free tenants. So the majority of our sample of rebels held land by disadvantageous tenures, often described as villein land, in a region where free tenants were very numerous. At least a tenth of our rebels (eight) were "serfs by blood" (*nativi de sanguine*).

The economic standing of our rebels is best indicated by the size of their holdings, of which we are given some indication in thirty-six cases. Of these, fifteen had holdings of 14 acres or more, of whom only two held more than 32 acres; nine held between 7 and 12 acres; and twelve were smallholders with 5 acres or less. In some cases the information is incomplete, so the figures represent minimum landholdings. Nor should the other rebels be assumed to have been landless—the great majority can be shown from references to rent payment or their attendance at manorial courts to have been tenants. An indication of the scale of the rebels' agricultural activities and of their wealth is provided by references to their animals. We find individuals owning flocks of as many as twenty-five, twenty-eight or eighty sheep; John Hermar of Havering-atte-Bower (Essex) had four oxen and a horse, while William Smyth of Ingatestone and Fryerning (Essex) owned six *avers* (draught animals), five calves and some pigs. Robert Wryghte from Foxearth (Essex), whose holding of land is not recorded, can be assumed to have had a strong interest in agriculture from references to his possession of three horses, two cows and six pigs. Rebels with smallholdings, and some sizeable amounts of land, would have had alternative sources of income from wage work or from the pursuit of crafts or trades. John Phelipp of Thorrington (Essex) was employed in fencing a park for 36½ days soon after the revolt. At least three of the rebels from his village cut wood for sale. Elsewhere individual rebels are known to have sold fish, and three are recorded as traders, as a fellmonger, draper and chandler. There were two carpenters, a miller, a cook and a barber. A subgroup among the rebels were brewers or close associates of brewers, for example one of the few women to be named as a rebel, Margaret Wright of Lakenheath (Suffolk), who helped to kill John Cavendish, the chief justice, appears in the court records before the revolt as breaking the assize of ale. The wife of Robert Wryghte of Foxearth brewed a good deal, and the father of William Metefeld junior was the chief seller of bread and ale at Brandon (Suffolk). Perhaps ale houses were especially suitable breeding grounds for disaffection, so that their keepers were drawn easily into rebellion, or perhaps brewers, like others involved in crafts and trades, were likely to be independent, articulate and aware. At the higher end of the scale of status and wealth was a franklin (Richard Baud of Moulsham, Essex), and two others who, judging from their wealth in animals and goods, clearly belonged to the top ranks of village society, perhaps on the fringe of the gentry.

In general the same seems to represent a wide spectrum of rural society, with a slight bias towards the better off. This could reflect the nature of the government sources, which tend to give the names of leaders rather than the rank and file, and the manorial records, which will tell us more about tenants than servants. The gentry will not appear in the sample because manorial documents will refer to them rarely, but rebels from this group were few in any case. There is nothing here to contradict the traditional identification of the rising as the "Peasants' Revolt."

The most striking common characteristic of our sample of rebels is their prominence in the government of their manor, village or hundred, either at the time of the revolt or within a few years of 1381. No less than fifty-three of them, out of seventy where we might expect to find evidence, are known to have served as reeves, chief pledges, affeerers, ale-tasters, bailiffs, jurors, constables or in other positions of responsibility. These offices were numerous, so that even a small village had to find more than a dozen officials at any one time, and we cannot regard the occupants of these positions as a narrow oligarchy. None the less every village had an élite, and it was evidently from this group that the leadership in the revolt was drawn. Office-holders in normal times and leaders in revolt both tended to have some maturity of years, and we can show that many of the 1381 rebels were middle-aged. Some estimate can be made of the age of twenty-two of our sample, and seventeen of them judging from their appearance in the court records in the years 1359–68, or from references to their mature children in the years around 1381, are likely to have been at least approaching forty at the time of the revolt. Most of the rebels came from families well established in their villages, and only two can be identified as recent immigrants, of which one was a special case. This was John Geffrey, a serf who had moved (or rather perhaps had been moved) from a Suffolk manor of the earls of Pembroke, Badmondisfield, 35 miles across the estate to their Essex manor of East Hanningfield to act as bailiff, presumably because of his administrative skills and trustworthy character.

It is typical of previous conceptions about the participants in the revolt that the editor of the *Essex Sessions of the Peace* has speculated that some of the criminals who were indicted before the J.P.s in 1377–9 would have joined the rising. In fact, none of those accused of felonies appear in the list of rebels; on the contrary, one of those helping to identify the criminals, a juror of Barstable Hundred in 1378, William Gildeborn of Fobbing, was hanged for his part in the revolt. Similarly, we might expect to find some of the many labourers hauled up before the justices for offences against the labour laws among the rebels. There is one, James atte Ford of Takelely, who took excessive wages in 1378, but he was exceptional, as he bought a large holding of 18¾ acres in 1380, and so had transformed his social position by the time of the rising. The other Essex rebel known to have fallen foul of the labour laws was an employer, William Bette of Elmdon, who lured two ploughmen with high wages—he may have been acting as a bailiff at the time. Two Suffolk rebels are known to have employed servants in their own right in the decade before the revolt.

The very different character of the Kentish manorial records makes similar analysis of our ten rebels from that county much more difficult. We can say no more than that three held office in seigneurial courts as borsholder (the Kentish equivalent of chief pledge), affeerer and juror; two of them were active in the landmarket, though the size of their holdings is not known; and three appear in the records in the 1360s, so in 1381 they were near to middle age. This suggests similarities with the rebels north of the Thames, but it must be said that rebels are more difficult to find in the manorial records in Kent. This could result from the peculiarities of Kentish customs and documentation, or may reflect the higher proportion of landless and poor among the rebels, already noted on the basis of the escheators' valuations.

In our concern to identify and learn more about the background of the named rebels, we are in danger of ignoring the participation of humbler and poorer men. For example, manorial *famuli*, full-time servants on the demesne, joined the rebel bands, like the servants of Coggeshall Abbey at Childerditch (Essex), who departed, supposedly against their will, on the encouragement of John Noreford, and at least five of the *famuli* at Wye (Kent) were "ensnared by Rakestrawesmayne" according to the manorial official who had to justify extra expenditure on replacement labour for the hay-making.

Although not all of the rebels were men of substance, occupying positions in seigneurial administration and as upholders of the law in their local communities, the presence of so many people of this kind must affect our assessment of the revolt. Experienced and well informed, they knew about the workings of law and government, and must have been aware of the risks of rebellion. In the event at least five of our sample were hanged, and another eight spent some time away from their homes as fugitives. Their revolt was not a temporary aberration, as some of them persisted in acts in defiance of authority long after the revolt, even to the point of personal ruin, like John Wylkyn of Fryerning (Essex), who lost his holding in 1382 for refusing to pay rent and carry out repairs after June 1381. It is difficult to believe that these leading rebels were acting on mere impulse, or that they were affected by collective delusions. We must conclude that they had substantial grievances, and that their experiences of the real world drove them to embark on the revolt. . . .

Rural unrest in the late fourteenth century can be readily explained in terms of the tension between entrenched lordly power and the changes, or potential changes, in peasant society. These tensions were felt acutely in the south-east because of the importance of the market economy in the region. Dissatisfaction with the government, especially with the administration of the law, was bound up with resentment against landlords. The outbreak of a major revolt came when the poll-tax provided the whole region with a single-common grievance. The specific form taken by the revolt, in terms of its organization and demands, reflected its origins in rural society. The village élite, acting from a position of confidence and authority, gave the revolt leadership and coherence. Out of the diversity of motives found in any popular movement emerged ideas and actions hostile not just to serfdom and servile tenures, but also to the very existence of lordship, championing the realizable goal of independent and self-governing village communities.

Mavis Mate

Daughters, Wives, and Widows After the Black Death

The conclusion to Mavis Mate's book sums up the effects the Black Death had on women. Overall, they experienced some improved opportunities like better wages and a greater likelihood of inheriting property. These changes, however, were quickly subsumed into the prevailing patriarchal structures. Thus, for example, even if a woman enjoyed greater economic power in the postplague era, this did not translate into the public recognition bestowed on her male counterparts. Mate also urges a close attentiveness to questions of class. The impact of the plague varied according to a woman's social status.

Women did make some gains as a result of the demographic crisis. They were likely to earn more money than in the pre-plague economy, but the kind of work available to them basically did not change. In the country-side they helped to bring in the harvest: they weeded, harrowed and winnowed and in pastoral districts they milked the cows and sheared sheep. In the towns they worked as servants in private houses, in inns, taverns, and shops, and in some industrial establishments like breweries and dye-houses. Women, in both urban and rural areas, also carded and spun on a piece-work basis, worked as independent traders, as brewsters, petty retailers, shepsters or dressmakers, and laundresses. At the same time, with the widespread availability of land, women, for the most part, retained their right to inherit real estate in the absence of male heirs. Thus daughters took over land when there were no sons, and sisters inherited if their brothers died without children. Urban tenements, which could be freely devised, were occasionally shared equally among sons and daughters and a few young women were granted a portion of the family estate at the time of their marriage. Yet these opportunities occurred

Source: Mavis E. Mate, *Daughters, Wives, and Widows After the Black Death* (Suffolk, UK: Boydell Press, 1998), 193–199.

within a society that remained strictly patriarchal and thus women benefited from them less than they might otherwise have done.

The economic changes that swept through late medieval society did
not alter its ideological structure. A hierarchal society in which children
were subordinate to parents, wives to husbands, servants to masters and
subjects to their king was seen as divinely ordained. Women, whatever
their rank, were left with the primary responsibility for child-care and domestic tasks and these tasks were accorded less value than the work carried out by men. In addition, male writers in literature and in moral and
medical treatises depicted women as less rational and morally and physically weaker than themselves. Daughters in the sixteenth century, as in
the fourteenth century, were taught to accept the authority of their fathers
and after marriage their husbands. The goal of female education was to
prepare women for their future roles of wife and mother. Young girls not
only learned domestic skills, but the importance of virtue—the need to
be chaste, faithful, obedient and above all silent. Although not all women
accepted these ideals, as the constant complaints of the moralists clearly
show, they remained in force throughout Europe, and may have been
intensified in some Protestant countries after the Reformation.

Historians like Hilton and Barron, who believe that the late Middle
Ages was to some extent a "golden age" for women, stress the independence enjoyed by married women and widows who worked as labourers
and traders. Barron, for example, believes that married women in London "were frequently working partners in marriages between economic
equals." There are some Sussex couples who might fit that description—the carpenter William Cole and his brewster wife Joan at Alfriston,
and within the town of Battle the butcher Richard Lole whose wife
Margery not only brewed but also borrowed and probably lent money. Yet
the economic contributions of these women did not lead to any public
recognition. Legally their husbands remained heads of household. Unlike in London, Battle women did not generally trade as *femme sole*. Thus
Richard Lole appeared in court to answer for his wife's debts and both he
and William Cole were generally presented for brewing even in years
when their wives were primarily responsible. Moreover, by the mid fifteenth century, when brewing had become professionalized, the number of women working as independent brewsters and thus capable of
producing an income in any way comparable to that of their husbands
was quite small. The majority of independent traders were hucksters,
who worked long hours to make small profits. Few of them could afford

servants, so this work had to be carried out in addition to their regular domestic tasks. Men who had other work were unlikely to take responsibility for laundry and child-care. Thus married women could well find that any economic independence was acquired at the expense of physical exhaustion.

However many Sussex women joined the labour force, they rarely achieved economic parity with men. Only for a few tasks such as weeding were women paid the same rate as men. By the fifteenth century, and perhaps earlier, female harvest workers were receiving lower wages than men and female dairymaids earned less than male shepherds. Management positions such as taking charge of a demesne dairy or supervising a harvest were always taken by men. No Sussex woman, not even a widow, is known to have controlled a lucrative business such as a tannery and there is no evidence that Sussex women were ever hired for such high-paid, high skilled jobs as carpenter, tiler or mason. Within the towns women primarily filled low-paid, low-status occupations in the victualling and textile industries. As the fifteenth century progressed and beer replaced ale as the favourite drink of the masses, the opportunity for women to work as independent brewsters diminished. A single women, without real estate, could survive on her own, either as a servant, or by combining spinning and carding with agricultural work, or occupations such as huckster, laundress and seamstress, but her standard of living was likely to be low and when the cloth trade was in recession, as in the mid fifteenth century, she could face poverty and destitution. For a married couple, a wife's earning undoubtedly provided a welcome, even essential, addition to the family's income, but did not necessarily give her any commensurate clout within the household. Her husband remained legally in control of the family's assets and if he wasted what she had earned, she had no recourse.

Likewise the money and goods that a woman brought to her marriage as her "portion" came under the control of her husband. He could sell or otherwise dispose of them as he wished without any consultation. A married woman could not make a will without her husband's consent since under common law she did not own goods of her own. Furthermore, apart from in a few towns such as London, a widow did not have any claim on the joint goods of the family. All that a husband was required to leave his widow in his will was her paraphernalia (the clothes on her back and the ornaments of her body). In practice, however, most Sussex widows received back all the goods that they brought to the marriage, plus a share of the family's goods. Thus the actual situation of some women was not nearly as bleak as their legal one. Yet this does not alter the fact that an extravagant and ungenerous husband could not only waste all her marriage portion, but also leave her very little of the family property, and she would have no legal remedy. The disabilities of being a *femme couverte* did not change in the post-plague economy. When a widow who had received a generous settlement from her first marriage remarried, these goods, like those of her original portion, came under the authority of her new husband. As Jane Lewkenore discovered, she could lose all that she had gained.

So too female inheritance of land did not generally lead to independence. Once a woman was married her husband took over the management and legal responsibility for her inheritance, although he could not sell it or alienate it without her consent. It was rare for an heiress to remain unmarried throughout her life and thus in full control of her estate. On the contrary wealthy heiresses were likely to marry at a younger age than their peers and to have less freedom of choice over their partners. They might even face abduction as in the case of the Wakeherst heiresses. Only as a widow did an heiress regain control over her inheritance. A widowed heiress with a large customary holding or in full control of several manors would have had sufficient resources to live independently and would not be faced with a seriously reduced standard of living. She had no economic need to remarry. Yet, in many cases, if she was young, she did remarry, and sometimes more than once. Only the more independent minded women, with a strong sense of their own identity, were able to ignore the prevailing ideology. Women had been taught that marriage was a natural state for women. It offered companionship, protection, status, and the opportunity for further children. For the majority of Sussex heiresses these advantages outweighed any loss of autonomy.

Non-heiress widows might receive land as their free-bench or as a result of a joint-tenure or deathbed transfer. They too were in a position to live independently, but did not always choose to do so. In pastoral districts—along the coast and in the Weald—some widows successfully reared cattle, horses, and pigs for the market and played an active role in the local courts, suing others for debt and trespass and answering for their own misdeeds. Other elderly widows kept their land, but eschewed a public role. They did not participate in the land market, contract debts, or trespass with their animals, and they regularly paid a fine to excuse themselves from attendance at the manorial court. Not all women,

however, were willing to remain on their own. In the early and mid fifteenth century a few widows voluntarily gave up their land to the heir or
others in return for maintenance. The difficulties of farming during the
mid century depression may have discouraged these women from continuing to live alone. Likewise remarriage was fairly common, with perhaps as many as two-thirds of the women who were widowed young
choosing to marry again. In addition to the other advantages of marriage
mentioned above a widow with a smallholding could hope for a higher
standard of living with the help of a second income produced by her husband. Independence was clearly less valued by fifteenth century Sussex
women than some modern historians have thought. Nothing in their
education had suggested that women were as capable as men of manag-
ing their own affairs. A few women, accustomed to taking charge in their
husbands' absences, may have delighted in their new found freedom;
most probably did not. If, because of their age, or an adverse sex-ratio,
they had no opportunity for remarriage, they managed as best as they
could. Unless their husband had been very tyrannical, they were unlikely
to see their widowhood as in any way liberating.

The rapid turnover in land was in the long run to have profound
effects on the lives of widows. On some Sussex manors a widow's claim
to her free-bench applied only to land that her husband had inherited;
any land acquired during his lifetime went directly to the heir. Thus
with the break-up and sale of customary holdings many widows lost
their free-bench rights. A husband could make alternative provision for
his wife, either during his lifetime by granting land to her jointly with
himself, or, on his deathbed, simply transferring land to her. Yet he was
under no obligation to do so. By 1500 when very few widows could still
claim their free-bench, they had become very dependent on the good-
will of their spouse. Some widows, who held land by joint tenure or a
deathbed transfer with no reversions, were able to keep this land if they
remarried and could even sell it or otherwise alienate it if they wished.
They were thus in a stronger legal position than widows who had held
customary land under their traditional right of free bench. But this group
was always a minority of widows. A woman who received no land to support her during her widowhood had to rely on house room and maintenance by the heir or the regular payment of an annuity. As has been
shown, not all heirs were trustworthy.

The greater availability of land was a mixed blessing for women.
Many lords reduced rents or leased out small portions of former demesne

land. Tenant holdings came on the market when the holder died with no surviving heirs or villeins illegally fled from the manor, never to return, leaving their land behind. Finally as family attachment to land weakened, tenants became willing to transfer land to non-kin during their lifetime. Yeomen and husbandmen built up large holdings of over 100 acres and many artisans—carpenters, tailors and the like—were able to acquire ten or more acres. So too many shepherds and ploughmen might not be unmarried, live-in, servants, but married smallholders. This extra land led to an improvement in the families' standard of living. In many cases they could eat more meat and afford larger and sturdier houses. But the land, at the same time, provided more work for women. In the case of the smallholders their other jobs would prevent the male members of the family from devoting very much time to their own land. Much of the day-to-day agricultural maintenance must have been undertaken by their wives and daughters. These women probably spent more hours on unpaid agricultural labour than the wives and daughters of cottagers in the pre-plague economy. This work, especially weeding and reaping with a sickle, was both tedious and back-breaking. When a woman worked for an outside employer in addition to her other responsibilities she may well have felt overburdened.

Likewise the wives and daughters of the yeomen and husbandmen were faced with a series of never-ending tasks, but in many cases enjoyed greater independence than in the pre-plague period. Although they did not work for wages, they had to feed an expanded household with at least some live-in servants. Furthermore with the general labour shortage the family may not have been able to hire all the servants that it really needed, leaving the women of the household to pick up the slack. Men, however, were likely to spend more time away from home than they had done in earlier periods, leaving their wives freer to make their own decisions concerning the management of the family land and its income. Widows, on the other hand, were more likely to be required to give up their holding in return for house room and maintenance when the heir came of age, and thus might be in a more dependent position than their peers several generations earlier.

For aristocratic women, like those in other social classes, the legal and economic changes occurring after 1348 brought benefits and losses. They probably benefited the most from the changes taking place in material culture. In late medieval society they were likely to eat a wider variety of foods, live in warmer surroundings and wear richer, albeit more restricting, clothes than their forbears in the twelfth and early thirteenth century. A greater number of them would be literate. Some widows, who had been granted a large portion of the family estates by their husband's feoffees, or who had secure possession of both dower and jointure, enjoyed a larger income than earlier widows relying on just their dower lands. Yet other widows with no more than a slim jointure that was considerably less than one-third of their husband's estates were obviously in a worse position. So too a widow who had to give up any land and estates that she had received in favour of an annuity when she remarried, or when her son came of age was less well situated than a widow who earlier had taken her dower lands to a second or third marriage. She no longer enjoyed any kind of seigneurial power, and she had no guarantee that the annuity would be paid regularly. Nonetheless no aristocratic widow was ever faced with the kind of poverty that was so often the fate of widows of labourers and artisans.

Class as well as gender controlled women's lives. Aristocratic wives during their husbands' long absences developed organizational and administrative skills, and exercised more power and influence than women of any other social group. Class also determined a woman's standard of living, and it influenced the age at which a young woman was likely to marry and the degree of freedom she might have over the choice of her partner. Her class also profoundly affected the kind of work that she would carry out as a married woman. On the other hand no woman could escape from the effects of gender. They were all vulnerable to rape and assault. All women watched their children or the children of friends die, and faced the possibility that they themselves might die in childbirth. The professions remained closed to them. However strong their piety, however great their intelligence, they could never dream of becoming a priest or a lawyer. The work that they did—whether in the fields, the market-place or the manor house—was less valued and given less recognition than the tasks performed by their men folk. Examples of companionate marriages and working economic partnerships cannot alter the fact that legally women were subordinate to men. Yet Sussex women, like women in other parts of medieval England, were by no means dowtrodden. In their husbands' absence, and in widowhood, some of them successfully controlled estates and businesses. Above all, women constantly talked to each other. Mother and daughter, mistress and maid, friends and enemies exchanged news, gossip, information and occasionally insults. Women also turned to other women for support at times of childbirth and death, in sickness and old age. Female networks paralleled male networks and gave women the strength to survive in a male-dominated environment.

Harry A. Miskimin

The Economy of Early Renaissance Europe: 1300–1460

The selection by Harry A. Miskimin looks at the twin issues of production and consumption. He demonstrates that the high mortality of the plague diminished the number of artisans and decreased productivity. In some instances, a smaller artisan pool also contributed to a decline in skill level. On the flip side of the equation, demand for certain goods increased in the postplague decades. The trade in luxury goods flourished. In addition, those with surplus capital tended to invest rather than save. Spurred on by the high toll disease was taking, some of these investments benefited the church, as testators sought to provide for their souls.

. . . Capital equipment in medieval industry consisted mainly of simple tools closely keyed to the man who used them; the skill of the individual artisan was of the utmost importance in the production process. These facts are crucial for understanding the impact of the vast late-fourteenth century population decline upon industry and the urban economy. In agriculture, the reduction of the rural population allowed the survivor to redistribute the land, to acquire larger holdings, and to abandon land that was not fully productive. For this reason, it is highly probable that the average productivity of agricultural workers rose substantially; the collective-inheritance effect gave each rural worker a larger and more fertile endowment of land whether he owned it or simply worked on it for others. In the towns, on the contrary, the inheritance effects on average productivity were far less noticeable. Where there was a one-to-one relationship between the worker and his tools, little additional benefit was gained from access to the capital goods left by victims of the plague. A farmer with twice as many acres as he held before the plague might be much, though probably not twice as much, more productive, but a carpenter

Source: Harry A. Miskimin, *The Economy of Early Renaissance Europe, 1300–1460* (New York: Prentice Hall, 1969), 82–89, 91–92.

with two hammers, or a shoemaker with two benches, gained little. Indeed, since the skill factor was crucial in medieval industry, it is very likely that the average productivity of artisans fell in the immediate wake of each successive visitation of plague or famine. The rapid increase in the death rate during such periods may well have outstripped the ability of society, hampered as it was by long terms of apprenticeship and limitations upon the number of apprentices, to train adequate replacements at the old levels of skill. During the slow process by which new entrants achieved technical competence in industry and manufacture, their contributions to the productive effort must have been less than those of experienced masters. Unlike the rural economy, the urban economy could not normally benefit from the greater per capita quantity of capital; technological factors prevented this, while the rapid attrition rates within the skilled labor force, resultant upon the high mortality levels of the fourteenth century, lowered still further the average level of productivity.

As in the case of all generalizations, some qualifications are necessary. Even in the Middle Ages, some industries were capital-intensive and consequently capable of reaping gains from the inheritance effects of the plague. The fulling process in the woolen industry—that is, the shrinking and felting of woven cloth—required major investment in fulling mills. The mills, in turn, since they had to be located on moderately swift and regular water courses, necessitated investment not only in money, but also in the commitment of choice sites that had alternative uses. Thus there was an opportunity cost in placing a fulling mill, rather than a grain mill, at a select spot on a water course. It is possible, therefore, that the fall in the demand for grain freed certain water courses for use as fulling mill locations. The success of Sir John Fastolf at Castle Combe in utilizing the water power on his estates indicates that in this one case, at least, the inheritance effects of plague, by reducing the demand for grain and consequently for scarce water power, worked to the benefit of the textile industry. It is equally possible that the location of fulling mills on the most favorable sites contributed to an increase in the average productivity of the fullers. In the salt trade also, technology may have favored increased productivity among the survivors of the plague. Since most salt was manufactured by evaporation of sea water in shallow pits along the coast, flat land close to the sea in places where the weather was normally fine and warm were at a premium. To the extent that the industry was able to abandon marginal locations and to concentrate in the most suitable sites, average productivity among the salt workers may have risen. In leather making, two factors may have worked in the same direction. The tanning process involved a substantial investment in an inventory of hides for the span of six months to two years during which the leather was soaked in a solution of oak bark and water. The fall in hide prices consequent upon the increased consumption of meat as consumers converted the gains obtained from falling bread prices into more protein-rich diets would have served to reduce the costs of carrying an inventory of hides through the tanning period. Since one man could handle large numbers of hides if he had the capital to buy them, it is again possible that average productivity in the leather industry rose as inventory costs fell.

Fulling, salt, leather—we might include some aspects of metallurgy and smelting in which reduced demands for building timber and the reversion of arable land to forest, as in Germany, may have increased fuel supplies—and a few other industries may have achieved gains in productivity, but we cannot be certain. The economic possibility was there, but without figures revealing total output and total employment in these industries, estimates of labor productivity remain no more than speculation. No weight of analysis, therefore, will be placed upon possible growth in productivity in these industries, but instead, the realization that gains may have occurred will be used to temper an analysis founded upon the absence of increases in productivity in the much wider group of industrial activities where the worker and his tools were so closely interrelated on a one-to-one basis as to preclude any inference of advantage from the inheritance effects of the plague.

In this group of industries, the first effect of higher mortality rates was to reduce sharply the number of artisans without increasing the productivity of those that remained. In some cases, levels of skill certainly fell. Medieval documentation provides few opportunities to evaluate comparative skill levels over time, but in the case of the scribes, the evidence has survived. Rolls of wills preserved in London illuminate two aspects of rapid demographic change; first, the accelerated speed with which scribal hands replace one another in the manuscripts after the middle of the fourteenth century testifies to heightened turnover as successive scribes succumbed to the plague. Second, the increasing irregularity and progressive disintegration of the script itself suggests that the replacements were less and less well trained. In this case, at least, the higher mortality lowered the level of skill to a demonstrable degree; it does not seem unreasonable to assume that the phenomenon was more general and that the difficulty of finding adequately trained artisans afflicted the entire range of industrial and commercial enterprise. Royal regulations in various regions confirm this view. In Paris in 1351, for example, King Jean le Bon issued a royal ordinance relaxing those guild restrictions that limited the number of apprentices in the shoemakers' craft. In another ordinance, he decreed freedom of contract in apprenticeship and ended the requirement of proof of capacity as a condition of entrance into any trade on a general basis. His son Charles V granted cloth workers who sought safety in Rouen during the Hundred Years' War the right to practice their craft without the formality of apprenticeship. Everywhere, after the first visitation of the plague, ordinances and statutes designed to regulate wages and to eliminate the labor scarcity multiplied; in 1366, Florence went so far as to allow the importation of pagan slaves. Such attempts usually met with little success, since it was an unalterable economic fact that labor, particularly skilled labor, was everywhere in short supply and likely to remain so because of the time required for training. The Paris ordinances cited were obviously intended to shorten the training period, but it is inconceivable that legislation alone could overcome the need for acquiring the skills of the craft. . . .

What, however, of the other side of the coin? What factors affected the market for manufactured goods? In dealing with this question, we may start with the initial presumption that the demand for manufactured goods of all classes was more elastic than that for the basic food grains. As declining grain prices freed money for other types of consumption, the per capita urban demand for manufactured goods grew. This pattern is identical to the shift in demand that led to greater per capita expenditures on meat, wine, butter, and certain spices; free funds sought new outlets in those commodities that did not satiate the appetite so readily as bread. Within the ample range of manufactured goods, many products fitted this category.

The sharp rise in mortality rates during the later Middle Ages diverted money from the bread grains into luxury foods and manufactured items, but this was not its only impact. There is an increasing body of evidence to show that individual preference patterns, both in consumption and in investment, were affected as well. Life was short and, to the medieval man who had endured plague, famine, malaria, and war, must have seemed to be growing shorter. The overriding presence of death appears to have had profound influence upon the demand for goods. Many men reasoned that what was not consumed today would be consumed by their heirs tomorrow; consequently, many turned to a life of worldly gratification. There was good reason for this view. Increased mortality, even discounting the desire to live for the moment, produced an immediate effect upon consumption patterns as many citizens inherited wealth from deceased relatives, while others simply helped themselves and scavenged the goods of the dead, whether related or not. The initial result of the series of plagues in the second half of the fourteenth century was a dramatic increase in the per capita wealth of the survivors; money, gold and silver plate, and durable goods of all sorts remained to be divided among perhaps one-third fewer people than before the plague. In the French town of Albi, the proportion of citizens with fortunes greater than one hundred livres doubled between 1343 and 1357; in the same period the percentage with less than ten livres dropped by half. At every social level, per capita wealth rose. In London, the enormous increase in the number of wills subjected to probate during the thirteen-fifties and -sixties reflects a similar concentration of wealth in the hands of the survivors, and there is no reason to suppose that experience differed in other cities of western Europe. In the south in 1351 Matteo Villani, describing Florence, put the case succinctly:

> No sooner had the plague ceased than . . . since men were few and since by hereditary succession they abounded in earthly goods, they forgot the past as though it had never been and gave themselves up to a more shameful and disordered life than they had led before . . . and the common people by reason of the abundance and superfluity that they found would no longer work at their accustomed trades; they wanted the dearest and most delicate foods . . . while children and common women clad themselves in all the fair and costly garments of the illustrious who had died.

Boccaccio's reference, in his introduction to the *Decameron*, to those who "thought the sure cure for the plague was to drink and be merry, to go about singing and amusing themselves, satisfying every appetite they could" and who "spent day and night going from tavern to tavern drinking immoderately" and "doing only those things which pleased them" provides additional literary evidence of the mutation of consumption patterns. Under the stress of plague, consumption had become for some an urgent matter. Wealth, or more accurately, the painful process of postponing pleasure while conserving or accumulating wealth, became for many an irrelevant act. Display, ornamentation, and the gratification of every personal desire seemed valid goals, doubly justified by increased funds and the nearness of death. Not all behaved in this fashion, of course, and even among those suddenly rich who did, reckless consumption could not last forever.

Substantial investment did occur, for example, in the agricultural regions of northern Italy, in the countryside surrounding French cities, and in the English textile industry, indicating that some entrepreneurs were paying more obeisance to the long future than to the immediate moment. But this was a phenomenon that attained its peak in the fifteenth century, well after the first shock of the plague had been absorbed.

Still others turned their attention entirely away from the things of this mortal world and sought to win grace in the next. If life was short, it was well to be warned and to prepare for judgment; the only sound investment in so troubled a world was in the well-being of the soul. As a result of the plague, investments in spiritual grace rose in three ways. First, the increase in the death rate automatically swelled the numbers of legacies to the Church, since it was customary to include provisions for the Church and charity in testaments of the time. Secondly, the elevated death rate, by destroying entire families and leaving many of the wealthy without heirs, encouraged larger individual bequests to the Church at the same time as it increased their number. Thirdly, since the incidence of death had risen so dramatically, many pious citizens endeavored to spend their remaining short span of years in preparation for the eternal life; among this group, increased bequests and gifts to the Church were common. Growing sums found their way into the coffers of the Church.

One effect of the plague, then, at least in the third quarter of the fourteenth century, was to reduce the desire to save and, consequently, to invest. Exceptions existed, of course, but the most striking feature of the period after the Black Death was a vast increase in consumption, particularly luxury consumption. In many countries, government policy may have contributed to this reaction. Growing demands for funds for use in war mobilized money that otherwise might have lain idle. The pressures of war in France and England drew money from the peasants in taxes, from the urban communities in both loans and taxes, and from bankers, both foreign and domestic. In France, during the fourteenth century, there were even several ordinances that required the nobles to carry specified portions of their bullion and plate to the mints for coinage into money; so far had fiscal necessity forced the mobilization of idle funds. Under the combined pressures of government finance, psychological reactions to the plague, and the inheritance effects of the resultant mortality, substantial demand for manufactured of the resultant mortality, substantial demand for manufactured goods was created. At the same time, the correlative reduction in both the desire for and the possibility of saving limited investment, while the increased mortality rates diminished the number of trained artisans capable of producing the goods that were demanded. Under these circumstances, we should expect to find boom conditions in the manufacturing sector of the late medieval economy. To some extent, this was the case, but the evidence requires many qualifications. Prices of manufactured goods rose sharply throughout Europe, and the wages of artisans rose with them. In England, for example, if we take average prices during the period 1261–1350 as a base of 100, price levels for the next 50-year period, 1351–1400, are as follows. For metals, including lead, tin, solder, pewter, and brass, the index rises to 176; for textiles—here canvas, linen, and two types of woolen cloth—the index is 160; and finally, for agricultural implements, clouts, cloutnails, two types of wheels, ligatures, greatnails, hurdles, horseshoes, horseshoe nails, ploughshoes, and ploughshares, the index mounts to the enormous level of 235. These figures may be compared to a price index of 99 for barley, peas, wheat, and rye, calculated on the same basis, for the second half of the fourteenth century. In the same period, the wages of building craftsmen increased by nearly 50 per cent. . . .

Changes in the levels of consumption were accompanied by changes in the objects desired. Within the spectrum of manufactures, some goods enjoyed more elastic demand functions than did others. Northern Europeans, catching up to the Italians, became extraordinarily fashion-conscious during the second half of the fourteenth century, under the combined influence of southern styles and the momentarily increased financial affluence inherited by the survivors of the plagues. More luxurious clothes, jewelry, and the like tended to find better markets than the more traditional products for two reasons. On the one hand, it had become possible for more people to emulate the very rich of former times. On the other, the diminutive scale of production of the most exotic goods meant that such goods did not depend upon large markets before the plague and hence, that they were more or less insulated against the demographic pressures of the plague. Prosperity, for these producers, did not require a wide market composed of many consumers, but rather, a small market composed of rich consumers. Pestilence destroyed large numbers of people but it did not, in its initial phases, destroy wealth. Indeed, to the extent that the figures from Albi reflect the general European experience, it would appear that the number of wealthy citizens in a position to buy costly luxuries grew as the total population declined. Consequently, luxury industries tended to flourish in the period following the demographic catastrophes, while those industries that had formerly served wide markets in a period of higher population density tended to fall rather quickly upon troubled times. . . .

Suggestions for
Further Reading

Because the scope of this volume is limited to the experience of plague in the late medieval period, the works cited do not typically extend into the early modern era. Additionally, even for the medieval period the scholarship on plague is vast. Thus, this bibliography is only a select sampling.

General studies of the plague include Philip Ziegler, *The Black Death* (Stroud, Gloucestershire, 1993); William G. Naphy and Andrew Spicer, *The Black Death: A History of Plagues, 1345–1730* (Stroud, Gloucestershire, 2000). For England see Colin Platt, *King Death: The Black Death and Its Aftermath in Late Medieval England* (London: UCL Press, 1996). David Herlihy's *The Black Death and the Transformation of the West*, edited with an introduction by Samuel K. Cohn (Cambridge: Harvard University Press, 1997) is less a survey of the Black Death and more the esteemed medieval historian's own hypotheses about the disease's identity and impact.

There is a rich literature about the "crisis" of the early fourteenth century. For one of the first comprehensive analyses of the famine in northern Europe, see Henry S. Lucas, "The Great European Famine of 1315, 1316, 1317," *Speculum*, vol. 5, no. 4 (October 1930): 343–377. A more recent examination and reassessment of the famine's impact in England appears in Ian Kershaw, "The Great Famine and Agrarian Crisis in England 1315–1322," *Speculum*, no. 59 (May 1973): 3–50. See, too, the collection of essays *Before the Black Death: Studies in the "Crisis" of the Early Fourteenth Century*, ed. Bruce M. S. Campbell (Manchester: Manchester University Press, 1991).

A good survey of medieval medicine can be found in Nancy G. Siraisi, *Medieval and Early Renaissance Medicine: An Introduction to Knowledge and Practice* (Chicago: University of Chicago Press, 1990). See also the collection of essays in *Practical Medicine from Salerno to the Black Death* (Cambridge: Cambridge University Press, 1994), particularly Jon Arrizabalaga, "Facing the Black Death: Perceptions and Reactions of University Medical Practitioners." For ideas about contagion, see Vivian Nutton "The Seeds of Disease: An Explanation of Contagion and Infection from the Greeks to the Renaissance," *Medical History* 27 (1983): 1–34, and "Contagion Theory and Contagion Practice in Fifteenth-Century Milan," *Renaissance Quarterly*, vol. 44 (1991): 213–256. See also Carole Rawcliffe, *Medicine and Society in Later Medieval England* (Stroud, Gloucestershire: A. Sutton, 1995). For Italy, the work of Ann Carmichael is indispensable; see her *Plague and the Poor in Renaissance Florence* (Cambridge: Cambridge

University Press, 1986). The best way currently to assess the impact of Samuel K. Cohn's controversial thesis is to read book reviews of his work. See, for example, Ann Carmichael, "Plague and More Plagues," *Early Science and Medicine*, vol. 8, no. 3 (2003): 1–14. There are also several other studies that challenge the plague's identity as bubonic plague; see, for example, Graham Twigg, *The Black Death: A Biological Reappraisal* (New York: Schocken Books, 1985) and Susan Scott and Christopher J. Duncan, *Biology of Plagues: Evidence from Historical Populations* (Cambridge: Cambridge University Press, 2001).

Other studies that look at the intersection of the plague and religious belief and practice include Samuel K. Cohn, *The Cult of Remembrance and the Black Death: Six Renaissance Cities in Central Italy* (Baltimore: Johns Hopkins University Press, 1992), and Robert E. Lerner, "The Black Death and Western European Eschatological Responses," *American Historical Review*, vol. 86, no. 3 (June 1981): 533–552. The literature on Jews in late medieval Europe includes Anna Foa, *The Jews of Europe After the Black Death*, trans. Andrea Grover (Berkeley: University of California Press, 2000), and Kenneth Stow, *Alienated Minority: The Jews of Medieval Latin Europe* (Cambridge: Harvard University Press, 1992). There is very little literature in English on the plague outside of western Europe in the medieval period. A few exceptions are Russell Zguta, "The One-Day Votive Church: A Religious Response to the Black Death in Early Russia," *Slavic Review*, vol. 40, no. 3 (Autumn 1981): 423–432, and O. Benedictow, *Plague in the Late Medieval Nordic Countries* (Middelalderforlaget, Oslo, 1992).

In addition to Louise Marshall's work there are several other important examinations of artistic production in the postplague era. They include Henk Van Os, "The Black Death and Sienese Painting: A Problem of Interpretation," *Art History* 4 (1981): 237–249, and Christine M. Boeckl, *Images of Plague and Pestilence: Iconography and Iconology* (Kirksville, Mo.: Truman State University Press, 2000). Remarkably, there are very few studies of the plague's impact on literature. Raymond Henry Payne Crawfurd, *Plague and Pestilence in Art and Literature* (Oxford: Clarendon Press, 1914) is quite dated. Two more useful pieces of scholarship are Renee Neu Watkins's "Petrarch and the Black Death: From Fear to Monuments," *Studies in the Renaissance*, vol. 19 (1972): 196–223, and Siegfried Wenzel, "Pestilence and Middle English Literature: Friar John Grimestone's Poems on Death," in *The Black Death: The Impact of the Fourteenth Century Plague*, edited by Daniel Williman (Binghamton: Medieval & Renaissance Texts & Studies, 1982).

Local studies of the plague and its impact focus overwhelmingly on England. A particularly good collection is W. M. Ormrod and P. G. Lindley, *Black Death in England* (Stamford: Paul Watkins, 1996). A few exceptions to this emphasis on England are Richard W. Emery, "The Black Death of 1348 in Perpignan," *Speculum*, vol. 42, no. 4 (October 1967): 611–623, and William D. Phillips, Jr., "*Peste Negra*: The Fourteenth-Century Plague Epidemics in Iberia," in *On the Social Origins of Medieval Institutions*, edited by Donald J. Kagay and Theresa M. Vann (Leiden: Brill, 1998), 47–62.

Our understanding of the institutional, political, social, and economic impact of the fourteenth-century plague is also dominated by studies of England. Some of the more noteworthy are R. A. Davies, "The Effect of the Black Death on the Parish Priests of the Medieval Diocese of Coventry and Lichfield," *Historical Research* 62 (1989): 85–90; Robert C. Palmer, *English Law in the Age of the Black Death, 1348–1381: A Transformation of Governance and Law* (Chapel Hill: University of North Carolina Press, 1993); L. R. Poos, *A Rural Society after the Black Death: Essex 1350–1525* (Cambridge: Cambridge University Press, 1991). Studies that focus particularly on the status of women in the postplague period are P. J. P. Goldberg, *Women, Work, and the Life Cycle in a Medieval Economy: Women in York and Yorkshire, c. 1300–1520* (Oxford: Clarendon Press, 1992), and Sandy Bardsley, "Women's Work Reconsidered: Gender and Wage Differentiation in Late Medieval England," *Past and Present*, no. 165 (Nov. 1999): 3–29. Analyses of the plague's impact in other parts of Europe include the review article by Judith C. Brown and Anthony Grafton, "Prosperity or Hard Times in Renaissance Italy?" *Renaissance Quarterly* 42, 4 (1989): 761–780. For clerical mortality, see Richard Gyug, "The Effects and Extent of the Black Death of 1348: New Evidence for Clerical Mortality in Barcelona," *Mediaeval Studies* 45 (1983): 385–398. See also the collection of essays, *The Black Death: The Impact of the Fourteenth-Century Plague* (Binghamton, N.Y.: Medieval and Renaissance Texts & Studies, 1982).

For additional studies of the English Peasants' Revolt, see R. H. Hilton, *Bond Men Made Free: Medieval Peasant Movements and the English Rising of 1381* (London: Temple Smith, 1973), E. B. Fryde, *Peasants and Landlords in Late Medieval England, c. 1380–c. 1525* (New York: St. Martin's Press, 1996), and R. H. Hilton and T. H. Ashton, eds., *The English Rising of 1381* (Cambridge: Cambridge University Press, 1984). For rebellions and uprisings not limited to the English Peasants' Revolt, see the essays in *Social Unrest in the Late Middle Ages: Papers of the Fifteenth Annual Conference of the Center for Medieval and Early Renaissance Studies*, ed. Francis X. Newman (Binghamton, N.Y.: Medieval and Renaissance Texts & Studies, 1986).

Credits

Part I

p. 13: Reprinted by permission of the publisher from "Bubonic Plague: Historical Epidemiology and the Medical Problems" in *The Black Death and The Transformation of the West* by David Herlihy, edited and with an Introduction by Samuel K. Cohn, Jr., pp. 31–38, Cambridge, Mass.: Harvard University Press, Copyright © 1997 by the President and Fellows of Harvard College.

p. 19: From Edward Miller and John Hatcher, *Medieval England: Rural Society and Economic Change 1036–1348*, Longman, 1978: pp. 241–251. Reprinted with permission of Pearson Education Limited.

p. 31: From William Jordan, *The Great Famine.* Copyright © 1996 Princeton University Press, 1998 paperback edition. Reprinted by permission of Princeton University Press.

Part II

p. 47: From John Henderson, "The Black Death in Florence: Medical and Communal Responses" in *Death and Towns: Urban Responses to the Dying and the Dead, 100–1600*, edited by Steven Bassett, 1992. Reprinted by permission of The Continuum International Publishing Company.

p. 59: From Samuel C. Cohn, "The Black Death: End of a Paradigm," *The American Historical Review*, Vol. 107, No. 3, June 2002. Reprinted with permission of The American Historical Association.

p. 65: From Michael McCormick, "Rats, Communications, and Plague: Toward an Ecological History," *The Journal of Interdisciplinary History*, 34:1 (Summer, 2003): pp. 1–25. Copyright © by the Massachusetts Institute of Technology and the editors of The Journal of Interdisciplinary History.

Part III

p. 77: From Louise Marshall, "Manipulating the Sacred: Image and Plague in Renaissance Italy," *Renaissance Quarterly*, Vol. 47, No. 3, Autumn 1994: pp. 488–506. Reprinted with permission of Renaissance Society of America.

p. 84: From Laura A. Smoller, "Plague and the Investigation of the Apocalypse" in *Last Things: Death and the Apocalypse in Middle Ages*, edited by Carolina Walker Bynum and Paul Freedman, 2000. Reprinted by permission of the University of Pennsylvania Press.

p. 99: From Richard Kieckhefer, "Radical Tendencies in the Glagellant Movement of the Mid-Fourteenth Century," in *Journal of Medieval and Renaissance Studies*, Volume 4: pp. 157–158, 160–165, 173–176. Copyright © 1974, Duke University Press. All rights reserved. Used by permission of the publisher.

p. 107: From David Nirenberg, *Communities of Violence*. Copyright © 1996 Princeton University Press. Reprinted by permission of Princeton University Press.

p. 115: From Michael W. Dols, *The Black Death in the Middle Ages*. Copyright © 1977 Princeton University Press, 2005 renewed PUP. Reprinted by permission of Princeton University Press.

Part IV

p. 126: From Anna Campbell, *The Black Death and Men of Learning*, 1931: pp. 109–112, 148–155.

p. 133: From William J. Courtenay, "The Effects of the Black death on English Higher Education," *Speculum*, Vol. 55, No. 4, October 1980: pp. 705–714. Reprinted with permission of Medieval Academy of America.

p. 143: From William M. Bowsky, "The Impact of the Black Death Upon Sienese Government and Society," *Speculum*, Vol. 39, No. 1, January 1964: pp. 23–24. Reprinted with permission of Medieval Academy of America.

p. 152: From William J. Dohar, *The Black Death and Pastoral Leadership*, 1995. Reprinted by permission of the University of Pennsylvania Press.

Part V

p. 165: From Paul Freedman, *The Origins of Peasant Servitude in Medieval Catalonia*, 1991: pp. 166–168, 171–178. Reprinted with permission of Cambridge University Press.

p. 173: From John Hatcher, "English in the Aftermath of the Black Death." This article first appeared in *Past and Present*, No. 144 (August 1994): pp. 3–35, and is reprinted here by permission of the Past and Present Society.

p. 181: From "The Social and Economic Background to the Rural Revolt of 1381," by Christopher Dyer in T. H. Ashton and R. H. Hilton, eds., *The English Rising of 1381*, 1991: pp. 9–10, 14–19, 41–42. Reprinted with permission of Cambridge University Press.

p. 187: Reprinted by permission of Boydell & Brewer Ltd. from *Daughters, Wives, and Widows After the Black Death*, by Mavis E. Mate, Boydell Press, 1998: pp. 193–199.

p. 194: From Harry A. Miskimin, *The Economy of Early Renaissance Europe, 1300–1460*, 1975. Reprinted with permission of Cambridge University Press.

without peasant revolt were they able to develop as a hole and Grow into this position of economic transformation?

In chapter 5 & Parsons to the top? "Social - Economic Impact of the Plague" and the common underlying question that is apparent.